Translanguaging i
Education

BILINGUAL EDUCATION & BILINGUALISM

Series Editors: **Nancy H. Hornberger**, (*University of Pennsylvania, USA*) and **Wayne E. Wright** (*Purdue University, USA*)

Bilingual Education and Bilingualism is an international, multidisciplinary series publishing research on the philosophy, politics, policy, provision and practice of language planning, Indigenous and minority language education, multilingualism, multiculturalism, biliteracy, bilingualism and bilingual education. The series aims to mirror current debates and discussions. New proposals for single-authored, multiple-authored, or edited books in the series are warmly welcomed, in any of the following categories or others authors may propose: overview or introductory texts; course readers or general reference texts; focus books on particular multilingual education program types; school-based case studies; national case studies; collected cases with a clear programmatic or conceptual theme; and professional education manuals.

Full details of all the books in this series and of all our other publications can be found on http://www.multilingual-matters.com, or by writing to Multilingual Matters, St Nicholas House, 31-34 High Street, Bristol BS1 2AW, UK.

BILINGUAL EDUCATION & BILINGUALISM: 104

Translanguaging in Higher Education

Beyond Monolingual Ideologies

Edited by
Catherine M. Mazak and Kevin S. Carroll

MULTILINGUAL MATTERS
Bristol • Blue Ridge Summit

Library of Congress Cataloging in Publication Data
A catalog record for this book is available from the Library of Congress.
Mazak, Catherine, editor. | Carroll, Kevin S., editor.
Translanguaging in Higher Education: Beyond Monolingual Ideologies /
Catherine M. Mazak and Kevin S. Carroll.
Bristol: Multilingual Matters, [2016] | Series: Bilingual Education & Bilingualism: 104 |
Includes bibliographical references and index.
LCCN 2016030411| ISBN 9781783096640 (hbk:alk. paper) | ISBN 9781783096633
  (pbk:alk. paper) | ISBN 9781783096671 (kindle)
LCSH: Language transfer (Language learning) | Education, Bilingual. | Language
  and languages–Study and teaching (Higher education) | Languages in contact. |
  Multilingualism.
LCC P118.25 .T72 2016 | DDC 418.0071/1–dc23 LC record available at https://lccn.loc.
gov/2016030411

British Library Cataloguing in Publication Data
A catalogue entry for this book is available from the British Library.

ISBN-13: 978-1-78309-664-0 (hbk)
ISBN-13: 978-1-78309-663-3 (pbk)

Multilingual Matters
UK: St Nicholas House, 31-34 High Street, Bristol BS1 2AW, UK.
USA: NBN, Blue Ridge Summit, PA, USA.

Website: www.multilingual-matters.com
Twitter: Multi_Ling_Mat
Facebook: https://www.facebook.com/multilingualmatters
Blog: www.channelviewpublications.wordpress.com

The policy of Multilingual Matters/Channel View Publications is to use papers that
are natural, renewable and recyclable products, made from wood grown in sustainable
forests. In the manufacturing process of our books, and to further support our policy,
preference is given to printers that have FSC and PEFC Chain of Custody certification.
The FSC and/or PEFC logos will appear on those books where full certification has been
granted to the printer concerned.

Typeset by Deanta Global Publishing Services Limited.
Printed and bound in the UK by the Short Run Press Ltd.
Printed and bound in the US by Edwards Brothers Malloy, Inc.

The editors would like to dedicate this book to our families, especially to the baby girls who arrived during our work on this volume, Kevin's daughter Emma Marie and Cathy's daughter Mariela Andrea.

Contents

Contributors

Sonja Barfod is a doctoral student at Roskilde University in the Department of Culture and Identity, where she also studied German and Danish. Since 2011, she has given lectures in the Department of German and since 2012 in the German Language Profile. Her doctoral thesis is about language choice in international workplace settings with a focus on German and the Scandinavian languages. She has also participated in Fehmarnbelt projects that aimed at enhancing the linguistic and intercultural skills of Danish employees.

Kevin S. Carroll is an Associate Professor in the Department of Graduate Studies in the College of Education at the University of Puerto Rico, Río Piedras and has also worked at Emirates College for Advanced Education in Abu Dhabi, United Arab Emirates. His research has used qualitative research methods to document language planning and policy efforts in Aruba, Puerto Rico, the United States and the United Arab Emirates. His research centers on issues of equity, college access and the use of language for empowerment.

Petra Daryai-Hansen is an Associate Professor at the Department of English, German and Romance Studies, University of Copenhagen, and at the Department of Research, Development and Internationalization, University College, Denmark. From 2012 to 2014, she was an Assistant Professor at the Department of Culture and Identity, Roskilde University, where she co-coordinated the Language Profiles, which are part of Roskilde University's plurilingual internationalization strategy. Her main research areas are internationalization of education, plurilingual education, content and language integrated learning (CLIL) and intercultural pedagogics. Daryai-Hansen has participated in a wide range of Danish and international collaboration research projects, among others the FREPA project, supported by the European Centre for Modern Languages of the Council of Europe. She is currently coordinating the project Developing the Language Awareness Approach in the Nordic and Baltic Countries.

Aintzane Doiz is Associate Professor at the University of the Basque Country UPV/EHU (Spain). Her research interests include cognitive semantics, contrastive linguistics and applied linguistics. Her latest research also includes multilingualism at pre-university and university levels, attitudes and motivation and the acquisition of an L3 in CLIL. She is part of the research group 'Language and Speech' at the UPV/EHU. Together with David Lasagabaster and Juan Manuel Sierra, she has edited the books *English-Medium Instruction at Universities: Global Challenges* (Multilingual Matters, 2012) and *Motivation and Foreign Language Learning: From Theory to Practice* (John Benjamins, 2014).

Bridget A. Goodman earned her MSEd in Teaching English to Speakers of Other Languages (TESOL) and her PhD in Educational Linguistics from the University of Pennsylvania. She is currently an Assistant Professor of multilingual education at Nazarbayev University Graduate School of Education in Astana, Kazakhstan. Her research interests include the medium of instruction policies and practices in multilingual contexts, language policy and practice in Ukraine and Kazakhstan and governance of higher education institutions in post-Socialist contexts. With the support of a social policy grant for preliminary research from Nazarbayev University, she is developing a comparative research study of English-medium education in higher education across post-Socialist contexts.

Cynthia Groff earned her PhD in Educational Linguistics at the University of Pennsylvania's Graduate School of Education. Her dissertation research focused on issues of language, education and empowerment as experienced and expressed by Kumauni young women and educators in North India. For this, she received the University of Pennsylvania's educational linguistics international award and the comparative and international education society's language issues dissertation award. Since graduating in 2010, she has conducted postdoctoral research through Université Laval in Québec and through Universidad Autónoma Metropolitana in Mexico. She has been awarded four foreign language and area studies fellowships, the American association of university women's dissertation fellowship and the national academy of education/Spencer postdoctoral fellowship. Her research interests include the adequacy of education for linguistic minorities and the experiences and discourses of minority youth.

Peichang He is a Research Assistant at the Faculty of Education, University of Hong Kong. She is currently a teaching consultant in a multilingual and multicultural partnership secondary school in Hong Kong. She has also been an ELT teacher and teacher educator in China for more than a decade. Her research interests include bi/multilingual education, CLIL, second language teacher education, teacher identity and pedagogical content knowledge.

Haiyan Lai is a PhD candidate majoring in English Language Education at the Faculty of Education, the University of Hong Kong. She has also been an English language training (ELT) teacher in China for more than five years. Her research interests include multimodal discourse analysis (MDA), systemic functional linguistics (SFL), English for academic purposes (EAP), genre-based pedagogy and CLIL.

David Lasagabaster is Associate Professor at the University of the Basque Country, Spain. He has published on second and third language acquisition, CLIL, attitudes and motivation and multilingualism. Among other works, he has coedited *Multilingualism in European Bilingual Contexts: Language Use and Attitudes* (Multilingual Matters, 2007), *English-Medium Instruction at Universities: Global Challenges* (Multilingual Matters, 2013) and *Motivation and Foreign Language Learning* (John Benjamins, 2014). Since 2008, he has been a member of the executive committee of the International Association for Language Awareness.

Angel Lin is a full Professor at the Faculty of Education, University of Hong Kong. She received her PhD from the Ontario Institute for Studies in Education, University of Toronto, Canada, in 1996. Since then, her research and teaching have focused on classroom discourse analysis, bilingual educa-tion, academic literacies and language policy and planning in postcolonial contexts. She has published six research books and over 80 research articles and serves on the editorial boards of leading international research journals including *Applied Linguistics*, *TESOL Quarterly*, *International Journal of Bilingual Education and Bilingualism*, *Language and Education* and *Pragmatics and Society*.

Leketi Makalela is a Professor and Head of the Division of Languages, Literacies and Literatures at the University of the Witwatersrand, South Africa. He is rated by the South African National Research Foundation on multilingualism, translanguaging, reading literacy and World Englishes. He also directs an innovative multilingual program, which includes nine indigenous African languages and English: Wits Abafunde-ba halalefe mul-tilingual literacy program (WAMLiP). He serves as an editor-in-chief of an ISI-listed journal, *Southern African Linguistics and Applied Language Studies*. His latest book is *New Directions in Language and Literacy Education for Multilingual Classrooms* (2015).

Catherine M. Mazak is Co-Director of CeIBA (*Centro para la investigación del bilingüismo y aprendizaje*/Center for Research on Bilingualism and Learning) and Associate Professor of English at the UPRM. She got her PhD in Critical Studies in the Teaching of English from Michigan State University and her MA in TESOL from the University of Arizona. She studies bilingualism in higher education using ethnographic and other qualitative research methods.

Her latest line of research explores translanguaging practices in science teaching at the UPRM. Her most recent article, 'Translanguaging practices at a bilingual university: A case study of a science classroom' appeared in the *International Journal of Bilingual Education and Bilingualism* 2015.

Fiorelys Mendoza is an English Professor at the University of Puerto Rico, Río Piedras Campus and an editor of the Puerto Rico Testsite for Exploring Contamination Threats (PRoTECT) Journal Publication Group at the University of Puerto Rico, Mayagüez. Some of her published works are 'The Only Portrait' on the website *Esta Vida Boricua* and *'Percepciones de género en las evaluaciones de asistentes de cátedra'* in *Actas del VIII Coloquio sobre las Mujeres.* She completed a Bachelor of Arts in Linguistics and a Master of Arts in English Education at the University of Puerto Rico, Mayagüez. She also received a Bilingual Education (K-12) certification from the Antillean University and is a state-certified secondary school English teacher.

Lauren Pérez Mangonez is a certified teacher of English and Spanish and graduated from the Universidad Pedagógica Nacional de Colombia. She is currently pursuing a Masters of Arts in English Education at the University of Puerto Rico (Mayagüez Campus), where she has also been working as a research assistant at CeIBA (*Centro para la investigación del bilingüismo y aprendizaje en Puerto Rico*). Her current interests are electronic literature and bilingualism in academic contexts.

Lena Schwarz is a student at Roskilde University. She is studying in her third semester in social science with a focus on pedagogy and work-life studies. She has a Danish-German background and has been attending the German Language Profile since her first semester. She is employed as a student assistant at the Language Profile.

Melanie van den Hoven is a PhD candidate at the University of Durham, England, and an instructor in the Culture, Society and Linguistic Education Department at Emirates College for Advanced Education in Abu Dhabi, United Arab Emirates. She has conducted qualitative research on issues regarding intercultural communication and the English as a foreign language (EFL) classroom, teaching English as an international language, perceptions of varieties of English and conceptions of English as a medium of instruction. She is a TIRF 2010 Sheikh Nahayan fellowship recipient.

Acknowledgements

The editors would like to thank Lauren Pérez Mangonéz and A.J. Rivera for their help with the compilation of this volume. We would also like to acknowledge the hard work of the following scholars who served as reviewers on this volume's chapters: Helena Guerrero, Nelson Flores, Janelle Johnson, Keith Kennetz, Daniel Kirk, Brian Meadows, Peter Sayer, Kate Seltzer and Sultan Turkan.

1 Introduction: Theorizing Translanguaging Practices in Higher Education

Catherine M. Mazak

Translanguaging is many things. It has become a rather trendy and at times controversial term as it has gained traction in academia over the last several years. However, the way in which it has been taken up by researchers, particularly in education, is evidence that it is filling a gap in our descriptions of language practices in educational settings. This introduction reviews the history of translanguaging as an evolving term, relates it to current thinking in socio- and applied linguistics and answers the question 'what is translanguaging?' as this author understands it. It then goes on to explain the importance of this volume's special focus on translanguaging in higher education and finally previews each chapter in the volume, particularly emphasizing what the chapter contributes to our ever-evolving understanding of translanguaging.

The Development of Translanguaging as a Term

The history of translanguaging is firmly rooted in the field of bilingual education, though it has developed alongside several other terms that use the prefix *trans-*, including translingualism (Canagarajah, 2014). The term *translanguaging* was first coined in Welsh as *trawsieithu* by bilingual education researcher Cen Williams (1994, 1996). Baker (2006: 297), in *Foundations of Bilingual Education*, states that when translanguaging in the classroom, 'the input (reading or listening) tends to be in one language, and the output (speaking or writing) in the other language, and this is systematically varied'. He further explains that Williams's research found that this type of translanguaging worked well as a teaching strategy in Welsh high schools to 'develop both languages successfully and also result in effective content learning' (Baker, 2006: 297). Research on translanguaging continues to be produced in the Welsh context, and scholars there have published several excellent reviews of the term and its development, including Lewis *et al.* (2012a, 2012b) and more recently Beres (2015). The definition of translanguaging that first came out of

Bangor, Wales, essentially described a *teaching strategy* that worked well in developing *both language and content knowledge*. This is part – but not all – of our current understanding of translanguaging. For that we need to turn to the work of Ofelia García.

García (2009: 45) first explained the concept of translanguaging in her book *Bilingual Education in the 21st Century* as the '*multiple discursive practices* in which bilinguals engage in order to *make sense of their bilingual worlds*'. This definition emphasizes existing bilingual *practices*, not *teaching strategies*, as in the work of Williams and Baker. Though it is often cited, the definition is rather broad and open to interpretation. Since 2009, García has worked to refine this definition, articulating the theory behind the term. She argues that 'language is an ongoing process that only exists as languag*ing*' (García & Leiva, 2014: 204; emphasis added). This ongoing process of languaging both shapes and is shaped by people as they interact in specific social, cultural and political contexts. The emphasis on process – the *–ing* – purposefully shifts the focus away from discrete 'languages' and makes the act of meaning-making central. Thus, García argues, translanguaging refers to the constant, active invention of new realities through social action.

Translanguaging and Poststructuralism

In *Translanguaging: Language, Bilingualism and Education*, García and Li (2014) attach translanguaging to recent shifts in the fields of socio- and applied linguistics. They situate translanguaging particularly within the poststructural turn that interrogates the notion of languages as discrete, separate entities. This notion is perhaps best articulated by Makoni and Pennycook (2007), who argue that the concept of a 'language' was an invention of colonialism. The Romantic notion that one state equals one culture equals one language was essential for nation-state building, and in that sense separate languages are 'inventions' that met the needs of the colonial project. The idea that languages are discrete entities is further questioned by Canagarajah (2014) in his theory of translingual practices, where he describes global semiotic practices that defy the supposedly rigid borders between languages. García and Li (2014) argue that in fact bilinguals do not have two distinct linguistic systems in the brain, but rather *one integrated repertoire of linguistic and semiotic practices* from which they constantly draw. Thus, the idea of 'code-switching' does not fit neatly into the theory of translanguaging because bilinguals are not shuttling between separate codes, but rather performing parts of their repertoires, which contain features from all of their 'languages'. The 'one system' idea is perhaps the most controversial aspect of current notions of translanguaging, particularly among linguists studying code-switching, but it is precisely where García and Li link translanguaging to the poststructural turn in applied linguistics.

This poststructural paradigm shift, also referred to as the 'trans turn' in applied linguistics, has refocused research away from 'homogeneity, stability, and boundedness as the starting assumptions' in favor of 'mobility, mixing, political dynamics, and historical embedding' as 'central concerns in the study of languages, language groups, and communication' (Blommaert & Rampton, 2011: 3). As a result, the ideology of 'one nation one language' has been critiqued as leading to monolingual ideologies of language and the 'two solitudes' approach to bilingualism (García & Li, 2014; Makoni & Pennycook, 2007). Canagarajah (2014: 6) claims that understanding translingual practice involves two key concepts: (1) 'communication transcends individual languages' and (2) 'communication transcends words and involves diverse semiotic resources and ecological affordances'. García and Li (2014: 21) posit that translanguaging 'refers to *new* language exchanges among people with different histories, and releases histories and understandings that had been buried within fixed language identities constrained by nation-states'. This definition captures the historical, political and social embeddedness of language practices and how these practices are and have been intertwined with ideologies. When we use the term *translanguaging*, we are indexing this poststructural paradigm shift in applied linguistics.

What is Translanguaging?

The previous sections help us to understand the theoretical underpinnings of translanguaging, but the question remains: What is translanguaging exactly? What do researchers actually mean when they use the term? The answer is, of course, that it means different things for different researchers in different contexts. Creese and Blackledge (2010) explore the relationship between translanguaging practices and identity in complimentary schools in the UK. They use the term *flexible bilingual pedagogy* and argue,

> This pedagogy adopts a translanguaging approach and is used by participants for identity performance as well as the business of language learning and teaching. ... we think the bilingual teachers and students in this study used whatever signs and forms they had at their disposal to connect with one another, indexing disparate allegiances and knowledges and creating new ones. (Creese & Blackledge: 2010: 112)

Thus, they argue that translanguaging is a *pedagogical approach* that at once serves to enhance teaching and indexes the speakers' shifting multilingual and multicultural identities.

Canagarajah (2011) investigates multilinguals' use of 'whatever signs and forms' are available to them and the deep connections that this use has to identity enactment in texts. In one of the few studies of translanguaging in texts, and one of even fewer looking at higher education, he explores how one graduate student used code-meshing to make meaning by employing Arabic, English, French and symbols in her academic writing. His emphasis on the process of the graduate student exploring the ways in which she could use all of her communicative repertoire as an integrated system shows how translanguaging in texts is strategic, and at the same time he raises important questions on how to assess translanguaging competence in academic settings. In Canagarajah's (2011: 408) synthesis of research on translanguaging, he notes that 'what current classroom studies show is that translanguaging is a naturally occurring phenomenon for multilingual students'. That is, in bi- and multilingual environments, translanguaging is *when students (and often teachers) use their entire linguistic repertoire strategically to teach and learn*, which they do with a keen awareness of the identity consequences of linguistic performance. Hornberger and Link (2012) reinforce this notion from a biliteracy perspective. They conclude,

> Two things are clear from the research though, in connection with fostering transfer, and both of them suggest the significance of translanguaging for biliteracy development: one, that individuals' biliteracy develops along the continua in direct response to contextual demands placed on them; and two, that individuals' biliteracy development is enhanced when they have recourse to all their existing skills (and not only those in the second language). (Hornberger & Link, 2012: 244–245)

Li (2011: 1233) describes translanguaging practices as 'creative', 'critical', 'flexible' and 'strategic' in his 'moment analysis' of multilingual Chinese youth in the UK. He describes translanguaging spaces as 'interactionally created' and emphasizes the performative nature of these spaces:

> For me, translanguaging is both going between different linguistic structures and systems, including different modalities (speaking, writing, signing, listening, reading, remembering) and going beyond them. It includes the full range of linguistic performances of multilingual language users for purposes that transcend the combination of structures, the alternation between systems, the transmission of information and the representation of values, identities and relationships. The act of translanguaging then is transformative in nature; it creates a social space for the multilingual language user by bringing together different dimensions of their personal history, experience and environment, their attitude, belief and ideology, their cognitive and physical capacity into one coordinated and meaningful performance, and making it into a lived experience. I call this space 'translanguaging space,' a space for the act of translanguaging as well as a space created through translanguaging.
> (Li, 2011: 1223)

Thus, for Li *translanguaging is linguistic performance* that not only includes the use of different features of the speakers' repertoire, but also creates something new that 'transcends the combination of structures' and creates a 'translanguaging space'.

In Sayer's (2013) ethnographic study of the classroom language practices of Mexican American second graders and their teacher in San Antonio, Texas, he refers to *translanguaging as method*. He argues that a

> translanguaging lens is less focused on language per se, and more concerned with examining how bilinguals make sense of things through language.... The excerpts illustrate how translanguaging through TexMex enables teacher and students to create discursive spaces that allow them to engage with the social meanings in school from their position as bilingual Latinos.   (Sayer, 2013: 84)

Although he emphasizes translanguaging as a method, he also argues that it is (1) 'a *descriptive label* that captures the fluid nature of [students'] language practices' and (2) 'a theoretical and *analytical tool* that allows researchers to portray the multifaceted ways that the children's bilingualism is not merely monolingualism times two' (Sayer, 2013: 85; emphasis added). Thus, Sayer includes multiple understandings of translanguaging: as a method, as a descriptive label for language practices and as an analytical tool.

In sum, based on the research cited here and my own work (Mazak & Herbas-Donoso, 2014a, 2014b, 2015), I see translanguaging as the following:

(1) Translanguaging is a *language ideology* that takes bilingualism as the norm.

(2) Translanguaging is a *theory of bilingualism* based on lived bilingual experiences. As such, it posits that bilinguals do not separate their 'languages' into discrete systems, but rather possess one integrated repertoire of languaging practices from which they draw as they navigate their everyday bilingual worlds.

(3) Translanguaging is a *pedagogical stance* that teachers and students take on that allows them to draw on all of their linguistic and semiotic resources as they teach and learn both language and content material in classrooms.

(4) Translanguaging is a *set of practices* that are still being researched and described. It is not limited to what is traditionally known as 'code-switching', but rather seeks to include any practices that draw on an individual's linguistic and semiotic repertoires (including reading in one language and discussing the reading in another, and many other practices that will be described in this book).

(5)   As such, translanguaging is *transformational*. It changes the world as it continually invents and reinvents languaging practices in a perpetual process of meaning-making. The acceptance of these practices – of the creative, adaptable, resourceful inventions of bilinguals – transforms not only our traditional notions of 'languages', but also the lives of bilinguals themselves as they remake the world through language.

Translanguaging in Higher Education

Even with the groundbreaking research described above, much remains in question about translanguaging. Almost no literature exists on translanguaging in higher education, since most (though not all) of the existing literature explores translanguaging in primary and occasionally secondary classrooms in the US and the UK. Thus, there is also a lack of research on translanguaging in global bi- and multilingual contexts. This volume hopes to fill this gap by showcasing the complexity and illustrating the various ways in which translanguaging practices exist within higher educational contexts around the world. Furthermore, the final two chapters from the United Arab Emirates and the Basque country of Spain remind us to think critically about the advantages but also the limitations of adopting a translingual approach and ideology.

In our compilation of this book, we sought to include studies that would both shed light on international contexts rarely discussed in the translanguaging literature and, by doing so, further contribute to the development of translanguaging as an educational and linguistic concept. Our selection of work from diverse sociocultural contexts necessarily employs many different types of research. The work collected here uses research methods that vary from ethnographic case studies to historical/social analysis. Data collection techniques include observation, focus groups, interviews and document analysis among others. Research stances range from advocacy research to ethnographic report. The incorporation of such a range of different research and rhetorical styles and approaches, we think, adds to the value of this volume as a truly diverse collection of deeply contextualized research on translanguaging.

Higher education is increasingly characterized by the global movement of people and ideas. For this reason, it is a particularly ripe context for translanguaging. English dominates as the indisputable international language of science and technology. In many institutions, publications in English are privileged as the only ones that 'count' for promotion and tenure. English-language texts and English-medium classrooms have become part of internationalization efforts meant to attract students from around the world for their higher tuition dollars. The privileging of English also means that even students who remain in their own countries may find themselves studying in higher education in English.

Combine this with monolingual ideologies that still dominate university language policies (even unwritten ones), and tensions often occur between the everyday multilingual practices of students and university classrooms that can become artificially 'monolingual'. In Chapter 2, Makelela addresses this by implementing the concept of *ubuntu* translanguaging pedagogy (UTP) in a Sepedi language course for preservice teachers in South Africa. He argues that UTP is meant 'to disrupt perceived language boundaries among preservice student teachers and to recreate complex multilingual spaces that reflect the *ubuntu* principles of ecological interdependence' (17). Central to his argument is that we 'need to reconceptualize classroom spaces as microcosms of societal multilingualism' (25). Thus, UTP is essential for higher education in the dynamically multilingual Limpopo Valley, where 'human and linguistic separations are blurred while interdependence is valued over independence' (25). Enacting UTP in a higher education classroom where preservice teachers are trained serves to break down monolingual ideologies for these teachers, who will then potentially enact UTP in their own classrooms.

In a similar effort to bring students' multilingual practices into the classroom and build on them academically, in Chapter 3 Daryai-Hansen and her colleagues in Denmark describe Roskilde University's 'language profiles' program. Created as a grassroots effort within the university and supported by the administration, the program is specifically designed to reinforce students' plurilingual and intercultural competences as students 'are invited to use translanguaging strategies in order to achieve interactional and social aims' (30). In the European context, where developing mobile, prepared students often – but not always – means English-medium instruction, students in this program choose to work with other students in their fields on projects using their choice of French, German or Spanish. The authors emphasize that this program challenges the prevailing monolingual ideology of higher education in Denmark and uses translanguaging to meet both language and content learning goals.

Monolingual ideologies of language also dominate in the Ukrainian university where Goodman's Chapter 4 study takes place. She explores translanguaging practices and attitudes within three languages: Ukrainian, Russian and English. As she documents the dominant use of Russian as an academic language in these contexts, she states, 'It is appropriate, however, to consider whether translanguaging practices in this context can serve as an act of resistance – or, at least, a counternarrative – to the hegemony of English as a global or international language' (52). Her findings suggest that the use of additional languages (other than English) through translanguaging in classrooms 'may not be a threat to multilingualism in the Ukrainian context' (52) as one might suspect.

In Chapter 5, my colleagues and I investigate the translanguaging practices of three professors at an officially bilingual university in Puerto Rico. In this context, English is both the colonial language and the privileged language of science and technology, though Spanish remains the language of everyday communication among students. We argue that the way in which these three professors navigate the complex waters of classroom language use in this context by using translanguaging respects students' entire linguistic repertoire and acknowledges Spanish as a legitimate academic language.

He *et al.* (Chapter 6) deeply explore a math education professor's translanguaging and trans-semiotizing practices during a tertiary mathematics education seminar in Hong Kong. One example of how translanguaging and trans-semiotizing practices worked together in the presentation was in the professor's explanation of 'scaffolding'. He *et al.* argue,

> translanguaging between Chinese and English, together with intercultural background knowledge (e.g. the comparison between mathematics education in mainland China and in the US), acted as a meaning-negotiation strategy to explain the intercultural differences between the Chinese concept *pudian* and the Western concept of scaffolding. (He *et al.*, this volume: 102)

Their chapter reminds us that translanguaging includes the use of many meaning-making resources to negotiate understanding in multilingual and multicultural higher education contexts.

In Chapter 7, Groff explores language in higher education in India, a context where monolingual ideologies are actually not as common as in other contexts in this book. She aims

> to describe multilingual language policies and practices in India within their historical and ideological context, showing that the use of multiple languages within one institution, within one classroom, and within one speech event is quite common in higher education in India. (Groff, this volume: 120)

In contrast to South Africa, for example, Groff argues that in India translanguaging in higher education is quite common and expected.

In contrast, Carroll and van den Hoven (Chapter 8) document the very strict – though unwritten – monolingual language policies in higher education in the United Arab Emirates (UAE). In the UAE, higher education classes are expected to be taught in English only, a belief reinforced by the hiring of many non-Arabic-speaking professors from abroad. Through interviews with professors and administrators, Carroll and van den Hoven explore the tension between the institutional pressure to give classes only in English and the demands of students who expect the professor to use some Arabic to help them succeed in the course. The authors paint a picture where translanguaging is actually prohibited, and the potential of using translanguaging to access students' entire linguistic repertoires goes largely untapped. The chapter asks us to examine the tensions between student expectations and administrative mandates when it comes to language use in classrooms.

In contrast to the UAE context, Doiz and Lasagabaster (Chapter 9) investigate professors' beliefs about translanguaging in English-medium classrooms at the University of the Basque Country. As part of a push toward internationalization, this university, which offers programs in both Basque and Spanish, is now offering English-medium programs. Since these courses are chosen by students specifically to help develop their content *and* language knowledge by using English-language instruction, many – though not all – professors in the study felt obligated to avoid translanguaging in class. This chapter presents a context that contrasts many others in this volume: students choose English-medium higher education rather than have it imposed on them. Thus, we are reminded that the use of translanguaging in higher education is highly contextualized and sometimes may not actually meet students' needs. In this sense, we must think critically about the use of translanguaging as always 'good' for students.

The conclusion of this volume (Chapter 10), written by co-editor Kevin S. Carroll, looks at translanguaging through a language policy lens. Carroll argues 'that one of the fundamental necessities in increasing access and equity in higher education is prestige planning among non-dominant languages' (175). Tying all the chapters together, he offers evidence from each to support his claim that translanguaging in higher education can help influence both primary and secondary education language policies and open space for non-dominant languages across levels of education. He also critiques translanguaging and reminds us that translanguaging itself is an ideology and must be examined through a critical lens.

Translanguaging as a concept shifts focus from the structural analysis of language itself to what people *do* with language in their everyday lives. But translanguaging does not stop there. It asks us to rethink bilingualism as the norm and take our analysis as socio- and applied linguists from that starting point. To do this, we as researchers, educators and policymakers need to put monolingual ideologies of language aside and adopt beliefs about language that put bi- and multilingual practices at the center of our investigation, teaching and policymaking. As we do so, we must consider critically the use of translanguaging for students in particular contexts with certain aims. We hope that this volume will contribute to this effort in the context of higher education worldwide.

References

Baker, C. (2006) *Foundations of Bilingual Education and Bilingualism* (4th edn). Clevedon: Multilingual Matters.

Beres, A.M. (2015) An overview of translanguaging: 20 years of 'giving voice to those who do not speak'. *Translation and Translanguaging in Multilingual Contexts* 1 (1), 103–118.

Blommaert, J. and Rampton, B. (2011) Language and superdiversity. *Diversities* 13 (2), 1–19.

Canagarajah, S. (2011) Codemeshing in academic writing: Identifying teachable strategies of translanguaging. *The Modern Language Journal* 95 (3), 401–417.

Canagarajah, S. (2014) *Translingual Practice: Global Englishes and Cosmopolitan Relations*. New York: Routledge.

Creese, A. and Blackledge, A. (2010) Translanguaging in the bilingual classroom: A pedagogy for learning and teaching? *The Modern Language Journal* 94 (1), 103–115.

García, O. (2009) *Bilingual Education in the 21st Century: A Global Perspective*. Oxford: Wiley-Blackwell.

García, O. and Leiva, C. (2014) Theorizing and enacting translanguaging for social justice. In A. Creese and A. Blackledge (eds) *Heteroglossia as Practice and Pedagogy* (pp. 199–216). New York: Springer.

García, O. and Li, W. (2014) *Translanguaging: Language, Bilingualism and Education*. New York: Palgrave Macmillan.

Hornberger, N. and Link, H. (2012) Translanguaging in today's classrooms: A biliteracy lens. *Theory into Practice*, 51, 239–247.

Lewis, G., Jones, B. and Baker, C. (2012a) Translanguaging: Developing its conceptualisation and contextualization. *Educational Research and Evaluation: An International Journal on Theory and Practice* 18 (7), 655–670.

Lewis, G., Jones, B. and Baker, C. (2012b) Translanguaging: Origins and development from school to street and beyond. *Educational Research and Evaluation: An International Journal on Theory and Practice* 18 (7), 641–654.

Li, W. (2011) Moment analysis and translanguaging space: Discursive construction of identities by multilingual Chinese youth in Britain. *Multilingual Structures and Agencies* 43 (5), 1222–1235.

Makoni, S. and Pennycook, A. (eds) (2007) *Disinventing and Reconstructing Languages*. Clevedon: Multilingual Matters.

Mazak, C. and Herbas-Donoso, C. (2014a) Translanguaging practices and language ideologies in Puerto Rican university science education. *Critical Inquiry in Language Studies* 11 (1), 27–49.

Mazak, C. and Herbas-Donoso, C. (2014b) Translanguaging practices at a bilingual university: A case study of a science classroom. *International Journal of Bilingual Education and Bilingualism* 11 (1), 27–49.

Mazak, C. and Herbas-Donoso, C. (2015) Living the bilingual university: Translanguaging in a bilingual science classroom from a student's perspective. In A. Fabricus and B. Preisler (eds) *Transcultural Interaction and Linguistic Diversity in Higher Education: The Student Experience* (pp. 255–277). Basingstoke: Palgrave.

Sayer, P. (2013) Translanguaging, TexMex, and bilingual pedagogy: Emergent bilinguals learning through the vernacular. *TESOL Quarterly* 47 (1), 63–88.

Williams, C. (1994) Arfarniad o Ddulliau Dysgu ac Addysgu yng Nghyd-destun Addysg Uwchradd Ddwyieithog. Unpublished PhD thesis, University of Wales.

Williams, C. (1996) Secondary education: Teaching in the bilingual situation. In C. Williams, G. Lewis and C. Baker (eds) *The Language Policy: Taking Stock* (pp. 193–211). Llangefni: CAI.

2 Translanguaging Practices in a South African Institution of Higher Learning: A Case of *Ubuntu* Multilingual Return

Leketi Makalela

Introduction

Recent scholarship on the nature of language has taken a 'multilingual turn' in response to the fluid and versatile discourses that 21st-century citizens practice (García & Li, 2014; Makalela, 2015; May, 2012). In particular, attention has shifted from what languages look like to what people do with them. This epistemological shift saw postmodernist scholars questioning the validity of language boundaries and recognizing the simultaneous use of languages for meaning making and for making sense both of the world and of who one is (García, 2009; Heller, 2007; Makalela, 2014; Shohamy, 2006).

While it is evident that what people do with languages cannot be successfully controlled through the separation of languages into sealable boxes (Makalela, 2015; Makoni, 2003), orthodox educational practices, especially in higher education, still treat languages as isolated units in learning and teaching worldwide. Most teachers often take this isolationist approach to guard against 'cross-contamination' between languages, usually in favor of the target language or the medium of instruction (García, 2009; Makalela, 2013; Ricento & Hornberger, 1996; Shohamy, 2006). As I have shown elsewhere, the persistence of monoglossic language 'policing' attitudes is the inheritance of one-nation-one-language ideologies that permeated the majority thinking in Europe as late as the 19th century, as well as the mistaken belief that using more than one language creates mental confusion (Makalela, 2013, 2015).

Contrary to isolationist teaching practices, research on multilingual classrooms has shown that monolingualism is ineffective in enhancing school experience or offering the pedagogic and cognitive support needed for multilingual children to succeed (e.g. Creese & Blackledge, 2010). In order to depart from the orthodox classroom practices that dominate contemporary language pedagogy, and to situate the notion of fluidity from an African epistemology that disrupts boundaries between cultural and linguistic systems, I have designed a language course around the concept of *ubuntu*[1] that is epitomized by the mantra *I am because you are, you are because we are*. *Ubuntu* as a plural way of life mirrors an ecological interdependence of languages where one language is incomplete without the other (Makalela, 2015). In this chapter, I report on the effectiveness of using *ubuntu* principles for teaching and learning an African language in a South African higher education institution. I consider recommendations for a multilingual (re) turn, as understood from what I have coined *ubuntu translanguaging pedagogy* (UTP), and conclude by highlighting directions for future research.

South African Multilingualism: An Unbounded Beginning

South Africa is endowed with dynamic multilingualism that can be tracked as far back as to what is referred to as the Limpopo Valley – the northern part of South Africa alongside the Limpopo River – where indigenous people of different ethnic affiliations developed the oldest form of civilization in southern Africa (Cox, 1992; Jackson, 2001). Evidence suggests that the Nguni, Sotho, Khoe and San language groupings formed part of a large Mapungubwe territory, using language systems that overlapped without boundaries (Khoza, 2013). The inhabitants of Mapungubwe, which borders South Africa, Zimbabwe and Botswana (three countries that are part of what is today known as the Southern African Development Community), traded minerals, had livestock, intermarried and formed an interwoven network that was guided by a worldview of belonging together despite differences. According to Khoza (2013), *ubuntu* has its origin in the African conception of being, which creates a common bond and destiny for humanity. Here, 'the individual is absorbed into the collective, yet retains an identity as an empirical being' (Khoza, 2013: xx). This communal way of life and philosophy finds full expression in the value of interdependence and the interconnectedness of human beings and their cultural products, as represented by the mantra *I am because you are, you are because we are*. The story of Mapungubwe is a useful barometer to understand that precolonial southern Africa did not have discrete language systems that operated in isolation; instead, there was an amorphous repertoire that stretched beyond current linguistic codes (Cox, 1992; Makalela, 2005). In shifting the paradigms from what languages look like to what people do with languages, the social practices embedded in *ubuntu* provide a gaze into porous multilingual encounters that, correspondingly, are relevant to shaping language use in the postmonolingual age.

It should be stated that *ubuntu* language practices suffered a violent history of colonization and linguistic control by the Dutch, British and Afrikaners for approximately 400 years, when South African multilingual resources were forced into 'boxes' (Makoni, 2003) by foreign nationalists to advance the mission of divide and rule. For example, foreign missionary linguists assigned different orthographic representations to mutually intelligible languages because of their mistaken belief that Africa was the Tower of Babel with innumerable language varieties (Prah, 1998). In South Africa, missionaries created artificial boundaries, used under the Dutch and British colonial projects and later under the apartheid system, that divided the speakers of these language varieties into linguistic tribes from 1948 until 1994. From 1953 until the early 1990s, there were 10 reserves[2] that were founded on perceived differences between Bantu[3] languages, as established by apartheid architect Dr H.F. Verwoerd's decree that 'those who speak different languages should stay in different quarters' (Alexander, 1989: 21).

While South African language boundaries have been officially eliminated in the new sociopolitical dispensation that started in 1994, discrete linguistic units are still used administratively as strong identity markers, which are enshrined in the official language policy and practiced throughout the schooling system. It should be stressed that some linguists predicted in the earlier years of the new sociolinguistic dispensation that the constitutional commitment to 11 official languages (nine indigenous African languages plus Afrikaans and English) would legitimize 'artificial constructions' (Makalela, 2005) and 'misinventions' (Makoni, 2003) of these linguistic entities and that the outcome would be pedagogical practices that were borrowed wholesale from Western monolingual practices.

In more than 17 years of the constitutional commitment to multilingualism and several legislative frameworks such as the Language Policy for Higher Education (LPHE), it has remained difficult to implement the objectives of the multilingual policy. The LPHE specifically decreed that higher education institutions should promote multilingualism by, among other things, establishing language policies to be submitted to the Minister of Education (Department of Education, 2002) for monitoring and evaluation. In particular, the institutions were tasked to develop any one or two of the nine indigenous African languages as languages of learning and teaching. This policy was intended to increase pathways to knowledge and transform the linguistic dispensation where only English and Afrikaans are used as the media of learning and teaching. The higher education sector has, however, seen a stalemate of multilingual practices in historically English-medium universities, even though there has been notable progress toward English–Afrikaans bilingualism in historically Afrikaans-medium universities (Du Plessis, 2009; Makalela & McCabe, 2013). More conspicuously, the pedagogy of African languages, especially teaching African languages to speakers of other African languages as second languages in higher education, is relatively unknown, to date. Where some teaching practices exist in the higher education sector, separatist and monolingual approaches are frequent.

Translanguaging Framework

The interdisciplinary school of thought that links sociology, political science, sociolinguistics and ecology has questioned our understanding of language as a static category with a clear boundary that separates it from other languages. Representative studies by García (2009, 2011), Hornberger and Link (2012), Makoni (2003), Makoni and Pennycook (2007), Shohamy (2006) and Li (2011) have all revealed that old notions of additive bilingualism and stable diglossia have lost space in the global world because of their separatist orientation toward languages. Translanguaging is regarded as an alternative paradigm to describe unbounded, fluid, mobile and versatile uses of languages in the 21st century.

As a pedagogic strategy in bilingual classrooms, translanguaging can be traced back to the work of Cen Williams, who studied Welsh–English bilingual secondary-school learners' language practices in Wales (Baker, 2011; Li, 2011). As understood in its earliest version, translanguaging referred to a communicative function of receiving input in one language and giving output in another. This process allowed bilingual learners to use their home language and develop positive experiences at school. García (2009: 40) extended this practice to include multiple discursive practices where, unlike a bicycle with two balanced wheels, the discursive practices are perceived as 'more like an all-terrain vehicle whose wheels extend and contract, flex and stretch, making possible, over highly uneven ground, movement forward that is bumpy and irregular but also sustained and effective' (García, 2009: 45). Li looked further at the creativity and criticality of multilingual speakers, using a psycholinguistic notion of 'languaging' (Swain, 2006), which refers to the process of using language to gain knowledge, to make sense, to articulate one's thoughts and to communicate about using language (Li, 2011: 1223). For Li (2011: 1223), translanguaging 'is going on between different linguistic structures and systems, including different modalities and going beyond them'. He refers to the social space for multilingual language users as 'translanguaging space', which is an ongoing space created for language practices where multilingual speakers are constantly involved in making strategic situation-specific choices about the language systems they use to achieve a communicative goal (Li, 2011: 1222). Taken together, languaging practices suggest that classroom language practices can no longer be restricted to monolingualism, which can limit transformative, creative and critical occupation of language spaces inherent in multilingual classrooms.

Noteworthy is that translanguaging assumptions depart from 20th-century views about classroom language practices of bilingual learners. Research shows that teachers, under the auspices of maintenance bilingual education, have always encouraged monoglossic classroom practices (e.g. Blommaert, 2010; Li, 2011). García (2011) compares teachers' and language practitioners' roles and the strict separation of languages to a flower garden, where each plot is differentiated according to the colors of the flowers. Just as a gardener would prune overlapping flowers, use of the learners' home languages in multilingual classes was devalued and prohibited. García (2011: 7) observes that such language separatism enables language minorities to preserve their 'mother tongues'. This means that a separatist view of language and classifications of 'first', 'second' and 'mother tongue' do not fit the sociolinguistic realities of the majority of speakers in the 21st century. In order to take a more complex account of language use and match multilingual spaces in this century, the classroom language practices of multilingual learners should be characterized by a discursive practice of 'languaging', which is described as the 'social features that are called upon by speakers in a seamless and complex network of multiple semiotic signs' (García, 2011: 7).

Within a translanguaging framework, scholars consider language shift and the loss of minority languages and the role the schools play in both, and they prefer to replace the term 'language maintenance' with the metaphor of language sustainability. From this perspective, the notion of language maintenance is not a desirable end in that it perpetuates strict definitions of language as autonomous and as used by a specific group of people whose identity depends on it (Shohamy, 2006). Maintenance also makes claims about the purity of a language before it came into contact with other languages and before associated diaspora came into being (García, 2011; Pennycook, 2010). Given that the conservation of languages in their purest forms is no longer tenable, there is a need for sustainable models of language. Sustainability, which is dynamic and future oriented, is an alternative to maintenance, and it refers to a renewal of past language practices to meet the needs of the present without making compromises to future generations (García, 2011).

As explained in previous studies, one important distinction made in translanguaging scholarship is its relationship with code-switching (García, 2009; Makalela, 2014). Unlike code-switching, translanguaging does not refer to the use of two separate languages or the shift of one language or code to the other (Hornberger & Link, 2012). In translanguaging, speakers 'select language features and soft assemble their language practices in ways that fit their communicative needs' (García, 2011: 7). It is instructive to note that code-switching, on the one hand, often carries language-centered connotations of language interference, language transfer or borrowing of codes, which all have a monolingual orientation where languages are treated as separate codes. Translanguaging, on the other hand, shifts the lens from a cross-linguistic influence to how multilingual speakers intermingle linguistic features that are administratively assigned to a particular language or variety (Hornberger & Link, 2012: 263). In other words, code-switching is language centered and treats language systems as discrete units, while translanguaging is speaker centered and assumes unitary language systems, or what can be referred to as fuzzy interdependence of language systems (see also Makalela, 2014).

Research shows that, despite restrictions placed on bilingual children by dominant monolingual practices, bilinguals can transform restrictive monolingual landscapes. For example, Li (2011) investigated translanguaging spaces, using observations of multilingual practices and metalanguage commentaries by Chinese youths in British schools. A moment analysis of the multilingual environment in this study revealed that the Chinese learners created critical and creative spaces for themselves using the resources they had (Li, 2011: 1234), despite the dominant monolingual context in which they operated. In a different study on complementary schools in Britain, schools that have accepted translanguaging reported the success of their programs, especially in the establishment of identity positions, the endorsement of simultaneous literacies and keeping the pedagogic task moving (Creese & Blackledge, 2010: 113).

While translanguaging presents an opportunity to understand the worldview of the speakers of African languages in their plurality and advance their pedagogy based on languaging practices, very little is known about innovative practices in higher education. There is, therefore, a need for a systematic inquiry into translanguaging practices to establish the extent to which these varieties have permeated into higher education classroom interactions. In particular, there is a need to conceptualize language use and practices from an African worldview and contexts in the postapartheid era. This study reports on the efficacy of the explicit use of *ubuntu* translanguaging techniques in teaching African languages to speakers of other African languages.

Research Methods

This is a practice-based inquiry that involved a population of Sepedi second language student teachers at the Wits School of Education, University of the Witwatersrand. The participants were 20 second-year students with a mean age of 19.4 years. Their home languages include all the Nguni languages, namely, isiZulu, siSwati, isiXhosa and isiNdebele. The majority of the students come from Johannesburg townships,[4] where it is common for them to have proficiency in more than four languages by the age of six (see Makalela, 2013).

In order to promote multilingualism as prescribed in the LPHE (Department of Education, 2002), the Division of Languages, Literacies and Literatures (LLL) at the School of Education has developed a comprehensive program that offers preservice teachers language-major options in any of these five official languages: English, Sesotho, Sepedi, isiZulu and Afrikaans. Language specialization is an elective that forms part of the general bachelor of education degree. In addition, the division offers second-language courses for all students who are required to take an additional language that is not in the same language cluster as their mother tongues. These students are further restricted from taking the languages in which they have had formal school exposure. The overriding goal of the new languages program is to ensure that every student teacher masters at least one new language so that they are prepared for diverse multilingual classrooms while in service. The new language-teaching focus provides the student teachers with basic conversational, reading and writing abilities so that they are equipped to work with learners from languages other than the ones in their own clusters. In this case, students with Nguni language backgrounds described here could take Sesotho, Sepedi or Afrikaans as these are in a different cluster from their own.

Ubuntu Translanguaging Pedagogy

I have designed a course in Sepedi, one of South Africa's 11 official languages, around the UTP concept to disrupt perceived language boundaries among preservice student teachers and to recreate complex multilingual spaces that reflect the *ubuntu* principles of ecological interdependence. I sought to explore how the idea of *ubuntu* can be used as a resource to enhance discursive language learning spaces for students who come from hybrid and linguistically complex contexts. I used this epistemological orientation to conceptualize a multilingual classroom as an ecosystem where both its biocultural and biolinguistic diversities are requisite conditions for survival: that is, one linguistic entity does not survive without the other, as is decreed in the *ubuntu* value system of existence: *I am because you are, you are because we are.* When framed in this light, multilingual classrooms become havens of fluid, unbounded and interdependent repertoires through which students make sense of the world and become who they need to become.

As stated earlier, the Limpopo Valley is instructive in organizing a multilingual classroom. We have learned that multilingual speakers in Mapungubwe used their complex linguistic encounters to develop one of the foremost civilization centers in southern Africa. They used varieties of the Nguni, Khoe, San and Sotho languages discursively, without one common language. These languages reflected mutual interdependence and a porous discursive system of existence through which I designed the Sepedi course and the intentional pedagogic practice of UTP. The two-semester UTP included the following activities:

- Multilingual lexical contrasts – explicit attention to vocabulary use in three to five languages.
- Use of more than two reading-comprehension materials: students reading texts in one language and responding to questions in a different language, and vice versa.
- Listening in one language and speaking in another.
- Reading in one language and writing and speaking in other languages.
- Comparing and contrasting various cultural constructs in multiple languages.

As a multilingual instructor, it was not necessary that I had to master all the languages brought to class by my students. I needed, instead, to enable the students to explore their ideas through the linguistic resources they possessed, and I relied on their input to explain some of the language- or culture-specific constructs that were discussed in their groups. The classroom discourses in this course were carried out in Sepedi, isiZulu, isiXhosa, SiSwati, isiNdebele and English and permitted overlap between and within students' utterances. To avoid focusing on language structure, as would be the case in grammar-translation pedagogy, I adopted a multilingual communicative approach where the emphasis was on what the students do with the language: greetings, introducing oneself and giving directions in more than one language, for example. This approach offered me an open-ended space to react to grammatical items as they emerged in situated language use and then use my instructor's intuition to determine whether the language error would impede mutual comprehension.

As a multilingual teacher of African languages and English, UTP transformed my practice from a monolingual grammar-translation method toward a communal space where languages of input and output were juxtaposed throughout the lessons. The students, for their part, were encouraged to think in at least two languages (something they already do in their daily practices) and explicitly draw comparisons and contrast ideas represented through the languages. This was not a direct reproduction of linguistic forms, as is the case with translation, but it was a development of meaning and overlapping of meaning units across a number of languages of writing and speaking.

Data Collection and Analysis

There were two phases of data collection to assess the effects of using UTP as a pedagogic strategy in the course. First, I asked 20 students to participate in two groups (10 each) of a focus-group discussion to reflect on the use of UTP. I used Sepedi and English in the conversations and allowed students to respond in any of the Nguni home languages they used during the classroom interactions. Second, I organized a follow-up interview schedule with six students who were purposefully selected on the basis of their previous comments in the focus groups. The purpose of this follow-up interview was to triangulate the data and to gain a deeper understanding of their metacognitive reflections about the use of UTP as a pedagogic tool in the course. In both phases of data collection, the student participants performed translanguaging (i.e. used more than one language while engaged in the meaning-making process) in their responses to questions and clarification of ideas throughout the discussions. After the audio-recorded data were transcribed, I used deductive and inductive thematic approaches where the coding and theme development were directed by both the content of the data and existing concepts (*ubuntu* translanguaging opportunities). This hybrid model of data analysis provided a rich base for assessment of how the student teachers experienced UTP as a meditating and socializing strategy for epistemic access and development of their identities.

Results

The results of the study show that *ubuntu* multilingualism is a useful classroom resource with multiple pathways for accessing a target language and culture and an inclusive act that valorizes what the students bring with them to class. The responses are broadly represented in the following themes: (i) linguistic *ubuntu*, (ii) the way we talk *ko kasi*, (iii) language continuum and (iv) fuzzy imagined community. Each of these themes is presented next.

Linguistic *ubuntu*

The results of the study show that UTP offers a unique space for students to transform their linguistic identities to a plural orientation of self. Mbali's reflection about the techniques used in class is a typical response:

Mbali: Well, at first I was not sure why we were asked to take African languages at university. It didn't make sense to me 'cause when you go to work only English will be used. We came to university to polish our English so we can get better jobs. You know even in schools, private schools and better-performing schools will hire someone whose English is good. I really thought that African languages have no chance and saw no reason to study an African language especially at varsity. You know, but now I realize that it is not necessary to treat English and African languages as completely different languages that cannot interact in class. Using all the languages while learning

Sepedi made me see that as speakers of these languages we are connected. *Ke ithutile* [I learned] something *ka classeng ye ya Sepedi* [in this Sepedi class], especially when we freely used other languages in the same lesson to think and express ourselves. Now I know *gore* [that] I can face *bana ba sekolo* [school kids] from different Sotho languages *ke sa tshabe* [without fear]

In this extract, Mbali reports on the stereotype she had about African languages and how she previously believed that English is the only language that should be learned at university in preparation for the world of work. In her analysis, the world of work includes the teaching profession, where English is used as the medium of learning and teaching. The UTP practice in this course has, however, made her realize the need to understand other languages and to access multiple languages in the same course. Her next focus is on how the course has enabled her to face the multilingual schools, where many languages coexist. What we see here is a change of attitude from negative stereotypes to an appreciation of African languages as vehicles for knowledge construction and identity affirmation at university. In the last part of the extract, Mbali performs translanguaging where English and Sepedi are blended in her argument about the benefits of using more than one language in a classroom. The UTP practices thus have the potential to instigate the appropriation of multilingualism and create spaces for more languages to be used in the same lesson. In this context, therefore, UTP serves as a catalyst for a transformative identity construction to shift students' lens toward an *ubuntu* orientation that is inclusive, flexible, broad and accommodative.

The way we talk *ko kasi*

The second observable aspect of the translanguaging class is the positive learning experience that the students had throughout the year. Most of the respondents reported that they had enjoyed the experience of learning an additional language because of the techniques that were applied in this class: giving output and receiving input in different languages. This response is represented in Extract 2:

Makhozi: This is different from learning in the language I don't understand. I never thought about it this way. It is my first time in the whole schooling life to attend a class where use of more than one language is appreciated and encouraged. I am used to hearing teachers saying we must not use other languages in their classes even though we would use them anyway. Just like where I come from, we just use any language we feel anytime. At my high school too I remember us using isiZulu, isiXhosa, and some Sesotho while discussing life science topics. No one gave us permission; it felt so natural because it is the way we talk *ko kasi* [in the location]. When I was using English, I felt so much like an outsider and half of the time I just switched off from the stuff I was learning. It felt so good to be able to use the languages I knew while learning a new language.

Makhozi provides a historical account of what learning a language looked like in her high school experience. She claims that while school policies gave preference to one language in their classroom, and some teachers tried to enforce a one-language-at-a-time rule, learners always 'language' privately in ways that connect them to the natural ways in which their communities communicate; in other words, using multiple languages in the same utterance, as in 'the way we talk *ko kasi*'. Instead of being constrained by language policing in their preuniversity education, Makhozi reports that this course gave them the freedom to use many languages and alternated them systematically to enhance access to learning Sepedi as a second language. Here, UTP resonates with natural communication strategies used in most Black townships where the languages of input and output are juxtaposed, as in this extract. The UTP techniques applied in this course are situated social practices that replicate both what is socially acceptable in these townships and the precolonial linguistic dispensation of language interdependence in Mapungubwe.

Language continuum

Previous research on classroom translanguaging (e.g. Li, 2011; Madiba, 2014; Makalela, 2014) showed that its discourse practices are indicative of a societal multilingualism where languages are embedded in speakers' everyday ways of meaning making. The results of this study affirm this viewpoint, as shown next in Nomfundo and Banele's dialogue:

Nomfundo: You know this style is same as the township lingo we use when talking to one another. It was frustrating at first and *nna* [me] I didn't know *gore* [that] it's possible to use many languages in the same class. I always thought I was wrong when I speak this way at school, but now I can be confident that it is possible to use it *ko classing* [in class]. *Yazi yini, nna* [you know what] I realized *gore* [that] I could use the Sepedi knowledge to talk with Basotho le Batswana *mang'fika elokshene* [when

I arrive at the location]. The speaking activities in class extended my use of Setswana and Sesotho with their speakers. They told me that they understood me when I try to talk. So the course helped me *kuthi ngi khulume* [so that I can speak] across. The course also just made it clear to me that it's normal to mix languages and that I understand better when more languages are used because I can compare.

Banele: *Le nna ke kgona ukukhuluma* [I too am able to speak] when I meet Tswanas, Sothos here on campus and if I visit with a friend over the weekend.

Nomfundo: *U hlalaphi wena?* [Where do you stay?]

Banele: *Ke tswa Ga-Maja* [I am from Ga-Maja] in Limpopo *mara* [but] I grew up in Attridgeville.

Nomfundo: *Mina* [Me] I'm from Alexander. *Si chizanyama* [We have meat barbecues] most of the time.

Nomfundo and Banele report on the experiences of using Sepedi across a wider spectrum of its sister languages, Setswana and Sesotho. When they meet speakers of these languages outside the classroom space, communication occurs fluidly despite the fact that they had no direct instruction in these sister languages. In addition, the UTP mode of mixing languages felt natural to Nomfundo and Banele, because it reflected familiar discourse patterns that are prevalent in their communities.

The dialogue shows a typical *ubuntu* translanguaging performance as follows: In the first extract, Nomfundo uses English but chooses words like the personal pronoun *nna* [me] and the preposition *ko* [at], which are derived from Sepedi and Sesotho languages. The next sentence begins with *yazini* for 'you know what?' and then *mangfike elokshene*, 'when I arrive at the location' and *kuthi ngi khulume*, 'that I speak', which are typical in all the Nguni languages. All of these utterances show that Nomfundo blends English, Sotho and Nguni languages through a continuum of meaning units that crosses preset linguistic boundaries. Banele uses three language units, Sepedi, isiZulu and English, to concur that she had similar language experiences in the class. For example, *'le nna ke kgona ukukhuluma'* has blended several Sotho languages and Nguni languages to mean 'I am also able to speak'. Nomfundo asks a question in isiZulu and receives a response in Sepedi, which is mixed with English in the same utterance. While the student teachers provide information about their experiences in the course that used UTP, their performance of languages shows that they use a repertoire that extends beyond the official language divisions. UTP thus provides spaces for students to behave, identify and reason through a continuum of their linguistic repertoires.

Imagined fuzzy community

The data sets show that one of the reasons the students learned Sepedi as a second language is that they had imagined they would be a part of the Sepedi community in a complex linguistic and cultural encounter that has no strict language boundaries. Norton (2000) and Pavlenko and Norton (2007) use the notion of identity investment to refer to language learners' views of themselves in relation to the social use of a language in the distant future. One distinguishing feature of the students' experiences in the UTP class was that the course changed their self-concept and their view on how the new language adds to their capital for use in the future. The following dialogue explicates this idea:

Jabulani:	I liked the way the class made me feel at home and belonging. It is always a struggle for me to change from who I am and become a different person in class. The class has for the first time in my life made it easy for me to feel I have brought myself in class and I love the feel of it.
Sipho:	Mina *ngi cabanga ukuthi* eclass ye ya Sepedi *e tla thusa hore ma ke ruta* as a teacher *ngi* teach in Sepedi schools here in Gauteng. I can talk to *abantwana ba* Sepedi and understand them very well. [I think this Sepedi class will help when I teach in Sepedi communities here in Gauteng. I can talk to children and understand them very well.]
Jabulani:	Yeah, I think so too.
Themba:	*Nna ke nahana gore nka thola le mosadi wa Mopedi* [I think I can find a Mopedi woman] if I use this language.
Jabulani:	How about a company where your clients *ba* [are] from all Sotho languages? *Nna ke batla ecompany ya* communications. [I need a communications company.]
Sipho:	*Mara ke the way re buang ka teng ge re le ka kasi. Nna ke bona gore a se Basotho fela re tla bolelang le bona*; it's everyone. Fine, I learned Sepedi, but *ko kasi ha gona motho yo a buang pure* Sepedi. Class *ye* helped me to be my true self when it comes to *amalanguage*. [But it is the way we speak in the location. I see that it is not only speakers of Sotho languages I am prepared for; it's everyone. I learned Sepedi, but the location does not have people who only speak Sepedi. The class helped me to be my true self when it comes to languages.]

In this extract, Jabulani, Themba and Sipho contemplate future uses of Sepedi in relation to the Sepedi communities where the language is predominantly used. They also report on how the course has opened a space where the capital of knowing Sepedi can be utilized. However, they are aware that it is virtually impossible to find a pure Sepedi community, and as a result they prepare themselves for a fuzzy space of translanguaging, which, for Themba, includes marrying a Sepedi-speaking woman. As seen in the previous extract, the interactions between the speakers show that there is variation within and between languages of input and output and that this type of interaction permits the flow of information between the speakers. The first utterance from Nomfundo is in English, but Themba responds in different languages (Nguni and Sotho language groups). Themba speaks in blended Sotho languages that follow the English utterance from Jabulani ('Yeah, I think so too'). Beyond this linguistic blending, the speakers imagine their future identities and imagine themselves among Sepedi communities. Themba, in particular, being able to use the linguistic capital he gained in this course, sees himself marrying a Sepedi-speaking woman. Sipho, on the other hand, observes that learning Sepedi in the fluid translanguaging space has prepared him for a more complex multilingual community. In a sense, he states that he is from this type of community and the class has valorized his experiences outside of school and given him confidence to be a translanguager. I refer to this concept as an imagined fuzzy community that begins with multilingualism as a norm, not an exception.

Discussion: *Ubuntu* Translanguaging

The main research question for the study was whether using UTP would be effective in enhancing preservice language teachers' acquisition of Sepedi as a second language in an institution of higher learning. The results of the study revealed positive experiences of adopting UTP principles that are oriented to the simultaneous use of more than one language in the same lesson and intentionally breaking boundaries between the target language and the linguistic repertoires that students bring with them to class. This potpourri of techniques to master language and cultural practices is at the core of the UTP approach, which goes beyond the exchange of one language of input and another of output as in the original conceptual framing by Cen Williams (Baker, 2011). The UTP approach demonstrated both a vertical and a horizontal phenomenon, where more than two languages were used for input and another two or more used for output as normal multilingual pathways to know and to be (García & Li, 2014).

One of the findings of the study is that translanguaging provided students with multilingual spaces to transform personal identities that had been curtailed by monolingual experiences prior to university. That is, the students gravitated from perceiving themselves as belonging to a particular language group to viewing themselves as users of languages that extend beyond discrete language boundaries. Their positive attitude toward another African language became a strong indicator of how well they performed in the language, without devaluing their own home languages. As shown in this chapter, it is important to restate that the interdependent nature of southern African societies and their linguistic repertoires are naturally endowed with dynamic multilingualism as found in the cradle of the southern African civilization, the Limpopo Valley, in which human and linguistic separations are blurred while interdependence is valued over independence (Khoza, 2013). I have referred to this system of communication where more than two languages are blended and used in horizontal and vertical pathways as a complex enactment of *ubuntu* translanguaging. When framed in this light, *ubuntu* translanguaging is based on human and linguistic repertoires that are porous, overlapping, fluid and flexible in an ecological system of interdependence.

The results of the study also point out the need to reconceptualize classroom spaces as microcosms of societal multilingualism. What was revealing in the results was that the translanguaging techniques validated what is already practiced in society and that many students saw, although in disbelief, that the classroom languaging experiences were not different from their own linguistic behaviors outside of class. In addition, their performances of translanguaging showed that the boundaries between traditional language labels such as home language and mother tongue are fluid (García, 2009; Hornberger & Link, 2012; Li, 2011). The conversations showed, in particular, that the boundaries between Sotho and Nguni languages no longer hold in the Black townships and that this linguistic complexity reflected their multilingual ways of meaning making and accessing knowledge about the world. In a nutshell, UTP facilitates a breakaway from artificial language boundaries and a reconnection with the African worldview of *ubuntu*, which propagates a communal orientation and a dynamic continuum of social and linguistic resources. The use of Sepedi in the context of other African languages typifies a return to this type of multilingualism, where more than two languages are used to enhance knowledge transmission and to become.

Finally, the use of UTP approaches in the Sepedi class has revealed that the student teachers' own identities as members of a Sepedi community have shifted and expanded. Some of the student teachers had imagined fitting into Sepedi culture and communities as understood alongside the identity-investment notion that learning a language has social capital that can be utilized in the future (Norton, 2000) and that language learners have an expectation to fit well within imagined communities of native speakers (Pavlenko & Norton, 2007). This type of investment is liberating for historically separated languages, and it affirms merging linguistic identities of contemporary multilingual speakers.

Conclusion

In this chapter, I have described both the recalled experiences of UTP and the translanguaging performances of university students in teaching Sepedi to speakers of other African languages at the University of the Witwatersrand. The results of the study show, first, that the preservice student teachers have adopted the UTP approach to increase their linguistic repertoires and assume multilingual identities that cut across their ethnolinguistic boundaries.

Second, the study shows that UTP can be used as a methodology that is linguistically and culturally transformative. This occurs by transforming the classroom space into a microcosm of societal multilingualism and offering constant affirmation of linguistic and cultural communities that are porous, fluid and versatile in language learning activities. Here, the interdependent nature of languages was conceived from the ancient African value system of *ubuntu*, where one language is incomplete without the other. The classroom space saw a rebirth of dynamic multilingualism that had been devalued throughout the colonial and apartheid periods. In other words, the classroom interaction epitomized *ubuntu* translanguaging as had been the case in Mapungubwe.

Beyond the use of UTP as a teachable technique, the results of the study show that translanguaging experiences in complex multilingual situations produce different identity investments from the ones postulated in previous studies (e.g. Norton, 2000; Pavlenko & Norton, 2007). Here, I have shown that there is both a vertical and a horizontal input–output exchange in more than two languages in either direction. In *ubuntu* translanguaging practices, the imagined communities in an *ubuntu* landscape are complex, concentrated and fuzzy in tandem with everyday ways of making sense of the world and complex identity constructions of the speakers. The use of UTP and other translanguaging discourse practices remain innovative steps toward a fully fledged multilingual return that counteracts monolingual bias in language and content classrooms in higher education. There is a need for further research on UTP in other complex multilingual contexts to fill in the void on transliteracies worldwide.

Notes

(1)   *Ubuntu* is a worldview and a way of life shared across a wider spectrum of speakers of Bantu languages in sub-Saharan Africa. The stem /-ntu/ refers to the interconnectedness of human existence as derived from the African mythology that human beings come from the reed. The sense of interconnection is found in the mantra *I am because you are, you are because we are*. The author has used this idea to coin the concept '*ubuntu* translanguaging' to stress the fuzzy interdependence (vs. independence) of human languages imbued by African multilingualism that predated European colonization.

(2)   Bantustan homelands were created on the basis of language difference and were extended into the labor reserves (townships), where speakers of 'different'

languages were assigned different geographical spaces. White people, in contrast, lived in the towns and cities reserved strictly for them.

(3) Bantu languages constitute about 80% of the languages spoken in sub-Saharan Africa. The nine indigenous African languages in South Africa belong to this group.

(4) Townships were created as labor reserves for Black people during apartheid. As with the Bantustan homeland system, the townships were segregated on the basis of language difference to divide and control the labor force.

References

Alexander, N. (1989) *Language Policy and National Unity in South Africa/Azania*. Cape Town: Buchu.

Baker, C. (2011) *Foundations of Bilingual Education and Bilingualism* (5th edn). Bristol: Multilingual Matters.

Blommaert, J. (2010) *The Sociolinguistics of Globalization*. Cambridge: Cambridge University Press.

Cox, G. (1992) *African Empires and Civilization: Ancient and Medieval*. New York: Pan African Publishing.

Creese, A. and Blackledge, A. (2010) Translanguaging in the bilingual classroom: A pedagogy for learning and teaching? *The Modern Language Journal* 94 (1), 103–115.

Department of Education (2002) *Language Policy Plan for Higher Education*. Pretoria: Government Printers.

Du Plessis, T. (2009) From monolingual to bilingual higher education: The repositioning of historically Afrikaans-medium universities in South Africa. *Language Policy* 5, 87–113.

García, O. (2009) *Bilingual Education in the 21st Century: A Global Perspective*. Malden, MA: Wiley/Blackwell.

García, O. (2011) From language garden to sustainable languaging: Bilingual education in a global world. *Perspectives* 34 (1), 5–9.

García, O. and Li, W. (2014) *Translanguaging: Language, Bilingualism, and Education*. New York: Palgrave.

Heller, M. (2007) Bilingualism as ideology and practice. In M. Heller (ed.) *Bilingualism: A Social Approach* (pp. 1–24). Basingstoke: Palgrave.

Hornberger, N. and Link, H. (2012) Translanguaging and transnational literacies in multilingual classrooms: A biliteracy lens. *International Journal of Bilingual Education and Bilingualism* 15, 261–278.

Jackson, J.G. (2001) *Introduction to African Civilizations*. New York: Citadel.

Khoza, R. (2013) *Let Africa Lead: African Transformational Leadership for 21st Century Business*. Johannesburg: Vezubuntu.

Li, W. (2011) Moment analysis and translanguaging space: Discursive construction of identities by multilingual Chinese youth in Britain. *Journal of Pragmatics* 43, 1222–1235.

Madiba, M. (2014) Promoting concept literacy through multilingual glossaries: A translanguaging approach. In C. van der Walt and L. Hibbert (eds) *Multilingual Teaching and Learning in Higher Education in South Africa* (pp. 68–87). Bristol: Multilingual Matters.

Makalela, L. (2005) 'We speak eleven tongues': Reconstructing multilingualism in South Africa. In B. Brock-Utne and R. Hopson (eds) *Languages of Instruction for African Emancipation: Focus on Postcolonial Contexts and Considerations* (pp. 147–174). Cape Town and Dar-es-Salaam: CASAS and Mkuki n Nyota.

Makalela, L. (2013) Translanguaging in Kasi-taal: Rethinking old language boundaries for new language planning. *Stellenbosch Papers in Linguistics Plus* 42, 111–125.

Makalela, L. (2014) Teaching indigenous African languages to speakers of other African languages: The effects of translanguaging for multilingual development. In C. van der Walt and L. Hibbert (eds) *Multilingual Teaching and Learning in Higher Education in South Africa* (pp. 88–104). Bristol: Multilingual Matters.

Makalela, L. (2015) Moving out of linguistic boxes: The effects of translanguaging strategies for multilingual classrooms. *Language and Education* 29 (3), 200–217.

Makalela, L. and McCabe, R. (2013) Monolingualism in a historically Black South African university: A case of inheritance. *Linguistics and Education* 24 (4), 406–414.

Makoni, S. (2003) From misinvention to disinvention of language: Multilingualism and the South African constitution. In S. Makoni, G. Smithermann, A. Ball and A. Spears (eds) *Black Linguistics: Language, Society and Politics in Africa and the Americas* (pp. 132–149). London and New York: Routledge.

Makoni, S. and Pennycook, A. (eds) (2007) *Disinventing and Reconstituting Languages*. Clevedon: Multilingual Matters.

May, S. (2012) The disciplinary constraints of second language acquisition and TESOL: Additive bilingualism and SLA, teaching and learning. *Linguistics and Education* 22 (3), 233–247.

Norton, B. (2000) *Identity and Language Learning: Gender, Ethnicity and Educational Change*. Harlow: Pearson Education/Longman.

Pavlenko, A. and Norton, B. (2007) Imagined communities, identity, and English language teaching. In J. Cummins and C. Davison (eds) *International Handbook of English Language Teaching* (pp. 669–680). New York: Springer.

Pennycook, A. (2010) *Language as Local Practice*. London: Routledge.

Prah, K. (1998) *Between Extinction and Distinction: Harmonization and Standardization of African Languages*. Johannesburg: Witwatersrand University Press.

Ricento, T. and Hornberger, N. (1996) Unpeeling the onion: Language planning and policy and the ELT professional. *TESOL Quarterly* 30 (3), 401–426.

Shohamy, E. (2006) *Language Policy: Hidden Agendas and New Approaches*. London: Routledge.

Swain, M. (2006) Languaging, agency, and collaboration in advanced second language proficiency. In H. Byrness (ed.) *Advanced Language Learning: The Contributions of Halliday and Vygotsky* (pp. 95–108). London: Continuum.

3 A Call for (Trans)languaging: The Language Profiles at Roskilde University

Petra Daryai-Hansen, Sonja Barfod and Lena Schwarz

Introduction

Translanguaging (García, 2009), *plurilingualism* (Moore & Gajo, 2009), *plurilanguaging* (Makoni & Makoni, 2010), *polylingualism* (Jørgensen *et al.*, 2011) – there exists a wide range of theoretical terms defining language competences as individualized, integrated, dynamic and contextualized (Daryai-Hansen *et al.*, 2015). Such sociolinguistically grounded conceptualizations are supported by psycholinguistic research in the field of language acquisition, emphasizing that languages are connected and integrated in one system (Herdina & Jessner, 2002). They are also promoted as part of a paradigm shift, such as by the Council of Europe's (2007, 2010) supranational plurilingual language policies.

In educational practice, however, ideologies of languages as segmented, pure entities are still dominant (Castellotti & Moore, 2010; Daryai-Hansen *et al.*, 2015). This is reflected, for example, as Candelier *et al.* (2012: 25) note, in the Common European Framework of Reference's 'scales of proficiency... considering each language individually'. The idea of monolingualism is also reflected on a language-policy level: Internationalization in Denmark – as in most countries – nowadays takes place within an English-only monolingual educational system. In Grin's (2013) terms, there is a strong tendency toward 'uniformization', and its effect, as Mortensen *et al.* (2012: 197) emphasize, is 'linguistic uniformity and cultural narrow-mindedness'. In Denmark, a so-called parallel language policy has been introduced, promoting English as the international language and Danish as the local language (Thøgersen, 2010). Other languages are excluded by this concept (Daryai-Hansen, 2010). Languages such as German and French, mandatory second foreign languages in Denmark, are suffering from a so-called transitional problem that manifests itself most strongly in the tertiary educational sector (Andersen, 2010: 4).

Because of global, national, institutional and individual needs, there is, as Risager (2012) points out, a need to implement a plurilingual language policy at 'international' universities that would recognize and develop the existence of linguistic diversity. Since 2012, Roskilde University (RUC), Denmark, has offered supplementary, curriculum-related courses in French, German and Spanish to all students in the bachelor's programs within the humanities and social sciences (Bojsen, 2015; Daryai-Hansen & Kraft, 2014) with the aim of promoting all students as 'multilingual subjects' (Kramsch, 2010). RUC's language profiles also put the aforementioned paradigm shift into educational practice, thereby bridging the gap between plurilingual theory and monolingual practice. The students in the program are explicitly asked to use *translanguaging* (García, 2009) in order to enhance their *languaging* (Jørgensen, 2010); in other words, they are invited to use translanguaging strategies in order to achieve interactional and social aims. We distinguish between these two concepts as follows: Languaging is the everyday communication practice, where individuals transcend norms and use language(s) in order to achieve interactional and social aims. Languaging can, from our perspective, be practiced integrating *intra*linguistic variation, without necessarily including other languages (*inter*linguistic variation). The concept of translanguaging is, in the following, defined as a languaging practice that integrates other languages, based on a pedagogical principle that deliberately draws on students' plurilingual competences.

The chapter will introduce the design and the learning objectives of RUC's language profiles and discuss, using the language profiles as an example, how translanguaging practices and policies can be described on supra, macro, meso, micro and nano levels. We focus on teachers' and students' translanguaging practices and their attitudes toward translanguaging in language teaching and learning. The content analysis (Mayring, 2000) is based on three data sets: (1) the audio record of students' and teachers' translanguaging practices, (2) questionnaires on students' attitudes toward translanguaging practices and (3) audio-recorded semistructured qualitative interviews with teachers. The research design can, in accordance with Grothjahn's (1987) types of research traditions in applied linguistics, be characterized as exploratory, qualitative and interpretive (Grothjahn's Paradigm 1). The data collection will be scrutinized to glean insight from different perspectives into these translanguaging practices and evaluations. We use theory dialogically to inform the data analysis. Our approach is both deductive and inductive. The focus is on further developing the theoretical understanding of translanguaging practices and attitudes toward these practices in a higher education context based on our data.

The Language Profiles at Roskilde University

In autumn 2012, RUC introduced French, German and Spanish language profiles based on a policy that was initiated by the teachers and strongly supported by the university management. The program aims at giving all students in the bachelor's programs within the humanities and social sciences the opportunity to reinforce their plurilingual and intercultural competences in a second foreign language related to their studies. The students choosing the program are, in the Common European Framework of Reference (CEFR) terminology, independent or proficient users of the profile languages. The program aims to develop the students' capacity to 'function as knowledge workers in a globalized, transnational and plurilingual context, both in public and private work settings' (Den humanistiske bacheloruddannelse, 2013: 2; Den samfundsvidenskabelige bacheloruddannelse, 2013: 39). The learning objectives are defined in terms of knowledge, skills and competences:

- Knowledge about and competences in text reading (reading strategies) and the ability to analyze social processes where several national, ethnic or social cultures are involved
- Knowledge about and competences in information searching within the language profile
- Competence to communicate and disseminate academic knowledge in French, German or Spanish, oral as well as written, and to continually improve these competences autonomously (Den samfundsvidenskabelige bacheloruddannelse, 2013)

The program is inspired by the Content and Language Integrated Learning approach, integrating both content learning and language learning focusing on the dimensions *language of learning, language for learning* and *language through learning* (Coyle *et al.*, 2010: 37). The program requires approximately 20 credit hours per semester (and a maximum of six semesters' attendance), in addition to which the students are encouraged to work independently with their profile language, linking the program to their project work. At RUC, 50% of the bachelor's program is based on interdisciplinary and problem-oriented academic project work in groups (Jensen & Olesen, 1999). The language profiles are designed for and benefit from this specific academic context. Students learn to find relevant theoretical, methodological or empirical literature for their project work in their profile language independently.

The language profiles' content is multifaceted. In the German profile, the content includes knowledge of significant theoretical perspectives in the humanities and social sciences, developed by German-speaking theorists (e.g. Gadamer, Honneth, Marx); knowledge about German-speaking countries (e.g. politics, economics, culture) and German languages; and skills to talk about German languages and cultures as well as to analyze and compare specific linguistic and cultural phenomena. It also includes general study skills such as reading, information searching and communication strategies, and a focus on attitudes. For example, students read articles about dominant attitudes toward Germany in Denmark (cf. Schramm, 2010) and reflect upon stereotyping, including their own. The program is based on collaborative learning (Wenger, 1999), where at the end of each semester, the students present and discuss this content with their peers and teachers at evaluation seminars.

The students define their progression themselves, choosing whether they want to make their presentations in the profile language or in Danish. In order to acquire a language profile certificate, the students have to demonstrate in the evaluation seminar that they have met all the learning objectives. In their final semester, the requirement is that both the presentation and the discussion are held in the profile language. Furthermore, in the evaluation seminars, the students evaluate and reflect on their learning process.

Translanguaging at Roskilde University

Translanguaging manifests itself at RUC at several levels. This can be elaborated on based on the Council of Europe's distinction between the *multilingualism of societies*, referring to 'a geographical area, large or small' (Council of Europe, 2014), and the *plurilingualism of individuals* (cf. Cavalli *et al.*, 2009). This distinction can be further elaborated through Beacco *et al.*'s (2010) five curriculum levels for the implementation of plurilingual and intercultural education:

> Development and implementation of a curriculum cover numerous activities on various levels of the education system: international (supra), national/regional (macro), school (meso), class, teaching group or teacher (micro) or even individual (nano). (Beacco *et al.*, 2010: 7)

Based on these supra-level conceptualizations of plurilingual education, we suggest distinguishing between the overlapping and interacting dimensions as follows: The development of individual plurilingualism lies at the center of the language profile (*nano level*). This development is supported by enhancing multilingualism at RUC as a geographical area, at the *meso level* through RUC's internationalization strategy and at the *micro level* through the implementation of the language profiles by the respective teachers. RUC's internationalization strategy is supported on the *macro level* through the Danish government's internationalization action plan, where the language profiles are represented – because of their plurilingual approach – as an innovation within modern language education in Danish higher education (Regeringen, 2013: 41).

On the basis of the aforementioned differentiation, translanguaging as pedagogical principle and practice can be described and investigated on different levels. The first level might be called a *translanguaging policy at the meso level*. RUC can be described as a multilingual geographical area with Danish and English as official academic languages. However, because of the plurilingual repertoire of students and teachers, other languages are, in practice, also represented in RUC's multilingual setting, such as in student–teacher and student–student interactions (cf. the CALPIU project; Hazel & Mortensen, 2013). With the language profiles, French, German and Spanish as academic languages are officially integrated outside language study programs and offered to all bachelor's students. These languages complement academic work in Danish and English.

At the second level, defined as a *translanguaging practice at the micro level*, the translanguaging policy is put into practice. For example, students search for literature in French, German and Spanish as a supplement to literature in Danish and English. They disseminate knowledge gained, both in the language profile context and in their primarily Danish- and English-grounded academic project group work.

Furthermore, students are explicitly asked to use translanguaging strategies to interact in their profile language. The emphasis on correctness and the monolingual ideology of pure and separate languages, which are still dominant in language learning and teaching, are replaced in the language profiles by an educational call for languaging and translanguaging. In their first semester, students are invited to reflect on monolingual ideologies. The teachers present this ideology as being in opposition to observable everyday practice in multilingual settings, where the interlocutors draw on their shared plurilingual repertoire to interact. In other words, translanguaging is represented as a common communication strategy implemented in the language profile program by the teachers, which the students are explicitly asked to draw upon. The program thus reflects on a meta level on language representations as constructions being produced and reproduced, and it thereby creates a space for metalanguage, which, as Jaworski *et al.* (2004: 3) state, 'can work on an ideological level, and influence people's actions and priorities in a wide range of ways'.

In the following, we will analyze data from the German language profile that shows how the translanguaging practice at the micro level is implemented and evaluated by individual teachers. Furthermore, we will focus on the third level, which might be called *translanguaging practice at the nano level*: Are the students of the German language profile using translanguaging practices? How do they embrace and implement multiple strategies for translanguaging?

Translanguaging Practices in the Language Profiles

From translanguaging policy to translanguaging practices

The following content analysis is based on audio data recorded during the evaluation seminars in the fall semester of 2013, containing 10:59 hours of 17 student presentations followed by discussions.

Our data show that students actively contribute to integrating German as an academic language into RUC's multilingual geographical area. In the first semester's evaluation seminars, students are not expected to make their presentation in the profile language. However, 11 of the 16 students did so. By choosing deliberately to use German to present the academic content they have investigated, the students implement RUC's overall translanguaging policy. The discussions were also started mostly in German, and some students spoke German almost exclusively. The teachers spoke German as the default interaction medium during the evaluation seminar.

In the evaluation seminars, both teachers' and students' interactions were based on the translanguaging principle. They used the language resources they had access to – primarily German and Danish – productively and receptively in their languaging practices. In the following, we will describe how this translanguaging practice within the translanguaging policy takes place at the micro level (teachers) and at the nano level (students).

To present these practices, we draw on Ferguson (2003), who, on the basis of a wider literature review, distinguishes between three broad categories to describe, at the micro level, pedagogical functions of language alternation (in Ferguson's terminology, code-switching, or CS) in classroom settings, where content subjects are taught through a foreign-language medium:

i.   CS for curriculum access. Basically, to help pupils understand the subject matter of their lessons.
ii. CS for classroom management discourse. E.g. to motivate, discipline and praise pupils and to signal a change of footing.
iii. CS for interpersonal relations. E.g. to humanize the affective climate of the classroom and to negotiate different identities. (Ferguson, 2003: 39)

In our data, very few examples of translanguaging practice attributable to classroom management discourse (ii) and interpersonal relations (iii) are to be found. This can be explained, concerning (ii), by the fact that we are in a higher education context and, in respect to (iii), by the fact that German, used as the default language by two teachers whose first language is German, also serves to establish interpersonal relations. Therefore, in the following, we focus on Ferguson's category (i), curriculum access. In contrast to Ferguson, who constructs students as objects to teach, the language profiles acknowledge students as co-creators of the curriculum. The students and their project work provide, to a large extent, the content of the language profiles. The curriculum used in the language profiles has two main dimensions: a content dimension and a linguistic dimension. To give students and teachers access to these two dimensions – the highly complex content and the language needed to interact with this content – both teachers and students use translanguaging practices.

Translanguaging is implemented in the language profiles as pedagogical principle. Thereby, the monolingual norm of language classroom interaction is avoided. In the following, we will, based on our data, show how this translanguaging teaching and learning environment is constructed by the teachers and students: What kind of translanguaging practices do they use? We will show how translanguaging practices are used to negotiate the principle of translanguaging, we will give examples of receptive and productive translanguaging practices and, finally, we will show how translanguaging is used by both students and teachers to facilitate the students' language learning.

Translanguaging practice to negotiate the principles of translanguaging

Both students and teachers use translanguaging strategies to reflect the translanguaging practice characteristic of the language profiles: They draw on languages' metalinguistic function or, in Cameron's (2004: 311) terminology, their 'metalinguistic potential'.

Some students use the introductory phase of their presentation to negotiate the language profiles' translanguaging concept. These students are, as the excerpts show, reassured by the teachers or by both teachers and students:

T:	Gut, jetzt kannst du anfangen. [Good, now you can start.] (German, GE)
S:	Jeg har lige et spørgsmål. [I just have a question.] (Danish, DA)
T:	Ja? [Yes?] (GE)
S:	Hvor meget må man gerne veksle mellem … [How often are you allowed to switch between…] (DA)
T:	Lige som du vil … [Just as you want …] (DA)

(18102013_1, 00:03:41)

S:	Hvis der er okay med jer, at jeg skifter mellem tysk og dansk? [If it is okay with you that I switch between German and Danish?] (DA)
Ss & T:	Ja! [Yes!] (DA/GE)

(15102013_1, 00:04:39)

One student uses the introductory phase to explain why, in contrast to most of the other students, he is not making his presentation in German, but in Danish. The teacher acknowledges the student's language choice by using the assessment 'godt' (good), thereby mirroring the student's language choice:

> **S**: Jeg ville gerne på tysk, men jeg følte ikke at jeg havde tid til at forberede det ordentlig på tysk, så det bliver på dansk. [I would like to make my presentation in German, but I felt that I did not have time to prepare it properly in German, so it will be in Danish.] (DA)
> **T**: Godt! [Good.] (DA)
> (01112013_1, 00:01:15)

Furthermore, both students and teachers explicitly refer to their translanguaging practice using metalinguistic markers (in italics in the following examples):

> **S**: Dann, dann kommt so eine Entehrung, aber.... *Jeg siger det på dansk*, hvis man på de store sådan regimer, hvor befolkningen har være undertrykt... [Then, then comes such a disgrace, but...] (GE) [*I say that in Danish*, if in such big regimes, where the population has been subjugated...] (DA)
> (01112013_2, 00:37:40)
> **T**: Kender I noget forskning, der arbejder lige netop med det, altså konstruktion af identitet i en gruppe in Abgrenzung zu... *Sprachenwechsel*... in Abgrenzung zu einer anderen Gruppe [Do you know any research that works right with that, that is the construction of a group identity in a group] (DA) [as a distinction from... *language alternation*... as a distinction from another group] (GE)
> (18102013_1, 00:53:08)

Receptive translanguaging practice

The teachers' default translanguaging practice reflected in our data is receptive translanguaging (cf. for receptive multilingualism: ten Thije & Zeevaert, 2007), or the teachers' facilitating and ensuring the overall translanguaging practice by using German productively, while students use Danish based on their plurilingual receptive competences. This kind of receptive translanguaging is mirrored in the language profiles' content-based foreign-language teaching settings, such as when discussing the students' project work:

> **T**: Mit welchen Machttheoretikern arbeitet ihr dort im Semesterprojekt? [With which theorists of power do you work in your semester project?] (GE)
> **S**: Det har vi ikke helt lagt os fast på endnu. [We have not defined that yet.] (DA)

T: Ja, ja... erstes Semester... [Yes, yes... first semester...] (GE)
    (students and teachers laugh)
S: Vi har 14 sider med magtteoretiker lige nu. [We have 14 pages with
    theorists of power so far.] (DA)
T: Und welche habt ihr da gewählt? [And which ones did you
    choose?] (GE)
S: Jamen det øh... det bliver i hvert fald. ... Vi kommer i hvert faldt til
    at kigge meget på Max Weber. [Well that is oh... that will in any
    case be. ... We will in any case look a lot at Max Weber.] (DA)
(01112013_2, 00:04:35)

Receptive translanguaging practice is reproduced not only in student–
teacher interaction, but also in student–student interaction, or the
collaborative learning established among the students:

S: ...ist aber nicht nur wie Max Weber sagt. Es ist auch Kultur. [...it is
    however not only as Max Weber says. It is also culture.] (GE)
S: Synes du så kultur, køn og religion skal ligestilles med de
    tre magtformer? [So do you think that culture, gender and
    religion should be put on the same level as the three forms of
    power?] (DA)
(01112013_2, 00:32:36)

Within the receptive multilingual setting, different language
proficiencies are represented, and the students also use translanguaging
practices to get access to content constructed by their peers:

S: Wobei hier kommen halt die, die aus Armut flüchten oder aus Krieg
    flüchten, die ökonomisch Unterstützung brauchen, denke ich.
    [Though here also come those who escape poverty or escape war,
    who need economic support, I think.] (GE)
S: Må jeg lige spørge om noget? Hvad var det lige helt, du sagde?
    [Could I ask something? What was all that you just said?] (DA)
(15102013_2, 1:28:58)

In the language profiles, the default mode is a receptive translanguaging
practice: The norm is established that everybody is allowed to speak
German, based on the assumption that German is understood, and those
who do not understand – in their construction of meaning – will ask for
help. This practice is, of course, realized in different ways: those who have
high-level German competences – this might be teachers or students –
primarily use the profile language, but the others also build on the receptive
translanguaging practice and thereby contribute to implement the language
profiles' overall translanguaging policy.

Productive translanguaging practices

In contrast to receptive translanguaging practice that is established as a norm (the students are obliged to be open toward understanding German), the students and the teachers are not forced to speak German and are explicitly encouraged to use productive translanguaging practices. In our data, productive translanguaging can be found on both micro and nano levels. The students mainly use productive translanguaging practice as a languaging strategy. In order to maintain the communication flow in German, Danish words and sentences are used extensively:

> **S:** Ich finde das Thema interessant, weil es gibt nicht, øh, nok Wohnungen für Studenten. [I find the theme interesting because there are not,] (GE) [oh, enough] (DA) [student apartments.] (GE)
>
> **S:** Das wir haben eine Beslussen in EU gemacht und øhm eine stärkere Interpendenz. Gensidig afhængighed zwischen die Europäische lande. Større behov for samarbejde. [That we have made a decision in the EU and, um, a stronger interdependency.] (GE) [Respective dependency] (DA) [between the European countries.] (GE) [A greater need for cooperation.] (DA)

German words are integrated primarily if the terminology is specific:

> **S:** Men det er om Max Weber og herskab eller øhm, magtanalyse og i forhold til de her Herrschaft-idealtyper. [But that is about Max Weber and dominance or, um, analysis of power in relation to those] (DA)]Herrschaft-] (GE) [ideal types.] (DA)

Furthermore, students and teachers do not translate titles and quotations, but use the original languages: either Danish or German. They also use words that are bound to the Danish context and can be categorized as difficult to translate, such as *hygge* (a Danish kind of cosiness) and *folkeskole* (the primary and lower secondary school in Denmark).

The productive translanguaging practice is not limited only to Danish and German. The students also use English (EN) words and expressions, expressing content and maintaining the communication flow:

> **S:** Das ist ein bisschen kompliziert, weil øhm similar culture... Kulturen und so... So man kann nicht separated. [This is a bit complex, because, um,] (GE) [similar culture] (EN) [...cultures and so... so one cannot] (GE) [separated] (EN).
>
> **S:** So man können nicht only auch eine Partei stimmen? [So one cannot] (GE) [only] (EN) also choose one party?] (GE)

Translanguaging practice to facilitate language learning

Within this context of receptive translanguaging practice (where German is used building on the others' receptive competences) and productive translanguaging practice (where German, Danish and sometimes English are used to achieve interactional and social aims), the students and teachers sometimes use translanguaging to facilitate the students' language learning. Translanguaging is used to enhance both receptive and productive competences and is triggered by both students and teachers.

In the language profiles, the students ask explicitly for linguistic help (underlined in the following examples). In order to facilitate the students' language learning, the teachers sometimes do not use their default mode, German, but use Danish:

> **T:** Und diese langsamen Änderungen von der Legimität – kannst du da vielleicht ein Beispiel bringen, zum Beispiel die Wahlbeteiligung? [And these slow changes of legitimacy – can you perhaps mention an example, for example, the *Wahlbeteiligung* [participation in the vote]?] (GE)
>
> **S:** 'Beteiligung' ist…? ['Beteiligung' is…?] (GE)
>
> **T:** 'Deltagelse'. ['Participation'.] (DA)
>
> **S:** Så die Probleme in der 'EU' – hvordan siger man det? [So] (DA) [the problems in the] (GE) ['EU' – how do you say that?] (DA)
>
> **T:** 'EU'. ['EU'.] (GE)

The students sometimes provide the word themselves (underlined in the following examples) but need a confirmation from the teacher to proceed:

> **S:** Ich glaube so, meine Eltern, die haben alle so demonstriert und gekämpft für Recht und besser Schule und besser ja… alle. Und die fühlen wirklich, dass man muss, øhm, samfundet… kan sige: 'Gesellschaft'? [I think that my parents, they have all demonstrated like that and fought for rights and better schools and better yes… all. And they feel really that one should, um,] (GE) [society… can say] (DA) ['Gesellschaft'?] (GE)
>
> **T:** Ja, 'Gesellschaft'. [Yes, 'Gesellschaft'.] (DE)

At the micro level, the teachers use translanguaging practice to explain differences between German and Danish:

> **T:** Wenn ihr jetzt da sagen wollt 'ikke'. Hvordan siger man 'ikke'? 'Ich liebe dich nicht'. Aber das ist: 'Det er ikke kærlighed'. Im Dänischen habt ihr beides Mal 'ikke'. Im Deutschen unterscheidet man 'nicht' und 'keine'. [Now if you would like to say] (GE) ['no'] (DA). How does one say 'no'?] (DA) ['I do not love you'. But you say:] (GE) ['This is not

love'.] (DA). [In Danish, both times you would use] (GE) 'not'] (DA). [In German one differentiates between 'not' and 'not any'.] (GE)

While discussing learning strategies, the teachers use their default mode, receptive translanguaging practice, and the students often resort to productive translanguaging practices, probably because their terminology within this field has not been sufficiently developed during secondary education:

T: Wie hast du deine Probleme gelöst? [How did you solve your problems?] (GE)

S: Ich habe viel Wörter opslag. Øhm ja. Det tog også lang tid. [I have] (GE) [looked up] (DA) [a lot of words.] (GE) [Um, yes. It also took a long time.] (DA)

Intermediate conclusion

To summarize, both teachers and students use translanguaging extensively in the German language profile's evaluation seminars, reflecting Ferguson's first category, curriculum access. Students and teachers use translanguaging to reflect at a meta level on the translanguaging principle. On the micro level, the teachers use German, drawing on the students' receptive translanguaging practice. They encourage the students' productive translanguaging practice as languaging strategy and use translanguaging to facilitate the students' language learning. At the nano level, students' participation in the highly complex discussions is enabled by both receptive and productive translanguaging practice. Furthermore, students use translanguaging practices to enhance their language learning.

The overall picture is that translanguaging practices provide a learning space for students to juggle languages in what seems to be both an unproblematic and an efficient way to achieve interactional and social aims. In the following, we will examine how teachers and students evaluate these practices.

Attitudes Toward Translanguaging Practices

Students' evaluations of translanguaging

In the following analysis, we discuss students' attitudes toward translanguaging in language teaching and learning by focusing on students' questionnaires, which were filled out in the fall of 2013 by students who participated in the German language profile's evaluation seminars. Nine evaluation questionnaires were collected (S1–S9).

The data show that the students' overall impression of the translanguaging policy implemented at RUC is positive. They appreciated that the language profile gave them the opportunity to experience German in a Danish university context at the meso level. In their evaluations, the students emphasized that the German language profile provided a learning environment where they had the chance to use languaging practices: having the possibility to speak 'freely' (S7) and 'impulsively' (S5) and 'not think too much before speaking' (S7), they developed the 'desire' (S4) and 'courage' (S7) to talk in German and to help each other (S4), and they became motivated to continue their learning process (S4).

In the evaluation questionnaire in which the students elaborated on their attitudes toward translanguaging, two questions, in particular, focused on translanguaging practices within the language profiles. In the first question, the students were asked to reflect on their own translanguaging practice at the nano level ('Which languages did you use: German, Danish, English'?) and to self-evaluate their translanguaging practices ('What do you think about this practice'?). In the second question, the students were asked to give recommendations at the micro level concerning language use with respect to the further development of the language profiles ('Which languages should be used by the students and teachers'?).

The data reflect strong individual differences. Furthermore, there is a discrepancy between the students' own experiences with the language profiles' translanguaging practices, on the one hand, and their ideological construction of 'good' language learning and language use, on the other.

Eight out of nine students were aware of their translanguaging practices in the language profile classes and the evaluation seminars. Most of the students acknowledged their use of linguistic features from both German and Danish to, in García and Sylvan's (2011: 389) terms, '"make sense" of and communicate in' the language profiles' learning context. Other than German and Danish, the students, despite their use of English in the evaluation seminars, mentioned no other languages.

Most of the students emphasized that they appreciated the translanguaging practice because it gave them the possibility and the courage to interact in the German language profile's learning context (the following italics are the authors' highlights):

> Jeg blander sprogene, hvilket helt klart er *den mest optimale løsning for mig, hvis jeg skal kunne bruge tysk.* [I mix languages, which is clearly *the best solution for me if I want to be able to use German.*] (S3)

> Det [translanguaging] kan jeg *ret godt lide.* ... Hvis man ikke har mulighed for at blande sprogene, *går man tit i stå og tør ikke prøve.* [I like that *quite a lot.* ... If you do not have the ability to mix languages, *you often freeze and do not dare to try.*] (S2)

Two students (S1, S5) represented the translanguaging practice as *befriende* ('liberating'). S5 emphasized that the translanguaging practices gave her the courage to continue her learning process within the language profile:

Det er *befriende* at det ikke er noget krav til udelukkende tysk. Det er nok *en af de største årsager til at jeg har mod til at fortsætte.* [It is a relief that it is not a requirement to use German exclusively. *It's probably one of the biggest reasons that I have the courage to continue.*] (S5)

Two students acknowledged their translanguaging practices but emphasized that they tried (S7), or will try in the future (S5), to speak as much German as possible. Only two students' evaluations reflected a strong monolingual norm: they reported that they used translanguaging practices but that they, in the future, want to use German *udelukkende* ('exclusively'). They used highly value-laden expressions as *tvinge mig selv* ('forcing myself') and *bandlyse* ('banish'), implying that, in the future, they would like to live up to the monolingual norm and impose this norm on themselves and others:

Jeg blandede tysk og dansk. Det er ok, men jeg vil gerne *udelukkende* tale tysk fremover. *Tvinge mig selv.* [I mixed German and Danish. It's okay, but I want to *speak only* German in the future. *Forcing myself.*] (S4)

Mest tysk – enkelte ord på dansk. *Vi burde bandlyse dansk.* [Most German – individual words in Danish. We should banish Danish.] (S6)

The overall positive evaluation of the language profiles, the evaluation seminars and their own languaging and translanguaging practices can be contrasted with the students' recommendations concerning language use with respect to the further development of the language profiles. Two students did not answer the question (S5, S9). Three students felt positive about the existing translanguaging practice and described different aspects of our methodological translanguaging approach:

Jeg synes det har fungeret godt med tyskundervisning, med opsummeringer på dansk. Det har også fungeret fint at de studerende selv har kunnet vælge om dialog skal fungere på tysk eller dansk. [I think it worked well with German lessons, with summaries in Danish. It also worked well that the students were allowed to choose whether the dialogue should be in German or Danish.] (S3)

The answers mirror the fact that the students experienced the language profiles' translanguaging practice as a possibility to acknowledge each student's linguistic competences and to implement differentiated instruction:

Godt at der veksles. Primært tysk, men at det kan oversættes til dansk hvis der er behov. *Det er fedt* at der er plads til mange forskellige niveauer. Man behøver *ikke at være vildt god* i forvejen. [*The switching is good.*

Mainly German, but it can be translated to Danish if needed. *It's great that there is room for many different levels. One does not have to be really good in advance.*] (S8)

In comparison with the description of their own experiences, there are more students who, in their recommendations concerning the further development of the language profiles, described good language learning and language use based on a monolingual norm. In five recommendations – including recommendations from students who answered the first question very positively – a monolingual German languaging practice is the preferred language teaching and learning form:

Tal tysk, også eleverne, når der er mulighed for det og i den bedste udstrækning eleverne kan [Speak German, and the students should too when possible and to the best extent that they can] (S7)
Tysk, tysk, tysk! [German, German, German!] (S2)

The data reflect that translanguaging, from the students' perspective, is acknowledged as a transitory phenomenon, a kind of interlanguage stage, and not represented as a stable phenomenon and common communication strategy. The students still represent the monolingual paradigm as valid and desirable. One student, being aware of everyday Danish–German communication practice outside the university context, suggested that, instead of Danish, English should be used in the translanguaging practices. This student thereby acknowledged the translanguaging principle but framed it as a transitory phenomenon:

Helt sikkert tysk – dansk skal helst slet ikke benyttes, hvis man går i stå brug engelsk. [Definitely German – Danish should preferably not be used; if you get stuck use English.] (S6)

Teachers' evaluations of translanguaging in language teaching

The following analysis of the teachers' attitudes toward the translanguaging practices is based on semistructured qualitative interviews (Kvale, 2009) with three teachers from the German language profile who were particularly involved in its design (T1–T3). The interviews with T1 and T3, who use German as their first language, were conducted in German. T2, who uses Danish as his first language, was interviewed in German, and he answered in Danish. The interviews were conducted in August 2014, and each lasted approximately 45 minutes.

All teachers answered that they used both German and Danish in the language profile classes. The data show that German, at the micro level, is used very differently, depending on the teachers' competencies in the two languages. This is a clear example of the nano level, the teachers' language competences, influencing the micro level, their teaching of the language profiles. The teachers who use German as their first language used German almost exclusively. T2, the teacher with Danish as his first language, primarily used Danish. T2 made a functional differentiation between German and Danish language use:

> Hvis tekstarbejdet var vanskeligt og kompliceret, læste vi på tysk og uddrog begreber og faglig forståelse på tysk, men samtalede om teksten først og fremmest på dansk. Men da vi så skulle lave en undersøgelse i stil med det, der var i teksten, så brugte vi tysk til at kommunikere med hinanden. [We used German and Danish and mixed them, depending on what we were working with. If the text was difficult and complicated, we read it in German and drew out concepts and technical understanding in German, but talked about the text primarily in Danish. But when we had to do a study similar to the one in the text, we used German to communicate with each other.]

T1, whose first language was German, had a rather different approach. She created a German-learning setting, where (trans)languaging practices were encouraged, referring to herself as a co-learner of Danish as the students' first language:

> Es war ein Vorteil, dass mein Dänisch begrenzt ist, und dass ich mich am Anfang vor die Klasse gestellt habe und auf Dänisch gesagt habe: So spreche ich Dänisch. Das heißt, euer Deutsch ist im Moment besser als mein Dänisch. ... Die Studierenden haben sehr gut drauf reagiert. Die haben konsequent Deutsch mit mir gesprochen. [It was an advantage that my Danish is limited, and that I put myself in front of the class at the beginning and have said in Danish: This is how I speak Danish. This means that your German is actually better than my Danish. ... The students responded very well to this. They consistently spoke German with me.]

T1 emphasized that the students' languaging was based on a translanguaging practice and represents this practice beyond the monolingual norm as fluent language use, which does not imply understanding problems:

> ... und wenn ein Satz mal schief ging, oder eine Formulierung nicht klar war, ohne Übergänge ins Dänisch gewechselt und einfach so dann weitergemacht und dann wieder zurück ins Deutsche, wenn der Satz zu Ende war, oder die Formulierung zu Ende war. Also wirklich fließend, ohne Probleme. [... and when a sentence sometimes went wrong, or

a formulation was not clear, they changed without transitions into Danish and simply went on with it and then returned to German when the sentence was done, or the formulation was at an end. Fluently, without problems.]

Although a translanguaging learning setting is constructed at the micro level, all three teachers emphasized that the language profiles' primary objective is to enhance the students' language skills in German in order to contribute to the translanguaging policy at RUC. T2 represented Danish as *hjælpesprog* ('auxiliary language') in this process and has, so far, not included other languages but is open to using other languages, such as Latin:

Jeg overvejede faktisk ikke at bruge engelsk. Jeg havde fokus på det tyske og brugte dansk som hjælpesprog. Man kunne også bruge flere sprog. Latin fx. [I didn't even consider using English. I focused on the German and used Danish as the auxiliary language. You could also use multiple languages. Latin, for example.]

T1 also represented Danish as the primary auxiliary language and used English as the common academic lingua franca:

Wenn die ein Wort auf Deutsch nicht wussten und mir es auf Dänisch nicht eingefallen ist, dann haben wir es auf Englisch gemacht, weil Englisch für uns alle die lingua franca, die Distanzsprache, war, in der wir manche akademische Wörter besser wissen als in unseren respektiven Muttersprachen. [If they did not know a word in German and I didn't know the Danish word, we used English, because English is for all of us the lingua franca, the language of distance, in which we know some academic words better than in our respective mother tongues.]

All three teachers saw it as an advantage to use all available linguistic resources when teaching languages. T3 commented:

Wenn man die Muttersprache der Studierenden kennt und kann, dann ist die Muttersprache auch eine Ressource im Unterricht, auf die man nicht verzichten sollte. Und auch andere Sprache können im Unterricht eine Ressource sein, auf die man nicht verzichten sollte. [If you know and speak the mother tongue of the students, then this is also a resource in teaching that you shouldn't do without. And different languages can be a resource in the classroom, which you should not do without.]

However, as stated previously, the practice and the norm within the language profiles' context seems to be a translanguaging practice based on German and Danish. For instance, T1, who normally teaches in English, reported that she often and unconsciously uses expressions that are common in a pedagogical context, like 'Let's go' and 'Five minutes left', in English. T1 emphasized that her impression is that the students' reaction toward this translanguaging practice is highly normative. The use of English seems to be inappropriate in this context, and the teacher's conclusion is that

> Der Kontext ist ganz klar Deutsch-Dänisch. [The context is clearly German-Danish.]

All three teachers defined translanguaging as a useful tool when teaching languages, and they all had the impression that the students also gain from it. As T1 phrased it,

> Das [translanguaging] hat gut funktioniert. Die Studierenden haben das auch in den Evaluation immer wieder gesagt, es ist gut einfach Deutsch zu sprechen in einem Umfeld, wo es okay ist, dass man Fehler macht. [That [translanguaging] worked out well. The students also repeatedly say in the evaluation, it is good just to speak German in an environment where it's okay that you make mistakes.]

T3 emphasized that this experimental environment is a very important aspect of (trans)languaging. To create a space where the students can, and dare to, try their language skills and where they learn how one manages several languages in the communication is demanding work, and the translanguaging practice needs to be explicitly encouraged by the teachers and conceptualized as, in Bourdieu's (1982) terminology, *legitimate* language use:

> Es ist und soll legitim sein, dass man auf Dänisch zurückgreift, und der Studierende hat immer das Recht auf Dänisch zurückzugreifen, denn das ist ja die Sprache, die alle verstehen hier in diesem Kontext... und der Lehrer soll das denn auch unterstützen, dass es legitim ist, die Muttersprache zu verwenden, beziehungsweise andere Sprachen, wenn das nützlich ist. [It is and should be legitimate to resort to Danish, and the students always have the right to do that, because that is the language that everybody understands in this context ... and the teacher has to support this legitimacy to use the mother tongue or other languages, if it is useful.] (Bourdieu, 1982)

Concluding Remarks and Perspectives

RUC's French, German and Spanish language profiles offer a setting where the predominant monolingualism or parallel English–Danish language use is challenged in a Danish higher education context. In order to enhance individual plurilingualism at the nano level, multilingualism is implemented on the meso level through RUC's internationalization strategy and at the micro level through the teachers' implementation of RUC's French, German and Spanish language profiles. At the macro level, the program is supported by the Danish governmental action plan for internationalization.

In RUC's language profiles, translanguaging represents a main strategy and practice. On the meso level, a translanguaging policy has been established that includes French, German and Spanish as academic languages in addition to Danish and English. Our data analysis focusing on translanguaging practices and evaluations at the micro and nano levels within the German language profiles showed that students and teachers embrace translanguaging in concept, method and practice. The teachers use this strategy actively in their conceptualization of teaching and learning to reflect real language use in multilingual settings. The teachers' main focus was to enhance the students' language competences in German. Through receptive translanguaging practice, they provided German language input, and through productive translanguaging practice the students were invited to use German in their interaction. The students used translanguaging practices, which enabled them to participate in the German language profiles' learning context to gain and share highly complex academic knowledge in a higher education context in their second foreign language.

Implementing the concept of translanguaging in the teaching and learning at RUC makes it evident how strongly language and norms are linked. The data reflect a tendency toward a monolingual norm in the students' ideal content-based foreign language classroom: In the students' recommendations for the further development of the language profile, a tendency toward strong monolingual norms emerges. Both students and teachers implement and acknowledge translanguaging practices integrating their second foreign language and other languages, primarily the students' first language but also English. At the nano level, the students experience translanguaging as liberating, with teachers strongly supporting the educational call for (trans)languaging at the micro level. However, Danish and English are represented as auxiliary languages. They are preferably not used and are supposed to pave the way for monolingual foreign language teaching and learning. While the translanguaging principle is acknowledged as being the norm and a 'natural' way of communication within the actual language profile settings, the pervasiveness of monolingual ideologies means that it may take time to acknowledge translanguaging as a resource, method and strategy in the future, inside and outside the foreign language classroom.

References

Andersen, M. (2010) Tysk i krise – tysk i det danske uddannelsessystem. In M. Andersen, K.S. Jakobsen, A. Klinge, J.E. Mogensen, A. Sandberg and D. Siegfried (eds) *Tysk nu* (pp. 4–15). Kopenhagen: Institut for Engelsk, Germansk og Romansk.

Beacco, J.C., Byram, M., Cavalli, M., Coste, D., Egli Cuenat, M., Goullier, F. and Panthier, J. (2010) *Guide for the Development and Implementation of Curricula for Plurilingual and Intercultural Education*. Strasbourg: Council of Europe.

Bojsen, H. (2015) The power of students' subjectivity processes in foreign language acquisition: The example of the language profiles at Roskilde University, Denmark. In S. Durrans (ed.) *(Se) construire dans l'interlangue/Subjectivity Processes in Interlanguage* (pp. 61–72). Villeneuve d'Ascq: Presses Universitaires du Septentrion.

Bourdieu, P. (1982) *Ce que parler veut dire: l'économie des échanges linguistiques*. Paris: Fayard.

Cameron, D. (2004) Out of the bottle: The social life of metalanguage. In A. Jaworski, N. Coupland and D. Galasinski (eds) *Metalanguage: Social and Ideological Perspectives* (pp. 311–322). Berlin: Mouton de Gruyter.

Candelier, M., Camilleri-Grima, A., Castellotti, V., de Pietro, J.-F., Lörincz, I., Meißner, F.-J. and Schröder-Sura, A. (2012) *FREPA: A Framework of Reference for Pluralistic Approaches to Languages and Cultures: Competences and Resources*. Graz: ECML.

Castellotti, V. and Moore, D. (2010) Capitalising on, activating and developing plurilingual and pluricultural repertoires for better school integration. Strasbourg: Council of Europe. See https://www.coe.int/t/dg4/linguistic/Source/Source2010_ForumGeneva/4-ValoriserCastellottiMoore_EN.pdf (accessed 8 July 2016).

Cavalli, M., Coste, D., Crisan, P. and von de Ven, P.-H. (2009) Plurilingual and intercultural education as a project. Strasbourg: Council of Europe, Language Policy Division. See http://www.coe.int/t/dg4/linguistic/Source/LE_texts_Source/EducPlurInter-Projet_en.pdf (accessed 8 July 2016).

Council of Europe (2007) *Guide for the Development of Language Education Policies in Europe*. Strasbourg: Council of Europe.

Council of Europe (2010) *Guide for the Development and Implementation of Curricula for Plurilingual and Intercultural Education*. Strasbourg: Council of Europe.

Council of Europe (2014) Council of Europe language education policy. See http://www.coe.int/t/dg4/linguistic/Division_en.asp (accessed 8 July 2016).

Coyle, D., Hood, P. and Marsh, D. (2010) *CLIL: Content and Language Integrated Learning*. Cambridge: Cambridge University Press.

Daryai-Hansen, P. (2010) Repræsentationernes magt – sproglige hierarkiseringer i Danmark. In J. Normann Jørgensen and A. Holmen (eds) *Sprogs status i Danmark 2021* (pp. 87–105). Copenhagen: Københavns Universitet.

Daryai-Hansen, P. and Kraft, K. (2014) Sproglige ressourcer, praksisser og profiler: RUC som internationalt universitet. *Rask* 41, 79–102.

Daryai-Hansen, P., Gerber, B., Lörincz, I., Haller, M., Ivanova, O., Krumm, H.-J. and Reich, H. (2015) Pluralistic approaches to languages in the curriculum: The case of French-speaking Switzerland, Spain and Austria. *International Journal of Multilingualism* 12 (1), 109–127.

Den humanistiske bacheloruddannelse (2013) Study regulation. Ændring af Studieordningen for Den humanistiske bacheloruddannelse. See https://intra.ruc.dk/for-ansatte/regelsamling/uddannelse/bachelorstudieordninger-knyttet-til-faellesreglerne-fra-2012/ (accessed 16 July 2016).

Den samfundsvidenskabelige bacheloruddannelse (2013) Study regulation. Studieordningen for Den samfundsvidenskabelige bacheloruddannelse. See https://intra.ruc.dk/for-ansatte/regelsamling/uddannelse/bachelorstudieordninger-knyttet-til-faellesreglerne-fra-2012/ (accessed 16 July 2016).

Ferguson, G. (2003) Classroom code-switching in post-colonial contexts: Functions, attitudes and policies. *AILA Review* 14, 38–51.

García, O. (2009) *Bilingual Education in the 21st Century: A Global Perspective*. Malden, MA and Oxford: Blackwell/Wiley.

García, O. and Sylvan, C.E. (2011) Pedagogies and practices in multilingual classrooms: Singularities in pluralities. *Modern Language Journal* 95 (3), 385–400.

Grin, F. (2013) L'anglais dans l'enseignement académique: le débat s'égare dans les clichés. *Le Temps* 13 June. See http://www.letemps.ch/opinions/2013/06/12/anglais-enseignement-academique-debat-s-egare-cliches (accessed 16 July).

Grothjahn, R. (1987) On the methodological basis of introspective methods. In C. Faerch and G. Kasper (eds) *Introspection in Second Language Research* (pp. 54–81). Clevedon: Multilingual Matters.

Hazel, S. and Mortensen, J. (2013) Kitchen talk – Exploring linguistic practices in liminal institutional interactions in a multilingual university setting. In H. Haberland, D. Lønsmann and B. Preisler (eds) *Language Alternation, Language Choice and Language Encounter in International Tertiary Education* (pp. 3–30). Dordrecht: Springer.

Herdina, P. and Jessner, U. (2002) *A Dynamic Model of Multilingualism: Perspectives of Change in Psycholinguistics*. Clevedon: Multilingual Matters.

Jaworski, A., Coupland, N. and Galasinski, D. (eds) (2004) *Metalanguage: Social and Ideological Perspectives*. Berlin: Mouton de Gruyter.

Jensen, J. and Olesen, H. (1999) *Project Studies: A Late Modern University Reform?* Roskilde: Roskilde University Press.

Jørgensen, J.N. (2010) *Languaging: Nine Years of Poly-lingual Development of Young Turkish-Danish Grade School Students*. Copenhagen: Det Humanistiske Fakultet.

Jørgensen, J.N., Karrebæk, M.S., Madsen, L.M. and Møller, J.S. (2011) Polylanguaging in superdiversity. *Diversities* 13 (2), 23–38.

Kramsch, C. (2010) *The Multilingual Subject*. Oxford: Oxford University Press.

Kvale, S. (2009) *Interview: Introduktion til et håndværk*. København: Gyldendal Akademisk.

Makoni, S. and Makoni, B. (2010) Multilingual discourses on wheels and public English in Africa: A case for 'vague linguistique'. In J. Maybin and J. Swann (eds) *The Routledge Companion to English Language Studies* (pp. 258–270). London: Routledge.

Mayring, P. (2000) Qualitative content analysis. *Forum Qualitative Sozialforschung/Forum Qualitative Social Research* 1 (2). See http://www.qualitative-research.net/index.php/fqs/article/view/1089/2385 (accessed 8 July 2016).

Moore, D. and Gajo, L. (2009) Introduction – French voices on plurilingualism and pluriculturalism: Theory, significance and perspectives. *International Journal of Multilingualism* 6 (2), 137–153.

Mortensen, J., Haberland, H. and Fabricius, A. (2012) Uddannelse on the move: Transnational studentermobilitet og uddannelseskvalitet. In H. Leth-Andersen and J.C. Jacobsen (eds) *Uddannelseskvalitet i en globaliseret verden: Vidensøkonomiens indtog i de videregående uddannelser* (pp. 197–209). Frederiksberg: Forlaget Samfundslitteratur.

Regeringen (2013) *Øget indsigt gennem globalt udsyn*. See http://ufm.dk/publikationer/2013/filer-2013/oget-indsigt-gennem-globalt-udsyn-1.pdf (accessed 8 July 2016).

Risager, K. (2012) Language hierarchies at the international university. *International Journal of the Sociology of Language* 216, 111–130.

Schramm, M. (2010) Tysk som trend: forandringer i det danske tysklandsbillede. In M.S. Andersen, K.S. Jakobsen, A. Klinge, J.E. Mogensen, A. Sandberg and D. Siegfried (eds) *Tysk nu* (pp. 34–37). Kopenhagen: Institut for Engelsk, Germansk og Romansk.

ten Thije, J.D. and Zeevaert, L. (eds) (2007) *Receptive Multilingualism: Linguistic Analyses, Language Policies and Didactic Concepts*. Amsterdam: Benjamins.

Thøgersen, J. (2010) 'Parallelsproglighed' i teori og praksis. *Nyt fra Sprognævnet* 4, 1–5.

Wenger, E. (1999) *Communities of Practice: Learning, Meaning, and Identity*. Cambridge: Cambridge University Press.

4 The Ecology of Language and Translanguaging in a Ukrainian University

Bridget A. Goodman

Introduction

As in many parts of the world today, English is a foreign language in Ukraine but is slowly emerging in higher education programs as a designated or primary medium of instruction – the language through which course content is taught (Cooper, 1989; Hornberger, 2003; Tollefson & Tsui, 2004). The option to study in English is still limited in the country but seems likely to grow, especially in private schools of economics and state medical schools. A Ukrainian university's choice to offer English as a medium of instruction (EMI) can be linked to general goals of social and economic integration with the European Union and to participation in the Bologna Process (Cots *et al.*, 2014; Phillipson, 2006), which promotes mobility and internationalization of higher education in Europe.

From an ecology-of-language perspective (Haugen, 1972 [2001]; Hornberger, 2003), the introduction of EMI has the potential to impact an already uncertain relationship between the Ukrainian and Russian languages in the country. Ukrainian has been the sole state language since Ukraine became an independent country in 1991. 'Ukrainianization' laws were passed in the 1990s and 2000s to promote the use of Ukrainian in multiple spheres of society, but these laws have not always been fully implemented in cities in eastern Ukraine with significant ethnic Russian and Russophone Ukrainian populations (Bilaniuk, 2010). In 2012, pro-Russian president Viktor Yanukovych passed a law allowing any language in the 2001 census that was declared a native language by more than 10% of the population in a region[1] to be an official, administrative language in that region. While this law has made space for the official use of Polish, Romanian and Hungarian in regions bordering their respective nations, the perceived primary purpose of the law was elevating the status of the Russian language, thereby threatening Ukrainian. As a result, the law sparked protests among Ukrainian speakers and Ukrainian nationalists across the country. Since the bloody 'Euromaidan' revolution of 2014 that drove out Yanukovych, pro-European leaders have acknowledged the need to respect the rights of Russian speakers (e.g. 'Yatseniuk says', 2014). Meanwhile, English is seen as a language of prestige that, at times, appears in public and educational spaces in place of Russian or in combination with both Ukrainian and Russian (Bilaniuk & Melnyk, 2008; Janmaat, 2008; Scollon & Scollon, 2003).

The Ecology of Language and Translanguaging

A complementary way to understand the shifting status of Ukrainian and Russian in the language ecology and the impact of English on this ecology is to look at translanguaging practices (Baker, 2001, 2003; Creese & Blackledge, 2011; García, 2009, 2011; Hornberger & Link, 2012; Williams, 1994) in a higher education site that is increasingly using EMI. Within such settings, translanguaging can refer to the communicative practices of emergent bilinguals in classrooms (García, 2009, 2011); the targeted, alternating use of one or more codes (languages or language varieties) in one or more modes (e.g. written, oral) for pedagogical purposes (Baker, 2001, 2003; Hornberger & Link, 2012; Williams, 1994); and the 'microalternation' of languages in moment-to-moment classroom discourse that 'allows educators to adjust language practices and content to the child' (García & Sylvan, 2011: 391). Previous studies in bilingual and multilingual contexts have shown that programs with a single designated medium of instruction can use the native language as well as the target language in classes (e.g. Bonacina & Gafaranga, 2011; Duff, 1995; Söderlundh, 2012; van der Walt, 2013). By exploring these manifestations of translanguaging, it is possible to index the current vitality (Stewart, 1968) of Ukrainian, Russian and English and project the future of these languages in Ukraine.

While translanguaging is a useful framework for exploring the ecology of language in Ukraine, Flores (2014: para. 4) warns us that 'translanguaging is not simply a research method but rather part of a larger political struggle of linguistic self-determination for language-minoritized populations'. However, Russian speakers in Ukraine are 'minority language' speakers who are not completely minoritized. Russian has a postcolonial legacy in Ukraine (see Pavlenko, 2008a, 2011) as the language of power under the Russian Empire and the Soviet Union from 1917 to 1991. The hegemony of Russian was especially prevalent in the large cities of eastern Ukraine (where this study was conducted) compared to rural areas nationwide or the western one-third of Ukraine, which entered the Soviet Union later, during World War II. Moreover, survey research indicates that Russian is spoken by at least 60% of the country and understood by an additional 20% (Pavlenko, 2008b). While it is true that in the 2001 census Russian speakers made up 29.6% of the national population, and the Russian language in

Ukraine is protected under the European Charter of the Rights of Minority Languages, applying a 'minoritized' lens to understanding Russian and Ukrainian language use in the current study is not appropriate.

It is appropriate, however, to consider whether translanguaging practices in this context can serve as an act of resistance – or, at least, a counternarrative – to the hegemony of English as a global or international language. With the implementation of the Bologna Process, there has been a concomitant rise of English-medium programs in European higher educational institutions (Mortensen & Haberland, 2012; Saarinen, 2012; Unterberger, 2012). Many linguists see the growing role of English in higher education as posing a threat to multilingualism in Europe (Huguet, 2007; Phillipson, 2006, 2013; Tosi, 2006). However, if teachers and students are using not only English but also one or more additional languages in the classroom, this would indicate that using EMI may not be a threat to multilingualism in the Ukrainian context.

It is also appropriate to consider the relationship between students' and teachers' translanguaging practices and ideologies of language purity. Bilaniuk (2005, 2009) found that, despite widespread examples in interviews and the media of the prevalence of *surzhyk* (a term denoting mixed forms of Ukrainian and Russian), Ukrainians still held to Soviet notions of the importance of language correctness or, in other words, that the two languages should be kept pure and separate. In classrooms, Friedman (2009) found that teachers also strove to socialize students away from mixing Ukrainian and Russian in their speech, as part of efforts to construct Ukraine's identity as a nation separate from Russia. Conversely, if students and teachers in the current study are mixing languages in classes, they may be implicitly accepting more heteroglossic norms, regardless of the designated medium of instruction. Moreover, multiple languages and mixed varieties may be said to be present in the language ecology.

Research Methods

The findings of translanguaging in a Ukrainian higher education context presented in this chapter emerged from an ethnographic case study of Alfred Nobel University, a private university in the eastern city of Dnipropetrovsk, Ukraine. Fieldwork was conducted at the university over the 2010/2011 school year and focused on three groups of students and their teachers: (1) a group of 25 students preparing to earn a joint degree from Alfred Nobel University and the University of Wales (or 'the Wales program'); (2) a group of 24 third-year students of international economics taking one subject in English; and (3) a group of nine philologists (language and literature majors). In addition to courses taught in English to these three groups, occasionally subjects taught in Russian or Ukrainian involving focal teachers and students were observed. These observations were supplemented by informal conversations before or after class with students and teachers. In addition, throughout the year, I attended school events such as conferences and holiday celebrations, took photos of signs in the university and collected hard-copy versions of school documents. Interviews were conducted with one-half of the students and four of the teachers in spring 2011.

As is customary in ethnographic research, data collection and data analysis were iterative processes (Creese *et al.*, 2008). For classes, conversations and school events, detailed field notes and transcripts with analytical reflections were written. Field notes, transcripts and selected photos were loaded into atlas.ti and open coded, starting in January 2011. These notes and transcripts were reviewed prior to finalizing interview questions. Interview questions were transcribed and coded in atlas.ti between February and July 2011. As recommended by Hammersley and Atkinson (2007), codes were combined into categories, and quotations within these categories were reviewed for patterns. This chapter will focus specifically on those patterns interpreted through the lenses of the ecology of language and translanguaging.

Policies and Choices of Medium of Instruction

Before elaborating on translanguaging practices within classrooms, it is important to unpack the concept of medium of instruction from an emic perspective, as one concerned less with national or even institutional language policy and more about choices and requests depending on the teachers, students and the language in question. With regard to Ukrainian and Russian in classes that are not designated English medium at the university, one teacher, Larisa Ivanovna,[2] said,

> I know that there are lecturers like Yaroslav Denisovich, you know him, he likes Ukrainian and he has lectures in Ukrainian. Of course students understand the information, but, if you ask them whether they want, or what language do they want, they will choose Russian. (Original language from audio file, 23 March 2011)

Larisa Ivanovna states that Yaroslav Denisovich has lectures in Ukrainian because he 'likes' it, indicating it is his personal choice (and not one necessarily shared by his students). Other teachers of academic subjects told me that they regularly choose Russian rather than Ukrainian as a medium of instruction because of their perception of students' language background, not their own background or preferences. Viktoria Sergeyevna said she allows her students to choose: 'I ask my students in which language they would like me to read, to give lectures in, either in Russian or Ukrainian, but they mostly choose Russian' (original language from audio file, 9 March 2011). Viktoria Sergeyevna comes from a Russian-speaking family and did not start to learn Ukrainian until she began to study at university, where she memorized poems. She still struggles to speak and write Ukrainian. It is possible here that her students' 'choice' is based on their perception of Viktoria Sergeyevna's Ukrainian language skills or even her decision to speak in Russian while making such an offer. However, other students told me they prefer to speak Russian to Ukrainian. Moreover, Viktoria Sergeyevna further noted that her choice of the medium of instruction was influenced by the presence of foreign students:

> We have a lot of students from Russia, from Russian-speaking countries such as Belorussia or Kazakhstan, post-Soviet Union countries where Russian is an international language. And of course it is easier to deliver knowledge in Russian, in the language they feel more comfortable to communicate in. And when it doesn't concern foreign languages and English in particular, my role is to develop, to deliver knowledge. ... So if they don't speak, for example, I had a group of students, uh, Georgian students or Armenian. They can hardly speak Russian, and I don't even mention Ukrainian, and what on earth should I force them to learn Ukrainian so that they could understand my lectures? (Original language from audio file, 9 March 2011)

In contrast, teachers framed their involvement in EMI teaching not as a choice they made or negotiated within the classroom, but as a request shaped by expectations external to the classroom and internal to the university. As Viktoria Sergeyevna said,

> Initially, it was the department of practical psychology who were supposed to arrange seminars and lectures and provide teaching staff, professors to read lectures in English, but as they don't have anybody who can read lectures and hold seminars in English at a good level, they asked Viktor Andreyevich to read lectures, and he asked me to hold seminars. (Original language from audio file, 9 March 2011)

Whereas Yaroslav Denisovich teaches in Ukrainian because he 'likes' it, Viktoria Sergeyevna teaches in English because she was 'asked' by a colleague, and he, in turn, was presumably asked by the university administration, since other faculty who were 'supposed' to teach in English could not. As for students in EMI classes, Alexander Nikolayevich said that now students have 'no choice. English is the language of teaching' (field notes, 25 March 2011).

Medium of Instruction and Mixed Language

One student I interviewed, Aleksandr, framed his teachers' choices regarding medium of instruction in terms of the intention to use a single language of instruction with a more heteroglossic result:

Mm, in most cases we use Russian, but some maybe tutors or teachers use Ukrainian, for example like [name], he speaks only Ukrainian. But he doesn't speak clear Ukrainian because he mixed words with Russian, with some, I don't know, uh, we call this *surzhyk*. (Original language from audio file, 29 March 2011)

Aleksandr's comment that the teacher 'doesn't speak clear Ukrainian' suggests that Aleksandr is ideologically opposed to mixing Russian and Ukrainian in this situation. He was also slightly opposed to the use of Russian in English-medium classes, saying, 'I don't like it much, but sometimes when maybe someone can't understand maybe the meaning of the word or something like this, it's better to explain [it to] him in Russian'. Yet, he also acknowledged more matter-of-factly that, at the university outside of classes, he mixes three languages freely: 'I can use some words in English just, just like *surzhyk*, but with Russian and English. But, um, we never speak Ukrainian, maybe just, a, quotation [or] maybe some, uh, phrases'. The ecological stance expressed here is that *surzhyk* can be a mixing of any two languages in one's repertoire, including English. The ideological stance expressed here is that mixing languages is more acceptable outside class than in class, unless it serves a particular communicative or pedagogical objective.

To sum up, it was clear from observations and interactions with teachers and students that Russian was the most prevalent medium of instruction. Yet, English was emerging as a more prevalent medium of instruction than Ukrainian. Moreover, the attitudes expressed by these teachers indicate that in the ecological hierarchy, English is positioned above Russian and Ukrainian at the university as expected and necessary. On the other hand, the choices regarding the medium of instruction in classes at this university also reflect a student-centered, goal-oriented approach. Nearly one-third of the students I interviewed attributed the choice to attend Alfred Nobel University to the university's English-language or EMI offerings, and it appears that students in non-EMI classes may be able to request their preferred language of instruction. These orientations to classroom medium of instruction as a matter of choice or request, as well as noted variations between plan and practice, suggest that at Alfred Nobel University there is considerable implementational space (Hornberger, 2003) for multiple languages and language forms in classes, regardless of the stated medium of instruction or prevailing language ideologies.

Translanguaging Practices in University Classrooms

In every class observed at Alfred Nobel University – regardless of whether the primary medium of instruction was English, Russian or Ukrainian – at least one additional language was used. In EMI classes, teachers frequently used Russian to provide equivalents of vocabulary words or to explain class procedures, while students often asked for help in Russian or switched to Russian if they could not remember an English word (see Tarnopolsky & Goodman, 2014). These uses of Russian indicate that Russian, not Ukrainian, is the default language supporting the acquisition of English.

In addition to microalternations between English and Russian in EMI classes, there were moments of simultaneous mixing of codes and modes. That is to say, teachers and students were occasionally observed speaking in one language to refer to words that were written in another language. For example, in an EMI class for Wales program students, Viktor Andreyevich was giving a lecture about continua of cultural behavior and attitudes. He wrote on the board the English words 'the attitude to uncertainty', stated them twice in English, then restated them in Russian as *otnoshenie k neopredelënnosti* (original language from video file, 8 December 2010). In a Russian-medium class, a Wales program student, Nikolai, had a company slogan in English in his PowerPoint slide that he explained in Russian.

What is striking about this translanguaging practice – in addition to its pedagogical utility (see Hornberger, 2003) – is that it was observed not only in individual classrooms but at university events as well. At a student conference, a presenter from a university in Kyiv had PowerPoint slides in English but spoke in Ukrainian. When Ukrainian representatives of international programs spoke on two occasions at the university, their slides were in Ukrainian, but they spoke in Russian. At least one of these shifts to Russian was based on a university administrator's request that the presenter accommodate the audience's preferred language. In each case, though, it can be said that the two languages being used in the presentation were expected or understood to be part of the audience's linguistic repertoire.

Another possible interpretation of Russian–Ukrainian translanguaging in these university events, however, is that Russian was supporting the acquisition of Ukrainian. In the Ukrainian language class I observed for Wales program students, the teacher occasionally translated words from the Ukrainian exercise book into Russian if students were unfamiliar with the word. The following field notes excerpt details the interpretation of the use of Russian and the overall pedagogical approach by the teacher, Ludmila Anatolievna, and me:

> Ludmila Anatolievna hands out a book of Ukrainian exercises to the students. As I understand the first exercise from reading the Ukrainian instructions in the book, students should rewrite a passage with the correct punctuation and explain why they used those punctuation marks. Students take turns giving answers which Ludmila Anatolievna comments on.
> Ludmila Anatolievna says in Ukrainian the second question/item is about dialogues. Students are assigned by name into pairs or groups of 3,

and each group gets one situation, e.g. *Vy zapiznylysia na zaniattia* [You are late to class]. She asks each pair to write one dialog. She clarifies that they only have the general situation (*zahalnaia sytuatsiia*).

It is at this moment I realize that this class feels more like a 'Ukrainian as a Foreign Language' class than a Ukrainian for native speakers class. Though punctuation can be hard for native speakers too, it's not normally taught like this. After class, I asked Ludmila Anatolievna (in a mixture of Russian and Ukrainian), what do you think? Do you think they study Ukrainian as a native language (*ridna mova*), or a second language, or something in between? She said I was absolutely right. They think in Russian and translate into Ukrainian. (Field notes, 16 May 2011)

Ludmila Anatolievna's belief that her students 'think in Russian and translate into Ukrainian' suggests that Ukrainian operates as a second language for her students. Therefore, Ludmila Anatolievna chose to give students instruction on the Ukrainian language using methods that are similar to the methods used, for example, to teach Russian to international students. Students' ideologies about Ukrainian (as expressed in interviews), however, were often more consistent with the notion that Ukrainian is their native language because they were born and raised in Ukraine (see also Arel, 2002, 2006; Bilaniuk & Melnyk, 2008; Friedman, 2006; Hrycak, 2006). Three Wales program students told me that they even spoke primarily Ukrainian (and some Russian) with family members at home.

As for Russian-medium classes, English appeared slightly more frequently than Ukrainian. In this case, however, English was not used to support learning in Russian; rather, it was part of the course content. For example, in a Russian-medium class for third-year economics students, the teacher's slides were sprinkled with English. The English word 'merchandising' appeared in Cyrillic as a calque, *мерчандайзинг* [*merchandaizing*], while the words 'above the line', 'below the line' and 'PR' were written directly in English. Like the term *kommiunikativnaia kompetentsia* [communicative competence], uttered by another teacher in a foreign-language teaching methods course, these concepts have been appropriated from English-speaking literature in the respective fields of study. Similarly, the student from Kyiv whose slides were in English noted that it was difficult to translate the source material, and, in principle, the material should be in the original (field notes, 16 December 2010).

The status of the original English can be interpreted in three ways. First, the need to present the 'original language' in English is consistent with Alfred Nobel University teachers' views that copying information and commenting on it – in English or Russian – is more important than presenting information in one's own words. Second, including English in one's presentation was described by people at the university as a mark of prestige and achievement. Third, students and teachers may see English-language resources as offering opportunities to obtain the knowledge of economics that will help them compete in the global marketplace or even integrate into European society. When I asked an economics teacher, Svetlana Petrovna, about the future of English in Ukraine, she replied,

> English will be the main language of conversation... because Ukraine have a strategic plan to implement all American and European technologies and education, and culture, and so on so. And the process of implementation of culture and technologies will be supported with the implementation of the language of those countries. So that's connected things. (Original language from audio file, 16 March 2011)

From an ecology-of-language perspective, these findings suggest that Russian is the predominant language of oral communication in classrooms, now followed by English and then Ukrainian. This indicates that English may pose a threat to Ukrainian in education in eastern Ukraine in the future. From a translanguaging perspective, however, one can see that at Alfred Nobel University, one language is not pushed out of the ecology completely at the classroom level by the choice of another language as the medium of instruction. There is a great range and fluidity among the three languages in moment-to-moment interaction. Moreover, using multiple codes in multiple modes affords students and adults a rich opportunity for dual input that – ideally – will facilitate their ability to acquire knowledge in multiple languages simultaneously.

Multilingual Repertoires of Translanguaging

While the initial impetus for this study was to explore the relative status of Ukrainian, Russian and English in the university, it became readily apparent that students and teachers had multiple foreign languages in their repertoires, which occasionally manifested through translanguaging practices in classrooms. According to Alfred Nobel University program guidelines, starting in the third year of study, students of international economics (including students in the Wales program) and philology are required to study a second foreign language in addition to English. The presence of foreign languages in students' repertoires is linked to this language-in-education policy. It was also found that these multilingual policies intersected with ideologies of language separation.

Three EMI teachers I interviewed who had educational backgrounds in philology also mentioned that they had studied a second foreign language, French or Mandarin Chinese, as part of their degree program. Two of these teachers even said that they were equally or more fluent in their second foreign language than in Ukrainian. These teachers, however, were never heard using these second foreign languages in their teaching. One of these teachers rarely spoke even Russian and regularly told her students during group work, 'I hope you are discussing everything in English, even thinking in English' (field notes, 9 September 2010). Another teacher, who told me he was more pragmatic in using Russian to support English learning, nevertheless expressed surprise at times when students or I used a language other than English when speaking to him in class (field notes, 10 and 29 September 2010).

Social sciences teacher Alexander Nikolayevich was not a philologist but frequently used quotations or phrases in Latin, Greek, German and French in both EMI and Russian-medium classes. He frequently expressed concern about his English, at one point saying, 'I'm not a professional English speaker. I didn't get linguistic training' (field notes, 18 February 2011). Thus, it is possible that he was invoking his multilingual repertoires to demonstrate his competency in other ways. However, the fact that he used these repertoires in both English- and Russian-medium classes suggests that it is an element of his individual personality. The 'professional' teachers with philology training, on the other hand, by omitting additional foreign languages from their communication, were reflecting an ideology that classes should be taught primarily in one language plus, perhaps, the first language.

The Wales program students I interviewed had either experience studying or plans to study a foreign language in addition to English (Chinese, French, German, Japanese, Polish and Spanish, to be exact). Ksenia, who was considering looking for work in China someday, talked about the importance of learning Chinese as a fourth language:

Bridget: Okay. Um, how important are these languages for finding work in the future?

Ksenia: I think that these languages are very important just for nowadays. Because when people apply for work, they have to know not less than three languages. For example, Ukrainian, Russian and German. Or, Ukrainian, Russian and [pause] English. Ukrainian, Russian or Spanish. Because you have to know one mother tongue language, but the other mother tongue language, Russian, in brackets of course. And the other foreign language. For example, I want to learn Chinese, to know four languages. To use them in future. I think it will help me to apply for work. (Original language from audio file, 24 February 2011)

While Chinese (Mandarin) is not part of her repertoire yet, the other three languages are, and at reasonably high levels, since Ksenia studied at a school that encouraged learning languages. Nevertheless, she expressed concerns that her language skills were not sufficient to prevent code-switching:

Ksenia: Um, for example, uh, my friends and I when we go something, somewhere to relax, to the cafe or the cinema, we sometimes just speaking and forget the Russian word, forget the Ukrainian word, we start to think about English words. And it's always we just speaking and using Ukrainian, Russian, English, three languages at all. We just forget a word in English, use Russian, use Ukrainian, forget the word in Ukrainian, use Russian, use English, forget the word in Russian, use Ukrainian, English all the time.

Bridget: Wow. So what does that mean for you in terms of your development in those languages?

Ksenia: It means that I need to learn more. To learn how to just, [pause] turn off English and start to speak Russian. Turn off Russian, and start speaking English. Not mix them at all.

Bridget: Okay. And how does taking classes in English affect that problem?

Ksenia: Mm, taking classes. [Pause] Uh...

Bridget: Does it make it harder to develop your Russian and Ukrainian? Do you worry that it's hurting your Russian or Ukrainian?

Ksenia: No, it's not hurting our language, it just makes us think on three languages. On the one time. We just think one idea on Russian, then we just automatically translate it on English, automatically translate it in Ukrainian. (Original language from audio file, 24 February 2011)

Like Aleksandr, Ksenia both code-switches outside of class and believes she needs better control over her language. Yet, at the same time, Ksenia acknowledges that during class, she uses and translates into three languages at once, even when the medium of instruction is 'only' English.

Another Wales program student, Evgeny, spoke Ukrainian with his grandmother and Russian with his parents and studied English and German in a school of foreign languages. In terms of speaking Russian at home, he said,

I speaking on Russian, but, uh, I don't think that it's correct. I'm ashamed of it. Because our national language is Ukrainian, and, uh, I think that, it's incorrect. But I can do nothing because my parents know Ukrainian very, really bad. (Original language from audio file, 3 March 2011)

In addition to these languages, he told me, 'it's my dream to study Chinese language or some of Asian languages' (original language from audio file, 3 March 2011). While he acknowledged his own multilingual repertoire and expressed interest in expanding it, he was concerned about knowing Ukrainian at a high level and about not using it sufficiently.

In contrast to Ksenia, students in one unique group-work session of a third-year EMI economics class I observed seemed to take a more playful attitude toward enacting multilingual repertoires. The teacher had asked these students to write questions in English for a multiple-choice quiz to be taken by their peers from other groups. They were told to have a statement or question with four possible answers – one correct and three incorrect. During the task, I observed and recorded one group of six students. They were speaking in English when Tamara (Line 11) asked, in Russian, for the translation of a word into English. While Tamara acknowledged the translation with the Russian word for yes, *da* (Line 14), Nadezhda inadvertently agreed in Spanish (Line 15). This triggered a playful switch to multiple languages and a discussion in Russian about which languages they were studying, before they returned to the primary task in English and Russian:

Line	Speaker and utterance	Language	English translation
1 2	**Lyuba:** I think it will be a very easy question.	English	**Lyuba:** I think it will be a very easy question.
3 4 5	**Tamara:** No, it's okay, no problem. From, more questions more better for us so.	English	**Tamara:** No, it's okay, no problem. From, more questions more better for us so.
6	**Anya:** But about this area.	English	**Anya:** But about this area.
7 8 9 10	**Lyuba:** We will give the one peculiarity and the question, 'What period of time this peculiarity, uh, is'.	English	**Lyuba:** We will give the one peculiarity and the question, 'What period of time this peculiarity, uh, is'.
11	**Tamara:** *Kak eto? Prinadlezhit?*	Russian,	**Tamara:** What is it? Belongs?
12	Depends?	English	Depends?
13	**Anya:** Depends to.	English	**Anya:** Depends to.
14	**Tamara:** *Da.* Depends to.	Russian, English	**Tamara:** Yes. Depends to.
15	**Nadezhda:** *Si.* Yes.	Spanish, English	**Nadezhda:** Yes. Yes.
16	**Yuri:** Yes?	English	**Yuri:** Yes?
17	**Tamara:** Yes.	English	**Tamara:** Yes.

(Continued)

Line	Speaker and utterance	Language	English translation
18	**Nadezhda:** *Si.* Yes.	Spanish, English	**Nadezhda:** Yes. Yes.
19	**Yaroslav:** *Ja.*	German	**Yaroslav:** Yes.
20	**Tamara:** *Si.* Yes.	Spanish, English	**Tamara:** Yes. Yes.
21 22	**Lyuba:** And one more question. *Oui. Oui.* [laughter]	English, French	**Lyuba:** And one more question. Yes. Yes.
23	**Nadezhda:** Shut up, please.	English	**Nadezhda:** Shut up, please.
24 25	**Tamara:** *Ty germanka, kak budet po-nemetski?*	Russian	**Tamara:** You are a German girl, how would you say it in German?
26 27	**Nadezhda:** *Kto germanka? Anya – germanka?*	Russian	**Nadezhda:** Who is a German girl? Is Anya German?
28	**Tamara:** *Nemetskyi uchish?*	Russian	**Tamara:** Do you study German?
29	**Lyuba:** *Frantsuzskyi.*	Russian	**Lyuba:** French.
30	**Anya:** *My nemetskyi uchim.*	Russian	**Anya:** We study German.
31	**Tamara:** *Ja, si, oui,* uh	German, Spanish, French	**Tamara:** Yes, yes, yes, uh
32	**Nadezhda:** *Ja!*	German	**Nadezhda:** Yes!
33	**Tamara:** *Ja!*	German	**Tamara:** Yes!
34	**Yaroslav:** *Ja!*	German	**Yaroslav:** Yes!
35	**Tamara:** *Tu es allemand?*[sic]	French	**Tamara:** You are German?
36 37	**Nadezhda:** *Est-ce que tu allemand?* [sic]	French	**Nadezhda:** Are you German?
38	**Tamara:** *Jo*	Swedish	**Tamara:** Yes
39 40	**Nadezhda:** *Eshchë est' takoe slovo kak spielt*	Russian, German	**Nadezhda:** There's another word that plays like that
41 42	**Tamara:** Sweden, *ser'ezno, Jo. Jo.*	English, Russian, Swedish	**Tamara:** Sweden, really, yes. Yes.
43	**Lyuba:** So, the next question.	English	**Lyuba:** So, the next question.

(Original language from audio file, 21 October 2010)

The instantiations of Spanish, German, French and Swedish all seem to be one-note citations, marked most often by the word 'yes' in multiple languages rather than extensive communication. These languages are not native languages that support the use of another foreign language. Yet, these one-word switches also triggered Tamara's sincere curiosity (expressed in Russian) about which languages students were studying; her questions were designed to account for her peers' linguistic behavior at that moment.

Moreover, that questioning process alternated between asking *what* students study and *who* students are. The focus on who students are could be either a means of jokingly suggesting that what you study is part of who you are, or a linguistic convention for asking in Russian what someone studies. On the other hand, the question 'are you German?' could also reflect the realization that some students have lived in other countries, an experience that influences their linguistic repertoires. In interviews with students from other groups, for example, it was reported that a Wales student lived in Germany in her early childhood and 'is speaking German much better than English' (original language from audio file, 24 February 2011). Another interviewee reported that a philology student attended school in Italy for a period of time and 'has a lot of difficulties connected with Ukrainian' (original language from audio file, 8 April 2011). Students' mobility (most likely a result of their parents choosing to move their families to other countries for work) thus increases their linguistic repertoire. Tamara, for example, has noted in social media posts that her mother is in Sweden and that she has traveled to Sweden to visit. This would account for her use of Swedish in that moment.

These multilingual repertoires, intertwined with the students' multilingual identities, emerged despite explicit efforts to keep the task in English. Before this multilingual exchange, the conversation about the task was entirely in English, until one student switched to Russian. Another student responded, 'Speak English, please'. After this multilingual exchange, students returned to switching freely between two languages, English and Russian. As the teacher came by to check on the group, she said, 'I hope you are discussing in English'. The English-only ideology competes with a multilingual reality, and in the context of classroom group work, the multilingual reality prevails. As a Wales program student, Pyotr, said about his use of Russian in group work, despite the presence of students from English-speaking Nigeria, 'I try to speak English more with everyone, but this is how it comes out' (my translation from Russian audio file, 10 March 2011).

Language in the Written Domain

A form of translanguaging found at Alfred Nobel University that could protect Ukrainian in the language ecology was the mesoalternation between languages in the oral and written domains. It was reported that, regardless of whether the medium of instruction is Ukrainian or Russian, Ukrainian is the only acceptable language for written assignments such as term papers (papers written at the end of a professional class) and diploma papers (papers written at the end of one's university study). For most students, and in most courses at the university, this constitutes an act of translanguaging in which course content is taught primarily in one language (Russian) through oral and visual modes, and students complete a summative assessment in another language (Ukrainian) through the written mode.

The expectation to write in Ukrainian was linked by teachers to broader social practices and expectations in Ukraine. Viktor Andreyevich told me that he writes books in Russian and Ukrainian, but 'you know, here, they prefer to publish books in Ukrainian' (original language from audio file, 25 January 2011). 'They', in this case, likely refers to Ukrainian companies and university organizations that print textbooks and research articles written by university professors. Viktoria Sergeyevna revealed that she is expected to publish articles in Ukrainian and uses Google Translate to help translate her Russian academic writings. Since publications can be both internal to the university and nationwide, the push to write in Ukrainian, while perhaps not in official legislation, is part of the linguistic culture (Schiffman, 2006) that has emerged in the post-Soviet era in Ukraine. These preferences and norms manifested themselves implicitly in classroom discourse in EMI classes. On those rare occasions when Ukrainian was heard in the classroom, it was used to refer to textbooks that had been published with Ukrainian titles, to printed government documents such as a visa or to the name of a TV show that appears in writing in the show's logo.

As English emerged as a medium of instruction, it also emerged as the expected language for written papers, potentially supplanting Ukrainian. Essays, final exams and term papers are written by Wales program students in English because, eventually, the evaluation team at the University of Wales needs to be able to read documents to confirm the students' progress toward the joint degree (Oleg Tarnopolsky, personal communication, 18 July 2012). For this reason, diploma papers of Wales students are also expected to be written in English. Larisa Ivanovna told the whole class about their final semester paper, 'This term paper should be written in English. It's very difficult to find information on internet on certain topics. You have to find in Russian, maybe translate. If you have problems I will try to help you' (paraphrased quote from original English, field notes, 16 February 2011). Larisa Ivanovna's comments indicate, however, that translanguaging is still encouraged. The difference is that, rather than translanguaging from Russian to Ukrainian, students were translanguaging from Russian (visual) to English (written).

In terms of student attitudes, these dynamics are exemplified again through Larisa Ivanovna's conversation with a student after an

English-medium class. When I asked Larisa Ivanovna what the conversation was about, she replied that the student wanted to know in which language she should write her report – Russian or English. Larisa Ivanovna told the student to write in Ukrainian, but she didn't want to (field notes, 11 November 2010). The student had, perhaps, become accustomed in this class to translanguaging between Russian and English, and was not as proficient in Ukrainian. The requirement to use Ukrainian, however, suggests that this report was likely a paper for the student's conference planned for the following month rather than for Larisa Ivanovna's course.

Even when papers are written in Ukrainian, another act of translanguaging favors English. University professors reported that some students defend their papers orally in English. Viktor Andreyevich said, 'Every year, about 100 students defend their diploma papers in English. It is quite welcome, it's considered as a kind of achievement' (original English from audio file, 21 February 2011). Larisa Ivanovna also referred to defending one's diploma paper in English as an achievement. After students defended their final course papers to the class in English, she said, 'Well, your presentations are very good, and I'm quite satisfied with your oral defense. …And I think you will defend your diploma in English because you proved them quite successfully' (original English from video file, 26 May 2011).

Overall, then, Ukrainian is reportedly preferred over Russian in the written domain at the classroom level – a sign that the change in Ukrainian's status and policy at the national level has impacted language use at the university. For students who study in Russian, writing in Ukrainian may offer a way to maintain both languages in their repertoire. Yet, English is also permissible in the written domain now, potentially limiting the development of Ukrainian in and through this domain. On the other hand, when the written domain is understood in combination with the oral and visual domains, it is clear that, when English is used, it is often in combination with at least one other language.

Implications for Theory and Practice of Translanguaging in Higher Education

The case of Alfred Nobel University is unique to Dnipropetrovsk and Ukraine as whole. More research is needed at other universities in the Ukrainian context and other post-Soviet contexts on translanguaging practices. In addition, more research is needed in these contexts on the impact of translanguaging on multilingual language acquisition in higher education (e.g. Lasagabaster, 2008). Nevertheless, the findings from this study offer insights into the possibilities afforded by translanguaging in higher education. In one Ukrainian university alone, Ukrainian appeared in English- and

Russian-medium classes, Russian appeared in Ukrainian-language classes, English appeared in Russian-medium classes and Spanish, French, German and Latin could be heard in English- and Russian-medium classes.

Not only were these languages and language varieties interwoven among the classes, there was evidence that the use of one or more languages in a classroom was generally aligned with pedagogical goals. In classes designated as English medium, teachers and students used Russian to ensure understanding of key course terms and concepts. While Ukrainian was much less frequent than Russian in classroom discourse, it emerged as more prevalent than both English and Russian in academic writing. This is true both for written assignments by students and for textbooks or other printed sources cited by teachers in Ukrainian. Additional foreign languages were expected to share a role in students' academic and future career development.

Translanguaging practices observed at the university were fluid, according to not only the choice and purpose of the languages but also the mode of communication. Teachers, students and outside guests showed PowerPoint slides or blackboard writings in one language while referring to those same texts in yet another language. The languages used in written and oral modes varied from moment to moment (English–Russian, Ukrainian–Russian, English–Ukrainian), but these choices can be understood in terms of the relative position of these languages in each moment.

From a more critical perspective, it is clear that the positioning of these languages is fraught with power issues. While students and teachers at Alfred Nobel have a choice in the language of oral classroom communication, writing was expected to be in Ukrainian. English was privileged over Russian, Ukrainian and additional foreign languages as an expected medium of instruction. However, even these constraints and hierarchies shifted from one language to another based on the communicative event at hand and, often, were connected to the use of one or more languages. Students and teachers alike expressed awareness of and, at times, concerns for the mixing of languages into 'impure' varieties.

This study demonstrates that studying classroom dynamics through a translanguaging lens yields insights into the status of languages in a particular language ecology. To turn a phrase from Cooper's (1989) questions about language planning, translanguaging scholars can ask: Who is translanguaging from which language to which language for what purpose? What modalities are being used in translanguaging? In which communicative events do certain forms of translanguaging occur? By asking and answering these questions, scholars can identify which languages need more pedagogical support and in which domains or contexts to ensure their future and can identify educational spaces in which multiple languages can, and will, continue to thrive.

Notes

(1) A *region* is an administrative territory of Ukraine that in other countries is referred to as a state, province, prefecture and so on. The term is an emerging English translation of the Ukrainian and Russian term *oblast*.
(2) All names of individuals from the university are pseudonyms. To be consistent with practices observed in classes, teachers are identified by a first name and a patronymic (a middle name derived from one's father's name). Students are referred to by first name only.

References

Arel, D. (2002) Interpreting 'nationality' and 'language' in the 2001 Ukrainian census. *Post-Soviet Affairs* 18 (3), 213–249.
Arel, D. (2006) Introduction: Theorizing politics of cultural identities in Russia and Ukraine. In D. Arel and B.A. Ruble (eds) *Rebounding Identities: The Politics of Identity in Russia and Ukraine* (pp. 1–30). Washington, DC: Woodrow Wilson Center Press.
Baker, C. (2001) *Foundations of Bilingual Education and Bilingualism* (3rd edn). Clevedon: Multilingual Matters.
Baker, C. (2003) Biliteracy and transliteracy in Wales: Language planning and the Welsh national curriculum. In N.H. Hornberger (ed.) *Continua of Biliteracy: An Ecological Framework for Educational Policy, Research, and Practice in Multilingual Settings* (pp. 71–90). Clevedon: Multilingual Matters.
Bilaniuk, L. (2005) *Contested Tongues: Language Politics and Cultural Correction in Ukraine.* Ithaca, NY: Cornell University Press.
Bilaniuk, L. (2009) Criticism and confidence: Reshaping the linguistic marketplace in post-Soviet Ukraine. In L.M.L. Zaleska Onyshkevych and M.G. Rewakowicz (eds) *Contemporary Ukraine on the Cultural Map of Europe* (pp. 336–358). Armonk, NY: M.E. Sharpe.
Bilaniuk, L. (2010) Cultural politics on Ukrainian television: Language choice and code switching on 'Khoroshou'. *Canadian-American Slavic Studies* 44 (1/2), 200–216.
Bilaniuk, L. and Melnyk, S. (2008) A tense and shifting balance: Bilingualism and education in Ukraine. *The International Journal of Bilingual Education and Bilingualism* 11 (3/4), 340–372.
Bonacina, F. and Gafaranga, J. (2011) 'Medium of instruction' vs. 'medium of classroom interaction': Language choice in a French complementary school classroom in Scotland. *International Journal of Bilingual Education and Bilingualism* 14 (3), 319–334.
Cooper, R. (1989) *Language Planning and Social Change.* Cambridge: Cambridge University Press.
Cots, J.M., Llurda, E. and Garrett, P. (2014) Language policies and practices in the internationalisation of higher education on the European margins: An introduction. *Journal of Multilingual and Multicultural Development* 35 (4), 311–317.
Creese, A., Bhatt, A., Bhojani, N. and Martin, P. (2008) Fieldnotes in team ethnography: Researching complementary schools. *Qualitative Research* 8 (2), 197–215.
Creese, A. and Blackledge, A. (2011) Ideologies and interactions in multilingual education: What can an ecological approach tell us about bilingual pedagogy? In C. Hélot and M. Ó Laoire (eds) *Language Policy for the Multilingual Classroom: Pedagogy of the Possible* (pp. 3–21). Bristol: Multilingual Matters.
Duff, P.A. (1995) An ethnography of communication in immersion classrooms in Hungary. *TESOL Quarterly* 29 (3), 505–537.
Flores, N. (2014) 'Let's not forget that translanguaging is a political act'. The Educational Linguist, blog post, 19 July. See https://educationallinguist.wordpress.

com/2014/07/19/lets-not-forget-that-translanguaging-is-a-political-act/ (accessed 21 June 2015).

Friedman, D.A. (2006) (Re)imagining the nation: Language socialization in Ukrainian classrooms. PhD dissertation, University of California.

Friedman, D.A. (2009) Speak correctly: Error correction as language socialization practice in a Ukrainian classroom. *Applied Linguistics* 31 (3), 346–367.

García, O. (ed.) (2009) *Bilingual Education in the 21st Century: A Global Perspective.* Malden, MA: Wiley-Blackwell.

García, O. (2011) Educating New York's bilingual children: Constructing a future from the past. *International Journal of Bilingual Education and Bilingualism* 14 (2), 133–153.

García, O. and Sylvan, C.E. (2011) Pedagogies and practices in multilingual classrooms: Singularities in pluralities. *Modern Language Journal* 95 (3), 385–400.

Hammersley, M. and Atkinson, P. (2007) *Ethnography: Principles in Practice* (3rd edn). London: Routledge.

Haugen, E. (2001) The ecology of language. In A. Fill and P. Mühlhäusler (eds) *The Ecolinguistics Reader* (pp. 57–66). London: Continuum. (Original work published 1972).

Hornberger, N.H. (2003) Multilingual language policies and the continua of biliteracy: An ecological approach. In N.H. Hornberger (ed.) *Continua of Biliteracy: An Ecological Framework for Educational Policy, Research, and Practice in Multilingual Settings* (pp. 315–339). Clevedon: Multilingual Matters.

Hornberger, N.H. and Link, H. (2012) Translanguaging and transnational literacies in multilingual classrooms: A biliteracy lens. *International Journal of Bilingual Education and Bilingualism* 15 (3), 261–278.

Hrycak, A. (2006) Institutional legacies and language revival in Ukraine. In D. Arel and B.A. Ruble (eds) *Rebounding Identities: The Politics of Identity in Russia and Ukraine* (pp. 62–88). Washington, DC: Woodrow Wilson Center Press.

Huguet, Á. (2007) Language use and language attitudes in Catalonia. In D. Lasagabaster and Á. Huguet (eds) *Multilingualism in European Bilingual Contexts: Language Use and Attitudes* (pp. 17–39). Clevedon: Multilingual Matters.

Janmaat, J.G. (2008) Nation building, democratization and globalization as competing priorities in Ukraine's education system. *Nationalities Papers* 36 (1), 1–23.

Lasagabaster, D. (2008) Foreign language competence in content and integrated language courses. *The Open Applied Linguistics Journal* 1, 31–42.

Mortensen, J. and Haberland, H. (2012) English – the new Latin of academia? Danish universities as a case. *International Journal of the Sociology of Language* 216, 175–197.

Pavlenko, A. (2008a) Multilingualism in post-Soviet countries: Language revival, language removal, and sociolinguistic theory. *The International Journal of Bilingual Education and Bilingualism* 11 (3/4), 275–340.

Pavlenko, A. (2008b) Russian in post-Soviet countries. *Russian Linguistics* 32, 59–80.

Pavlenko, A. (2011) Language rights versus speakers' rights: On the applicability of Western language rights approaches in Eastern European contexts. *Language Policy* 10 (1), 37–58.

Phillipson, R. (2006) English: A cuckoo in the European higher education nest of languages? *European Journal of English Studies* 10 (1), 13–32.

Phillipson, R. (2013, April) English as a threat: Reality or myth? Paper presented at English in Europe: Opportunity or Threat? Conference, Copenhagen, Denmark.

Saarinen, T. (2012) Internationalization of Finnish higher education – is language an issue? *International Journal of the Sociology of Language* 216, 157–173.

Schiffman, H. (2006) Language policy and linguistic culture. In T. Ricento (ed.) *An Introduction to Language Policy: Theory and Method* (pp. 111–125). Malden, MA: Blackwell.

Scollon, R. and Scollon, S.W. (2003) *Discourses in Place: Language in the Material World.* London: Routledge.

Söderlundh, H. (2012) Global policies and local norms: Sociolinguistic awareness and language choice at an international university. *International Journal of the Sociology of Language* 216, 87–109.

Stewart, W. (1968) A sociolinguistic typology for describing national multilingualism. In J. Fishman (ed.) *Readings in the Sociology of Language* (pp. 531–545). The Hague: Mouton.

Tarnopolsky, O. and Goodman, B. (2014) The ecology of language in classrooms at a university in Ukraine. *Language and Education* 28 (4), 383–396.

Tollefson, J.W. and Tsui, A.B.M. (eds) (2004) *Medium of Instruction Policies: Which Agenda? Whose Agenda?* Mahwah, NJ: Lawrence Erlbaum Associates.

Tosi, A. (2006) The devil in the kaleidoscope: Can Europe speak with a single voice in many languages? In C. Leung and J. Jenkins (eds) *Reconfiguring Europe: The Contribution of Applied Linguistics* (pp. 5–20). London: Equinox.

Unterberger, B. (2012) English medium programmes at Austrian business faculties: A status quo survey on national trends and a case study on programme design and delivery. *AILA Review* 25, 80–100.

van der Walt, C. (2013) *Multilingual Higher Education: Beyond English Medium Orientations.* Bristol: Multilingual Matters.

Yatseniuk says no one is prohibiting people from freely using Russian language in Ukraine (2014). *Interfax-Ukraine* 18 March. See http://en.interfax.com.ua/news/general/196505.html (accessed 21 June 2015).

Williams, C. (1994) *Arfarniad o ddulliau dysgu ac addysgu yng nghyd-destun addysg uwchradd ddwyieithog* [*Evaluation of Teaching and Learning Methods in the Context of Bilingual Secondary Education*]. Bangor, Wales: University of Wales.

5   Professors Translanguaging in Practice: Three Cases from a Bilingual University

Catherine M. Mazak, Fiorelys Mendoza and Lauren Pérez Mangonéz

Introduction

This chapter compares three professors at a bilingual university in Puerto Rico who teach using what García and Li (2014: 92) call a translanguaging pedagogy. The three cases compared here show a range of practices implemented by the three professors, who have very different linguistic and cultural backgrounds but who all enact a flexible bilingual pedagogy (Blackledge & Creese, 2010) while teaching university-level academic content to Spanish–English bilingual students who have a range of different language proficiencies. We argue that the professors and the practices that we describe here are leveraging students' bilingual resources to create affordances for students to develop their understanding of the academic subject matter. By doing this, these professors also create opportunities in the classrooms for students to develop their academic language in both Spanish and English.

The bilingual university in the context of Puerto Rico

The use of English in classrooms in Puerto Rico has been highly contested since the US invaded the island in 1898 and, soon after, implemented English-medium instruction in the schools (Schmidt, 2014). Because this English-medium instruction was explicitly meant to 'Americanize' Puerto Ricans (Algren de Gutiérrez, 1987), and because it failed to do so, Puerto Ricans, in general, have been resistant to the idea of English-medium instruction in the public schools. Vélez (2000: 75) asserts that 'Puerto Ricans for the most part enthusiastically support the concept of individual bilingualism... But the concept of societal bilingualism is certainly much more controversial'. Many parents who have the economic resources to do so choose bilingual private education for their children in hopes of developing this individual bilingualism, which is seen as beneficial for competitiveness in the job market and useful for the ever-looming possibility of migration to the US. However, the language of everyday communication remains Spanish for most Puerto Ricans.

The role of English in higher education is somewhat less controversial, since ideologically it is believed to be the 'language of science' and, thus, accepted as part of university study, particularly in its written form (Mazak & Herbas-Donoso, 2014a). Even courses such as 'The History of Spain' are taught using English textbooks, and the use of English texts is normalized in many science and engineering classrooms. In this way, the context of higher education in Puerto Rico mirrors other higher education contexts around the world: English is the taken-for-granted 'international language of academia' (Phillipson, 2009), but it coexists with the local vernacular (Spanish) in classrooms.

The ideologies surrounding English in higher education in Puerto Rico, then, are multilayered. These layers are influenced by Puerto Rico's sociopolitical relationship with both the US and the world. English is a colonial language (Puerto Rico is still a US territory, with the US Congress in control of its sovereignty) and, thus, has been constructed as the enemy in a long history of resistance against Americanization (Algren de Gutiérrez, 1987; Torres Gonzalez, 2002). English also has an intricately intertwined relationship with Puerto Ricans at every socioeconomic level, as migration and return migration create a continuous flow of people between Puerto Rico and the US in search of jobs (Duany, 2002). This 'nation on the move', as anthropologist Jorge Duany (2002) has called it, brings English linguistic practices back and forth between Puerto Rican communities in the US and the islands. In addition, English is a global language, associated particularly with technology and science, and this additional meaning permeates Puerto Rican society alongside resistance to English as a tool of Americanization. This complex push-pull of Puerto Rico's relationship with English creates a perfect storm for the development of translanguaging practices, as does most higher education language policy in Puerto Rico.

Language policy in many institutions of higher education in Puerto Rico is 'open', that is, there are few explicit policies requiring courses to be taught in Spanish or English (Carroll & Mazak, forthcoming 2017). This opens the door for translanguaging practice in higher education classrooms as professors and students navigate the push-pull of English and Spanish that is characteristic of the Puerto Rican context. For example, the university where this study takes place calls itself, in the undergraduate course catalog, a 'bilingual university'. The only identifiable written language policy (also in the undergraduate catalog) goes on to state, 'Spanish is the language of instruction in most courses at UPRM [University of Puerto Rico at Mayagüez], but students are required to have a working knowledge of the English language. The individual professor decides the language used in class lectures and in student evaluation activities' (UPRM, 2013: 69). Thus, it is really up to individual professors to make choices about how to use Spanish and English in their classrooms.

Translanguaging as Pedagogy in Higher Education

According to García and Li (2014: 92), 'Translanguaging as pedagogy refers to building on bilingual students' language practices flexibly in order to develop new understandings and new language practices, including those deemed "academic standard" language practices'. Importantly, this definition emphasizes the development of both new understandings and new language practices. That is, the goal of using two languages in translanguaging pedagogy is, simultaneously, to teach content knowledge using all of the students' linguistic resources and to further develop those linguistic resources. In higher education, this development often means apprenticing students in the linguistic and rhetorical structures of specific fields of study. In the three cases presented here, the fields of study are agriculture (specifically weed science), evolutionary biology and abnormal psychology.

This chapter focuses on professors' translanguaging practices and seeks to show how these practices constitute a translanguaging pedagogy specific to the higher education context. Lewis et al. (2012: 665) explain teacher-directed translanguaging as 'a planned and structured activity by the teacher'; for example, deliberately alternating the language mode in class (reading in English and presenting about the reading in Welsh in one class; reading in Welsh and presenting in English in another class). We agree that translanguaging pedagogy is intentional, but we will show that it is often not quite as structured or planned as Lewis et al. imply. Rather, the translanguaging pedagogy that we saw in our three cases developed quite organically, based on professors' keen understandings of students' sociolinguistic, cultural and historical backgrounds. In this sense, translanguaging as pedagogy is more of an attitude or stance that sees the value of using all of students' linguistic resources and takes steps (some more deliberate than others) to use and develop those resources. It enacts a translanguaging ideology (García & Li, 2014) or a multilingual orientation (Blackledge & Creese, 2010) that results in the implementation of certain teaching strategies and practices. Thus, 'translanguaging as pedagogy involves *leveraging*, that is, *deliberately* and simultaneously merging students' repertoires of practice' (García & Li, 2014: 93).

Translanguaging pedagogy has consequences for classroom dynamics. Students will read professors' translanguaging differently, depending on the professors' own cultural and linguistic backgrounds. A Puerto Rican professor (such as the agriculture professor we describe below) asking students to discuss English academic articles in Spanish is perceived differently than an Anglo professor from the US with emerging knowledge of Spanish doing so (such as the biology professor in our study). García and Li (2014: 93) argue that 'the teacher who uses translanguaging gives up her authority role in the classroom', particularly if the teacher's linguistic repertoire does not exactly mirror students' repertoires. However, as we will show in our examples, not all teachers give up authority by translanguaging; some actually gain authority. By translanguaging, they enact an identity as professors who relate to students, strategically positioning themselves as authorities who can successfully apprentice college students in the discourses of their respective disciplines. So, though we agree with García and Li (2014: 94) that 'a teacher who uses translanguaging as pedagogy participates as learner; that is, she adopts a multivoicedness, a *raznoglosie*, in Baktin's terms', that multivoicedness indexes different cultural meanings and has different identity consequences, depending on professors' linguistic and cultural backgrounds and the context in which they work.

Previous work in the Puerto Rican university context has shown that though many professors held monolingual views about language, specifically claiming English to be 'the language of science', they enacted translanguaging ideologies in the classroom (Mazak & Herbas-Donoso, 2014a). In other words, the power of English as an academic language is not great enough in the Puerto Rican context to make most professors give all their classes only in English, even though many have been trained in the US and have the language proficiency to do so. The resulting classroom practices thus chip away at monolingual ideologies as they legitimize bilingual practices and alternative voices in academia. 'By exposing alternative histories, representations and knowledge, translanguaging has the potential to crack the "standard language" bubble in education that continues to ostracize many bilingual students' (García & Li, 2014: 115).

Research Methods

This study is a cross-case analysis of three case studies conducted by the three authors of this chapter at the same university, the UPRM. Each was conducted as an ethnographic case study including classroom observations, an interview with the professor, interviews with the students (in the case of the biology and agriculture professors) and surveys of students (in the case of the psychology class). The agriculture professor was observed 11 times (50 minutes per observation), the biology professor was observed 20 times (1 hour and 15 minutes per observation) and the psychology professor was observed 9 times (1 hour and 15 minutes per observation). The case studies were not designed as part of one comprehensive cross-case study, which accounts for some discrepancy in the data collected. Instead, they were designed as individual case studies by the authors of this chapter that took place over the course of a number of years (2009–2013) and that were then combined and reanalyzed across cases. Cross-case analysis of these particular professors was warranted, because they each had different linguistic and cultural backgrounds, yet they all used translanguaging practices in their classrooms in ways that benefited students.

For the cross-case analysis, we relied on the ethnographic field notes taken in each class over the course of a semester and interviews with the professors. Field notes, and their corresponding audio recordings for the psychology and agriculture professors, were analyzed and coded for the professors' translanguaging practices. Interviews were also analyzed specifically for the professors' reflections on their translanguaging practices. We were guided by the research question: How are translanguaging practices used to create affordances for students to both learn content and develop their academic language in Spanish and English? Once these translanguaging practices and reflections were initially coded, named and described, they were compared across the three cases to explore similarities and differences. We explain these similarities and differences, taking into consideration the different linguistic, social and cultural backgrounds of the professors. In this section, we describe the professors in detail before going on to describe, compare and contrast their translanguaging practices in the subsequent sections.

Víctor, the agriculture professor

At the time of the classroom observations, Víctor was an assistant professor who had recently returned from studying for his doctoral degree in weed science at a large agricultural university in the southern US. His bachelor's and master's degrees were from the UPRM in the department in which he teaches. Víctor is Puerto Rican, and the fact that, as an undergraduate, he had taken the same weed-science course that he was observed teaching positioned him well to relate to the students in the class. Víctor's teaching persona was professional yet easygoing. He took time to check for student understanding and carefully created PowerPoint presentations for all of his lectures, which he made available through the online course software Moodle. Students liked the fact that they could download the class materials ahead of time, and it was important to Víctor to provide students with careful explanations of the main concepts of the course, as evidenced by the time he took to stop and ask students whether they understood and to field questions. He communicated his excitement about his profession by sharing conference presentations he had delivered, which included photos of his research with aquatic weeds where he appeared waist-high in water, taking samples in the field.

Víctor learned English as many of his weed-science students did through mandatory English class in K-12 school in Puerto Rico. Through undergraduate internship opportunities with federal agriculture programs in the US, he was able to further develop his spoken English and his professional knowledge in the field. He received a special university scholarship from the UPRM, which financed his doctoral study in return for a set number of years of service as a professor at the university. This program was designed to train and retain promising Puerto Rican academics. Though Víctor had very well-developed academic English, he spoke with students mostly in Spanish.

Ray, the biology professor

Ray was a junior faculty member at the time of data collection and had recently obtained his PhD in the US. He had taught at the UPRM for just over a year and a half. Born and raised in the US, Ray's decision to come to Puerto Rico was thrilling for him. He thought it was 'the perfect job', given the fact that he had visited Latin America and had studied some Spanish and that his dissertation was about tropical birds in Panamá. Ray was a self-reflective pedagogue who realized his weaknesses in the classroom and tried to make them better. To keep students interested, he said, 'I vary my tone of voice; use my hands, and the whiteboard. I also address students directly, by name or eye contact. Especially when people are falling asleep or not paying attention. I start lecturing them or walk over to their desks'. He knows when such techniques work, usually because of the immediate response he gets. Additional approaches are guided more toward getting students involved in the class. He comments, 'I give participation points. Some students don't like it, but I want students to feel like they are learning actively, they are involved'. The rationale behind the participation points is getting the shy people to talk. The professor mentioned, 'You spread the talking around the classroom. Plus, opening your mouth makes students feel involved'. The participation points go hand in hand with Friday class discussion activities, which are held because 'some students just can't be talked at for such a long time'. He also thinks it is great to encourage the sharing of ideas and develop a sense of community in the classroom. It also helps students develop public-speaking skills, makes them responsible for their ideas and encourages them not to get behind in the reading. Another tool used is Moodle; like Víctor's, the presentations are prepared and uploaded beforehand, so students can study them. Mock exams are also provided for practicing, and there is exam review on the day of the exam at a separate hour. Ray specifically seeks to improve his pedagogy, assessing his sections to see what needs to be changed or modified to address students' specific needs.

Though he was not the only professor who taught evolutionary biology at the UPRM, Ray was the only one who conducted this particular class in English and used a textbook written in English. Despite the fact that all classes, materials and tests were in English, Ray could understand Spanish very well. He makes it clear to students that they are expected to understand English to take the class and do well. However, he also makes them aware that questions can be asked and answered in Spanish. He is also aware of how he makes lots of jokes that nobody understands, so he tries to consciously drop in Puerto Rican words, names of local species or a culturally relevant example to get an immediate reaction from students. When asked about his ability to hold a conversation in Spanish, he felt confident: 'I've gotten better every day'. However, despite the fact that he speaks Spanish in casual conversations, he is very emphatic about the language used in the classroom: 'Students need competence in English to pass my class'. Although he is eager to help and even uses Spanish to communicate with his graduate students, especially those who have trouble speaking English, he feels that there has to be a certain competency in English.

Alison, the psychology professor

Alison was a highly sought-after psychology professor. Her cheerful, caring disposition and enthusiastic, energetic demeanor encouraged students to attend and participate in class. Alison was always professional, but also funny, looking for ways to relate the abnormal-psychology material we observed her teaching to the lives of college students through movies and popular culture. Her pedagogy engaged students through heavy emphasis on group work and discussion. She also required students to present and to incorporate engaging activities into their classroom presentations, such as psychological tests, physical exercises and YouTube videos. It was not unusual for Alison's class to engage in beginner's tai chi routines in relation to a lesson on anxiety disorder or sing along with a music video during a lesson about suicide and self-esteem. She required students to change their thinking by writing down three positive things that happened to them every day. Always one to practice what she preaches, Alison, who encouraged students to exercise to battle stress, was an active marathon runner.

Born and raised in Alaska, Alison had learned Spanish through extensive time living abroad, including in Colombia on a Fulbright scholarship. An associate professor, she has won numerous awards for her teaching and research. Alison's academic bilingualism in English and Spanish was very well developed. She was perfectly comfortable giving class in both English and Spanish and corrected students' writing in both languages.

Translanguaging Pedagogy in Practice

The goal of translanguaging pedagogy, as stated above, is twofold: (1) to teach content knowledge using all of the students' linguistic resources and (2) to create opportunities for students to further develop those linguistic resources, particularly in relation to the academic field of study. In this section, we describe the translanguaging practices of each of the three professors, before comparing and contrasting these practices in the final section.

Víctor: Translanguaging practices in a Spanish-dominant agriculture class

As mentioned above, Víctor conducted class mostly in Spanish. However, he used English materials such as academic articles and diagrams labeled in English, which led to translanguaging practices (for a fully detailed account of Víctor's translanguaging practices, see Mazak & Herbas-Donoso [2014b]). In our analysis of the observational data, we identified Víctor as using the following translanguaging practices:

(1) Using key English terminology in discussion of scientific content in Spanish.
(2) Reading text in English and talking about it in Spanish.
(3) Using Spanish cognates while referring to English text.
(4) Talking about figures labeled in English using Spanish.
(5) Using English acronyms (some pronounced in English, some pronounced in Spanish).

The following field note excerpts will illustrate how these practices worked together in translanguaging events.

Víctor Excerpt 1:

Víctor gave a class using a presentation that had been written in and delivered in English for an academic conference. For the class, he used the same slides but talked about them in Spanish. Víctor began the lecture by clearly stating that the entire PowerPoint presentation was in English. He acknowledged that students might have to put extra effort into following it, saying, *'Quiero que le presten mucha atención'* ['I want you to pay a lot of attention'], and he facilitated the classroom's ambiance by turning off the lights for students to see the slides better, saying, *'El background es negro, y necesito que vean bien'* ['The background is black, and I need you to be able to see well'].

He began talking about the slide's title, which was also a key term. While the slide was projected, he said, 'Remote sensing *o percepción*

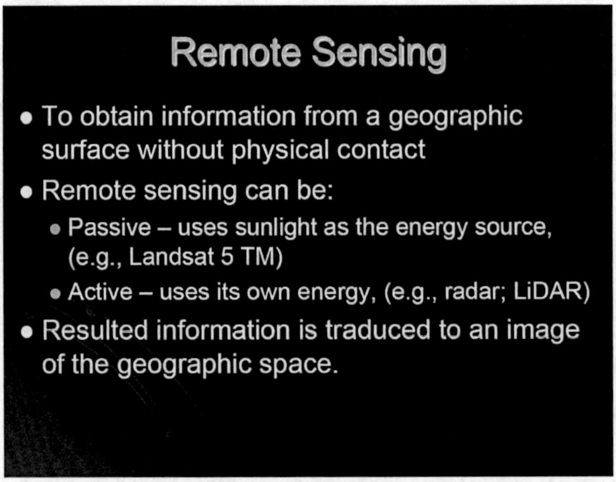

Figure 5.1 Remote sensing slide

remota, utilizando equipo multiespectral o hiperespectral' ['Remote sensing or remote perception, using multi- or hyperspectral resolution'].

The slide (Figure 5.1) was completely in English, with a key term at the top: 'Remote Sensing'. The professor kept the key concept in English, translated it and then explained its function. While keeping key technical and scientific terms in English, he also sought to ensure that the concepts were explained and understood by students using Spanish. This weaving of English and Spanish occurred in relation to the projected English text. By using this translanguaging practice, he provided opportunities for students to build content knowledge and facilitate their access to the scientific discourse of his field.

Víctor's slides were not usually in English, however. Most days, they were translanguaged: a combination of English, Spanish and graphics that required students to draw on all of their linguistic and semiotic resources to make meaning. Víctor created these slides himself by combining graphics he found in books or on the internet with labels or titles in Spanish. Excerpt 2 shows how Víctor used cognates to help students make meaning from this translanguaged text.

Víctor Excerpt 2:

Víctor's lecture was about the different types of aquatic weeds and how different methods are needed to control them. Part of his lecture was a slide (Figure 5.2) that contained a graphic titled in Spanish, *'Tipos de crecimiento'* ['Types of growth'], but which was labeled in English with the key term 'Littoral Zone' in large letters at the bottom.

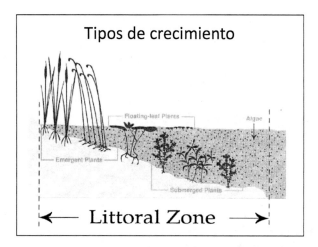

Figure 5.2 Littoral zone translanguaged slide (Image from http://www.identifypond weeds.com/functions-of-aquatic-vegetation)

Víctor pointed to the words 'Littoral Zone' on the slide and said, '*Aqui tenemos la zona litoral*' ['Here we have the littoral zone'].

In Excerpt 2, Víctor is using a translanguaging practice that draws on his students' knowledge of cognates. By pointing at the words 'littoral zone' and saying '*zona litoral*', he establishes a connection between English text and spoken Spanish that needs no further explanation. This is translanguaging: It activates students' entire linguistic repertoire in the process of teaching and learning. It is also important to point out that the slide itself relies on the teacher and the students using both Spanish and English to get the point of the diagram. The labeled diagram without the title would not fit into Víctor's lecture about the different types of growth and the different strategies to approach these types when trying to manage aquatic weeds. Therefore, Víctor's translanguaging here is integral to his pedagogy.

As part of his delivery of content material, Víctor often used acronyms. When he did this, he sometimes pronounced these acronyms in English and sometimes in Spanish. For example, he pronounced USDA by saying the letters in English U-S-D-A, while EPA he pronounced /epa/ (in English it would be E-P-A). We asked, in our interview with the professor, about this constant use of acronyms during delivery of content material. He replied,

> *Es que como es un vocabulario que es bien usado, como por ejemplo todo el mundo ahí en agricultura debería conocer que es el* USDA, United States Department of Agriculture, *igual que* EPA, Environmental Protection Agency.... *Es algo que para mí es normal, no sé si a lo mejor yo pretendo que ellos lo vieran bien normal. ... Cuando yo recibo emails de otras personas de*

Estados Unidos, de otros lugares siempre han adoptado tantos acrónimos que yo me he tenido que acostumbrar y no sé a lo mejor pretenden conscientemente que los estudiantes también se acostumbren a ellos. [It is a vocabulary that is often used, common, for example everybody there in agriculture should know what the USDA is, United States Department of Agriculture, the same with EPA, Environmental Protection Agency. ... It is something very normal for me, I don't know, maybe I intend that they [students] see it that way too. ... When I get emails from different people from the US, from other places, they have always adopted many acronyms and I've had to get used to that and I don't know, maybe they assume consciously that students should also get used to it.]

Here, Víctor explains that keeping acronyms in their English form – whether pronounced in English or Spanish – is very similar to teaching a key vocabulary word in English (as in Excerpt 1). He explains that it is necessary to use these acronyms because they are *'bien usado'* ['commonly used'] and 'normalized' in the field. By teaching his students these acronyms, he is making sure that, in their searches for and communications about the terms, they can communicate with the larger scientific community. When he says, *'Es algo que para mí es normal, no sé si a lo mejor yo pretendo que ellos lo vieran bien normal'* ['It is something very normal for me, I don't know, maybe I intend that they [students] see it that way too'], he shows his awareness of this translanguaging practice in the discourse community and his motivations behind using it.

Ray: English-dominant biology learning with a translanguaging disposition

As mentioned above, Ray's evolutionary biology class was the only section that offered the course in English medium with English textbooks. Two other professors offer the course in Spanish with a Spanish textbook. Because Ray was explicitly open to Spanish, and the students knew it, he was enacting a translanguaging pedagogy. In addition, the classroom excerpts detailed below show how this translanguaging pedagogy provided opportunities for students to learn content material and develop their academic English in relation to the field of evolutionary biology. In our analysis of the observational data, we identified Ray as using the following translanguaging practices:

(1) Facilitating the students' translanguaging.
(2) Explaining in Spanish when students got stuck.

Ray actively encouraged students to translanguage in class. That is, if a student could not express himself or herself in English, Ray asked him or her to please use Spanish. In this way, Ray actively sought to have students use their entire linguistic repertoire, even as he also emphasized their need to practice using English. Many of these events took place on what the professor called 'Discussion Fridays'. On these days, students got into small groups to answer discussion questions about the material. Then, students answered the questions in front of the whole class for points. The following field note excerpts show how Ray drew on students' entire linguistic repertoires during these interactive class sessions.

Ray Excerpt 1:

The professor asks a student to answer the question. The student starts talking but is really struggling with his English. When the professor sees it is difficult for him to even utter a word he jumps in and suggests, 'You can say it in Spanish if you want'. The student immediately switches to Spanish with no problem and waits for the professor to answer. After the professor hears the student's question, he answers the question in English.

Ray Excerpt 2:

Another question is projected on the screen: 'What causes convergent evolution?' A student without raising his hand immediately began answering, 'It is when they *evolute* [evolve]. Ahhhh', he uttered, demonstrating some frustration in his face and tone of voice. The student summarized, '*Es cuando se unen por presión ambiental*' ['It's when they unite because of environmental pressure']. Ray exclaims, 'Great! You actually answered the question and went on to talk about it'. He seems pleased and continues asking the students whether they remembered other examples of similar ecological pressure.

In both Excerpts 1 and 2, Ray demonstrates his disposition toward translanguaging. What is important to him is student participation, and encouraging this participation in Spanish meets his pedagogical goals. By being open to listening to students' Spanish, he is able to assess their understanding and encourage them when they are correct, as in Excerpt 2 when he says 'Great!' and goes on to explain in English what the student had accomplished in Spanish: 'You actually answered the question and went on to talk about it'. In this way, students understand that they can bring all their linguistic resources to bear on their learning of evolutionary biology.

Ray not only encouraged students to speak in Spanish with him, but he also encouraged them to use each other as linguistic resources as they learned evolutionary biology together, as in Excerpt 3.

Ray Excerpt 3:

The professor entered the classroom and began setting up the presentation. As the computer started, he used the time to answer students' questions. However, he also prompted students to answer their peers' questions.

One student asked a question, and the professor referred it to another student to see whether that student could answer. Another student jumped in and answered the question. The professor replied, 'Great'. Another student asked in English, 'What is an ecological niche?' Another peer immediately jumped in and answered in Spanish; yet another student added an example regarding birds and their niche, also in Spanish. The professor watched and listened. When the students had finished he said, 'The only thing I would add is not to limit you to geographical settings. Humidity, heat, and others are all parts of its niche'.

In Excerpt 3, Ray supervises a volley of students answering questions about content in Spanish. He starts the volley by tossing a student's question back to the group to see whether another student can answer. This exchange happens in English, but, as students continue to answer each other's questions, the talk switches to Spanish, which Ray continues to evaluate for content correctness. To conclude the event, he adds information in English, showing that he has followed the Spanish turn in the conversation and is responding in English. This use of translanguaging again shows Ray's disposition toward the practice and his ability to accept his students' use of their bilingual resources to learn content.

Occasionally, but very rarely, Ray also used Spanish in class himself.

Ray Excerpt 4:

Ray begins class by giving students the grades for the exams and discussing them. Most of the class time is spent talking about the questions and answering the students' doubts. A student asks the professor about parsimonious phylogeny. Ray asks another student to answer the question, but a third student jumps in and tries to explain it to the student in Spanish. The student who originally asked the question still seems a bit confused. Ray interrupts and tells the other students to allow him to explain. Ray explains in English, and when he finishes the students summarize his explanation in Spanish. The professor sees that the student still looks unsure. The professor tries to explain it in English again, but the student does not understand. Then the professor begins explaining the concept in Spanish. He is very slow and struggling a bit, but he uses his hands and looks directly at the student when explaining. Once he is done, Ray asks the student to repeat what he understood back to him in Spanish. When he does, the professor seems satisfied with the answer and continues around the room answering other questions.

As mentioned in the previous section, Ray's Spanish was still developing, though he did use it to talk with his graduate students. Ray was emphatic that his class was English medium and made sure students knew that they needed to understand English to do well in the course. However, Ray's translanguaging pedagogy would not let a student stay confused if using Spanish was going to get the message across, as seen in Excerpt 4. After he had used his method of having other students try to explain the concept of parsimonious phylogeny to the confused student, he decided to take matters into his own hands and explain it himself in Spanish. To double-check, he insisted that the student explain it back to him in Spanish. This use of translanguaging assured Ray that the student was no longer confused, and he could move on to other questions.

Ray's willingness and ability to connect to students using translanguaging helps to create a teaching persona that encourages students to use their entire linguistic repertoires. This is not true of other professors who give their classes in English medium; many of these professors have been known to pretend that they do not understand students' Spanish and to actively quiet their Spanish speaking with one another. Ray is deliberately creating a very different teaching persona here using a translanguaging pedagogy, as we have seen in the previous excerpts.

Alison: Mixing it up in a bilingual psychology classroom

In contrast to Víctor, who mainly used Spanish in class, and Ray, who mainly used English in class, Alison used both. That is, English and Spanish coexisted easily and without tension in her pedagogy. While Víctor apprenticed students in the use of English through key terms, and Ray pushed their limits by operating almost entirely in English (though with a disposition toward translanguaging that made it acceptable to students), Alison used Spanish and English in parallel most of the time. By using both the English and Spanish terms for abnormal-psychology concepts and giving explanations in both English and Spanish, she effectively repeated key concepts throughout the course. This may have acted to solidify the content material for her bilingual students while simultaneously modeling a fluid academic bilingualism that could serve them well in their further studies and their professional lives as psychologists. In our analysis of the observational data, we identified Alison as using the following translanguaging practices:

(1) Restating in English or Spanish (for instructions, definitions, clarifications, key terms).

(2) Drawing attention to English–Spanish vocabulary contrasts.
(3) Identifying with students' everyday situations bilingually.
(4) Using English fillers within Spanish discourse ('so', 'right', etc.).

Alison used the translanguaging practice of translation and repetition often, as in Excerpt 1.

Alison Excerpt 1:

While explaining the triggers of stress, Alison says, '*¿Qué más les estresa?* What else causes you stress? Some of you guys have like the world's longest list'. The students laugh. 'You don't sleep, you don't eat, you cry all the time, right? ... *No duermen, no comen, están llorando todo el día*' ['What else stresses you? What else causes you stress? Some of you guys have like the world's longest list. You don't sleep, you don't eat, you cry all the time, right? ... You don't sleep, you don't eat, you're crying all day']

In this excerpt, Alison is repeating the same content information about the causes of stress in both English and Spanish by translating it exactly. This characterizes much of her spoken discourse in class, which means that through this translanguaging practice, students are getting double the explanation of key concepts.

In addition to translations, Alison often restated (rather than directly translated) the content, as in the following excerpt.

Alison Excerpt 2:

Alison is talking about the timeline for psychological treament. '*Como todo tratamiento psicológico, la mayoría de los medicamentos, cambios de dieta, de sueño, de ejercicio, enamorarse, conseguir un trabajo, graduarse de la universidad, no pasan de la noche a la mañana*, right? You guys are doing this for four of five years, okay? So, *para cambiar la manera en la cual uno piensa sobre su vida se pueden imaginar que es todo un proceso, ¿verdad?*' ['Just like all psychological treatments, the majority of medicines, changes in diet, in sleep patterns, in exercise, to fall in love, to get a job, to stay in the university, don't happen from one day to the next, right? You guys are doing this for four of five years, okay? So, to change the way you think about your life you can imagine that it is really a process, right?']

In Excerpt 2, Alison uses a long list of examples in Spanish and further explanation in English to explain, in depth, how changing psychological processes takes time. Here, Alison is not directly translating but, rather, is drawing on all of her linguistic resources to explain her point to her students. In this way, her translanguaging pedagogy works to explain the concept in depth.

Though most of Alison's translanguaging was seen in the process of teaching content knowledge, she also occasionally shared her bilingual knowledge by specifically drawing attention to Spanish–English vocabulary contrasts, as in Excerpt 3.

Alison Excerpt 3:

'Personas con ansiedad tienden de mirarlo todo como si fuera un catástrofe. Right? They tend to catastrophize; that's the word in English, too. They look at everything like "that's it, that's the end. I'll never ever be good at having a diet, or making a diet, or going on a diet, whatever"'. [*'People with anxiety tend to look at things like everything is a catastrophe. Right? They tend to catastrophize; that's the word in English, too. They look at everything like "that's it, that's the end. I'll never ever be good at having a diet, or making a diet, or going on a diet, whatever"'.*]

'*Catástrofe*' is a cognate of the English word 'catastrophe', and so it is likely familiar to students. However, the verb 'catastrophize' merits some explaining, which Alison does elegantly, using both languages. Her first sentence in Spanish sets up the definition of catastrophize, and then she gives examples of what it means in English. Specifically, she draws attention to the fact that 'that's the word in English, too', which draws on students' knowledge of cognates to teach a new key vocabulary word in English.

Alison was adept at identifying with students' everyday situations to relate the academic material to their everyday lives. As usual, Alison did this while translanguaging.

Alison Excerpt 4:

Alison is talking about appreciating and recognizing small happy things in order to change one's thinking to be more positive. *'Si una flor le cae al parabrisas del carro hace una pausa y diga "wow, hoy es mi día",* right? *Yo lo hago. Una cosa pequeña, ¿no? Hay papel higiénico en el baño,* wohoo!' Students laugh. *'Estamos* ... this is the best day of the week! *Y si hay toallas de papel,* wow, *estamos'.* At this point she raises her right hand and makes the thumb-up gesture. *'De verdad* ...' ['If a flower falls onto your car windshield take pause and say, "wow, today is my day!" I do it. A small thing, no? There's toilet paper in the bathroom, wohoo!' Students laugh. 'You're with me ... this is the best day of the week! And if there are paper towels, wow, we're set'. At this point she raises her right hand and makes the thumb-up gesture. 'Truthfully']

In Excerpt 4, Alison refers to a common occurrence at the university – the lack of paper products in the bathrooms. The idea of changing one's thinking by purposely thinking positive thoughts every day was a main theme in the class, and students were even required to turn in an assignment where they wrote three 'happy things' every day. Thus, while she was definitely being funny, she was also connecting to students' everyday lives and demonstrating the process of changing one's thinking, a key component in abnormal psychology. But, as usual, she did so while translanguaging, showing again that translanguaging was key to her delivery of content material.

Comparing and Contrasting Three Professors

The three professors described here had very different linguistic backgrounds, and students read their translanguaging in the classroom differently. As a Puerto Rican and with a linguistic and cultural background more in common with his students, Víctor's use of English text immersed in Spanish talk and translanguaging of key words and acronyms is not threatening to students. Rather, it is par for the course in this particular sociocultural context. Because they are not Puerto Rican, Ray and Alison could be taking a risk when they use English in class in this context. As mentioned previously, English is more commonly accepted in higher education than it is in other educational arenas in Puerto Rico. However, the kinds of gestures toward Spanish that Ray makes go a long way to helping his students accept his use of English. In an interview, one of his students commented about his class, *'Debido a que como vivimos en un país cuya lengua primera es el español, el estudiante se siente con más confianza de decir algo que no sepa decirlo en inglés'* ['Given that we live in a country whose first language is Spanish, the student feels more confidence to say something that he doesn't know how to say in English']. Ray's students knew that they were at liberty and, in fact, often encouraged to use Spanish to participate in the content learning. Another one of Ray's students mentioned, *'Si es un profesor extranjero, hacer referencias a las situaciones que pasan en Puerto Rico lo hace más fácil de relacionar'* ['If the professor is foreign, making references to the situations that happen in Puerto Rico makes it easier to relate']. Ray was conscious of this and used it to establish his translanguaging pedagogy.

When we first began talking about observing her class, Alison said that she delivered the class in Spanish. It is evident from the field notes, however, that she delivered the class bilingually. The types of translanguaging practices that she engaged in, like giving examples and explanations in both English and Spanish, require an extreme amount of preparation and effort. In other semesters, when Alison has taught multiple sections of the same class, she has polled her students to find out their preference for the medium of instruction (English, Spanish or, as she calls it, 'Spanglish'), and she has actually prepared the same content in these three different media of instruction. For this reason, we can say with confidence that Alison is exemplary, because she is in tune with her students' needs and uses translanguaging to meet them.

By translanguaging, these three professors enacted identities that related to students, strategically positioning themselves as authorities who can successfully apprentice college students in the discourses of their respective disciplines. So, though we agree with García and Li (2014: 94) that 'a teacher who uses translanguaging as pedagogy participates as learner; that is, she adopts a multivoicedness, a *raznoglosie*, in Bakhtin's terms', that multivoicedness indexes different cultural meanings and has different identity consequences, depending on the professors' linguistic and cultural backgrounds. In particular, Ray, by accepting and encouraging a language that he did not feel 100% confident in, opened himself up to the vulnerability of participating as a learner in his own classroom. But, this did not cause him to give up authority (as García and Li suggest) as much as gain authority and respect from students. Alison's use of English and Spanish worked in a similar way. She projected herself as open, confident, a professor who 'wields her field' in two languages. This translanguaging gives her authority in the context because students can approach her in either language and benefit by her use of English for their own language development. Víctor's translanguaging pedagogy positions him as a gateway for students to access larger scientific discourses, which are, most often, in English and, thus, gives him authority as a person who can apprentice students in those discourses. This he does strategically and purposefully, as he stated in his interview. In sum, translanguaging pedagogy works to position these professors in different ways, but all, we argue, in ways that benefit their students in this bilingual context.

It is clear from the excerpts presented here that the dual functions of translanguaging pedagogy in this context are to use students' entire linguistic repertoires to teach content and to provide opportunities to further develop those repertoires. When Ray turns over the conversational volley to students and encourages them to use Spanish, he helps them get over language-related confusion about content and keeps them moving forward in their learning of the material. Even when Ray and Alison use translanguaging to relate to students, they are doing so to relate *ideas about content* to the lives of students. Only Alison translanguages discourse markers, and even these are discourse markers used to double-check information ('right?') and connect ideas ('so...') and are related to the content she is teaching. All of Víctor's translanguaging was meant to deliver content about weed science to his students.

But, the professors' translanguaging pedagogies also set up affordances for students to develop their linguistic repertoires. In each of the three cases, translanguaging was used in different ways to help students acquire the ability to engage in academic discourse about their fields. In his interview, Víctor confirmed that his use of English terms and acronyms was strategically meant to connect students to the larger scientific discourse community by giving them the vocabulary items they would need in internet and library searches and when talking to people in the field.

> *Trato de mantener mucho de los conceptos en el idioma inglés porque sino se pierde el significado del concepto como tal. .... Si tú buscas eso [el termino en español] en cualquier libro o en el internet como tal nunca lo vas a encontrar.* [I tried to keep much of the concepts in English, otherwise the meaning of the concept as such is lost. ... If you look it up [the term in Spanish] as such in any book or on the internet, you will never find it, because it doesn't appear like that.]

By letting students use their strong language (Spanish) to access academic discourse in their developing language (English), Ray also set up affordances for students to acquire English through translanguaging. His translanguaging leveraged all students' linguistic resources to continue learning content and, in this way, moved them forward in learning the discourse of evolutionary biology. Alison had moments when she specifically drew attention to language (as in her Excerpt 4). But, her use of further explanations and restatement, both in written texts and spoken explanations, again created affordances for students weak in English to develop that English in relation to the subject of psychology.

Conclusions and Implications

In translanguaging pedagogy, 'The teacher sets up the affordances for students to engage in discursive and semiotic practices that respond to their cognitive and social intentions' (García & Li, 2014: 93). This does not always mean that translanguaging practices are structured or planned but, rather, that teachers have a disposition or openness toward translanguaging – a translanguaging ideology – that allows these practices to develop organically, based on professors' keen understandings of students' sociolinguistic, cultural and historical backgrounds. The three professors whose practices we describe here have done that through their use of Spanish and English in higher education classrooms in Puerto Rico. For example, Ray's use of Spanish to explain the concept of 'parsimonious phylogeny' in Excerpt 4 was an impromptu response to a particular student's confusion, in contrast to the very purposefully set up lecture in Spanish with English slides that Víctor delivered. But, even though not all translanguaging practices were set up ahead of time, they were all motivated by a translanguaging pedagogy that allowed professors to take a stance in class toward bilingual repertoires as strategic resources in learning. According to Blackledge and Creese (2010: 213), this 'flexible bilingual pedagogy is used by teachers as an instructional strategy to make links for classroom participants between the social, bicultural, community, and linguistic domains of their lives'.

The excerpts from the three case studies described here show these three professors doing just that.

García and Li (2014) state,

> [T]he translanguaging pedagogy of the teacher creates a new reality because neither English nor Spanish is seen as static or dominant, but rather operates within a dynamic network of cultural and linguistic transformations. It is not two fixed identities or languages that are combined. Translanguaging opens up the space to talk about this dynamic relationship, and to actualize it in the classroom. (García & Li, 2014: 98–99)

In the context of Puerto Rico, with its complex dynamic tension between English and Spanish and the layered meanings that accompany these languages into the classroom, translanguaging pedagogy is a useful tool for professors to employ to both teach content and provide students with opportunities to expand their linguistic, academic and meaning-making repertoires. We have seen three very different instantiations of this pedagogy in the three cases described here and have gotten a glimpse of the possibilities for translanguaging pedagogy in a bilingual university context such as that found in Puerto Rico. We agree with García and Li (2014: 94) that 'More difficult ... is how to educate teachers to be taught to use translanguaging strategically *moment-by-moment* and as a *critical gesture*', and perhaps even more difficult is how to help university professors to do so. One start, however, is to document translanguaging pedagogies as we hope we have done here.

References

Algren de Gutiérrez, E.A. (1987) *The Movement Against Teaching English in the Schools of Puerto Rico.* Lanham, MD: University Press of America.

Blackledge, A. and Creese, A. (2010) *Multilingualism: A Critical Perspective.* London: Bloomsbury Academic.

Carroll, K. and Mazak, C. (forthcoming 2017) Language policy in Puerto Rico's higher education: Opening the door for translanguaging practices. *Anthropology & Education Quarterly* 48 (1).

Duany, J. (2002) *The Puerto Rican Nation On the Move: Identities on the Island and in the United States.* Chapel Hill, NC: University of North Carolina Press.

García, O. and Li, W. (2014) *Translanguaging: Language, Bilingualism and Education.* New York: Palgrave Macmillan.

Lewis, G., Jones, B. and Baker, C. (2012) Translanguaging: Origins and development from school to street and beyond. *Educational Research and Evaluation* 18 (7), 641–654.

Mazak, C. and Herbas-Donoso, C. (2014a) Translanguaging practices and language ideologies in Puerto Rican university science education. *Critical Inquiry in Language Studies* 11 (1), 27–49.

Mazak, C. and Herbas-Donoso, C. (2014b) Translanguaging practices at a bilingual university: A case study of a science classroom. *International Journal of Bilingual Education and Bilingualism* 18 (6), 698–714.

Phillipson, R. (2009) English in higher education: Panacea or pandemic? In P. Harder (ed.) *Angles on the English-Speaking World: English Language Policy, Internationalization, and University Teaching* (pp. 199–216). Copenhagen: Museum Tusculanum Press.

Schmidt, J.R. (2014) *The Politics of English in Puerto Rico's Public Schools.* Boulder, CO: First Forum Press.

Torres-Gonzalez, R. (2002) *Idioma, bilinguismo y nacionalidad: La presencia del ingles en Puerto Rico.* San Juan: Editorial de la Universidad de Puerto Rico.

University of Puerto Rico, Mayagüez Campus (2013) *2013–2014 Undergraduate Catalogue.* See http://www.uprm.edu/cms/index.php?a=file&fid=2552 (accessed 3 July 2015).

Vélez, J.A. (2000) Understanding Spanish-language maintenance in Puerto Rico: Political will meets the demographic imperative. *International Journal of the Sociology of Language* 142, 5–24.

6 Translanguaging in a Multimodal Mathematics Presentation

Peichang He, Haiyan Lai and Angel Lin

Introduction

This research investigates the translanguaging and trans-semiotizing practices of Professor Liu (a pseudonym),[1] a mathematics education professor from mainland China, during his presentation at a tertiary mathematics education seminar in Hong Kong. Because of the international background of the university, the majority of the audience was Chinese professors and students in mathematics education, but there were also some international students who did not understand Chinese. Among the Chinese audience, some were Hong Kongers who speak Cantonese and read and write in 繁体字 (complex Chinese characters), whereas others were mainland Chinese who speak Putonghua and read and write in 简体字 (simplified Chinese characters). This formed a linguistically complex community, since there are conspicuous discrepancies between the two languages in both oral and written communication (Li & Zhu, 2013). For instance, the Putonghua pronunciation (pinyin) of the concept 'variation' in Professor Liu's presentation is *bian shi*, while its pronunciation in Cantonese is *bin sik*; and the simplified version of the characters of the term in mainland China is 变式, whereas the traditional complex version of the characters of the term becomes 變式. Although some characters remain the same in both simplified and complex versions, like 式, others can be very different, like 變 and 变. Such a complicated linguistic background might hinder the communication between Professor Liu, who came from mainland China and delivered the presentation mainly in Putonghua with simplified Chinese characters in his PowerPoint slides, and the audience, who were international non-Chinese students or local Hong Kong professionals who did not have much exposure to Putonghua or simplified Chinese characters in daily life. To tackle the linguistic barriers in the bi/multilingual multimodal mathematics presentation, Professor Liu tried to facilitate meaning making by translanguaging and trans-semiotizing between diverse semiotic resources such as Chinese and English, mathematics symbolisms, PowerPoint slides, blackboard layouts, pictures, graphic organizers and gestures.

Literature Review

Before introducing Professor Liu's mathematics presentation, we shall review the key notions 'translanguaging', 'trans-semiotizing', 'multimodal' ('trans-semiotics'), 'mathematics discourses' and 'PowerPoint design', which constitute the conceptual framework of the present study. These concepts are elaborated in the following sections.

Translanguaging and trans-semiotizing in bi/multilingual multimodal communication

'Translanguaging', according to Ofelia García, refers to 'multiple discursive practices in which bilinguals engage in order to make sense of their bilingual worlds' (García, 2009: 45). Although definitions overlap in recent publications, 'languaging' is generally viewed as a holistic process during which people use language to express their thoughts, obtain knowledge and experience, make sense and communicate with each other (Li & Zhu, 2013), and the prefix trans- is used to emphasize three dimensions (trans-system/ structure/space, transformative and transdisciplinary) that reflect the flexibility and dynamicity of multilingual practices (Li, 2011). In the face of increasing linguistic complexity in 21st-century communication, García (2009: 54) proposes the 'dynamic model of bilingualism', which highlights language practices at different planes, including 'multimodalities' (different modes of language, visuals, sound and gestures, etc.) and 'multilingualism'. This dynamic model of bilingualism is applicable to multilingual Asian contexts in which communicators take part in multiple discursive practices that draw on various semiotic repertoires to which they have access. Being 'the enactment of ... dynamic bilingualism', translanguaging is defined as 'the repertoire of bilingual language practices that can only emerge and expand in interrelationship with each other and through practice and socialization' (García, 2011: 4). In translanguaging practices, the linguistic repertoire of bilinguals is viewed as a 'language continuum' (García, 2009). Translanguaging, thus, goes beyond the traditional, static linguistic term 'code-switching' and is different from Cummins's cognitive view on the interdependence among the languages of bilinguals (García, 2009). Drawing on a holistic perspective, García and Li (2014) conclude, 'Translanguaging, as we have said, liberates language from structuralist-only or mentalist-only or even social-only definitions. Instead, it signals a *trans-semiotic* system with many meaning-making signs, primarily linguistic ones that combine to make up a person's semiotic repertoire' (García & Li, 2014: 42; emphasis added). Such dynamic bilingualism resonates with Halliday's (2013) 'trans-semiotic' view, drawing on which Lin (2015) proposes the notion of 'trans-semiotizing' as a new perspective of conceptualizing bi/multilingualism in the globalized world. While translanguaging performs a fundamental role in plurilingual and multimodal ('trans-semiotic', in Halliday's term) backgrounds, the proposal of trans-semiotizing as a communicative strategy broadens our horizon about bi/multilingual communication, since languages (as a central semiotic) not only interact with each other but also intertwine with other semiotics (e.g. visual images, gestures, sound and music) in human communication practices during which the common semiotic repertoire expands under the contributions of communicators.

Mathematics discourse

Mathematics discourse is multimodal in nature, and mathematical meaning is realized through the codeployment of multiple semiotic systems (Lemke, 2003; Moschkovich, 2010; O'Halloran, 2005; Schleppegrell, 2007) that are in the forms of mathematic symbolism (e.g. formulas, equations and clusters), visual displays (e.g. tables, graphs and drawings) and natural language (e.g. verbal explanations and written instructions). A mathematics presentation is a dynamic meaning-making process and a microecological academic mathematics discourse scaffolded by bilingual repertoire (e.g. English and Chinese) and multimodal resources (e.g. PowerPoint, visual displays, verbal explanations and gestures) in the mathematics education context.

Mathematics discourse is inquiry based, which involves mathematical reasoning and problem solving of mathematical concepts such as geometrical relationships and algebraic rules (Lemke, 2003). Mathematics symbolism, visual displays and natural language have their own unique ways of meaning making via lexico-grammatical systems. For instance, mathematical language has its own lexico-grammatical patterns such as technical vocabulary (e.g. 'conceptual variation' and 'procedural variation'), dense noun phrases (e.g. 'trilogy with variation'), V+ing forms (e.g. 'applying the solutions to different situations'), conjunctions with technical meanings (arrows indicating logical relations) and implicit logical relationships (e.g. mathematical signs $\because$ and $\therefore$) (Schleppegrell, 2007). This unique mathematics register is distinct from everyday language because it poses linguistic challenges and demands additional semantic, thematic and generic efforts from mathematics teachers and learners. The mathematics register consists of a set of mathematics terminologies and symbols to make mathematical meanings. Previous studies have shown that mathematical understanding is closely associated with mathematics vocabulary learning (Schleppegrell, 2007; Thompson & Rubenstein, 2000). Learning mathematics means learning how to operate both the language system and meaning system of mathematics (Chapman & Lee, 1990). The social context of mathematics inevitably affects its interactional and thematic patterns of language use, register and genre features. In this study, multilingual and multimodal (bi) literacy practices construct the bilingual identity of the professor and the social relations between the professor and the audience.

PowerPoint design

Academic discipline-specific presentation is a kind of genre with its own unique features. PowerPoint is an important digital instrument in academic presentations to achieve effective communication between the speaker and the audience. It is regarded as a genre of 'semiotic artifact' that incorporates multiple semiotic modes such as verbal language, visual images, sound, color and layout (Kress & van Leeuwen, 2001). According to Martin (1992: 505), genre is 'a staged, goal-oriented social process'. Thus, the design of an academic PowerPoint presentation usually consists of five goal-oriented stages: introduction, outline, presentation of study, references and thanks.

Previous literature reveals that little research has been conducted on the analysis of PowerPoint from a multimodal perspective (Djonov & van Leeuwen, 2013). Drawing on Halliday's (1994) systemic functional theory, Kress and van Leeuwen (2006) set up a descriptive framework of multimodality and assigned representational, interactive and compositional meanings to images. These three visual metafunctions deal with modeling material reality, constructing viewer-image relations and creating coherent visual composition in visual communication. In terms of the compositional meaning, there are three elements in the analysis of multimodal layout: information value, salience and framing. Information value refers to page layout and how multimodal elements are positioned on the page. It consists of three structures: left-right, top-down and center-margin. Salience deals with creating visual hierarchy to attract viewers' attention by using visual cues such as color, size, distance, sharpness of focus, placement of object and perspective (e.g. foreground vs. background). Framing involves the degree of connectedness between the visual elements on the multimodal page. Grounded in Kress and van Leeuwen's (2006) visual grammar, the present study focuses on the presentation-of-study stage of Professor Liu's PowerPoint and scrutinizes how the presenter employed multiple semiotic resources including Chinese, English, mathematics symbolism, diagrams, pictures and graphic organizers to make mathematical meanings coherent.

The Study

A review of the literature shows that most of the existing studies on translanguaging deal with face-to-face oral interactions, while studies that explore how translanguaging works in other genres and modalities of communication are still lacking (Canagarajah, 2011b). In mathematics education, although previous literature has documented bilingual studies at the elementary (August & Shanahan, 2008), secondary (Rubinstein-Avila *et al.*, 2014) and tertiary levels (Mazak & Herbas-Donoso, 2014), little research has been done on the role of translanguaging in the academic presentation genre of multimodal mathematics discourse at the tertiary level (Moschkovich, 2010). Thus, this study sets out to address the following research questions:

(1) How does translanguaging facilitate intercultural communication in a bi/multilingual multimodal tertiary mathematics presentation?
(2) How does translanguaging interplay with trans-semiotizing between diverse semiotic resources to achieve meaning making in an intercultural bi/multilingual multimodal tertiary mathematics presentation?

The data collected include the PowerPoint slides and the audio recording of Professor Liu's presentation. Both were analyzed based on García's (2009) conceptualization of translanguaging, O'Halloran's (2005) multimodal mathematics discourse and Kress and van Leeuwen's (2006) visual grammar. A fine-grained analysis of the speaker's PowerPoint slides and the audio recording of his presentation provided a lens to observe how translanguaging and trans-semiotizing interplayed to facilitate communication at the intercultural, bi/multilingual multimodal tertiary mathematics seminar.

Research Methods

To explore the research questions, a basic interpretative qualitative study (Merriam, 2002) focusing on text analysis (Marshall & Rossman, 2006) was adopted to explore the translanguaging and trans-semiotizing strategies employed in a multilingual multimodal tertiary mathematics presentation. One of the authors attended Professor Liu's presentation during which she took notes and made observations. With the consent of the speaker, she also collected both the PowerPoint slides and the audio recording of the presentation. The PowerPoint slides were analyzed according to O'Halloran's (2005) multimodal mathematics discourse, and Kress and van Leeuwen's (2006) visual grammar. The audio recording was transcribed and coded according to the overall structure of the presentation and the themes of the PowerPoint slides. The PowerPoint text and the audio recording transcription were matched and compared, and then analyzed based on both García's (2009) conceptualization of translanguaging and Lin's (2015) notion of 'trans-semiotizing'. After the first analysis of both the visual presentation (i.e. the PowerPoint text) and the oral presentation (i.e. the audio recording), the research findings were further discussed according to García and Li's (2014) interpretation of the nature of translanguaging, Lin's (2012) framework of Bridging Multiple Resources, and Lim's (2004) integrative multi-semiotic model (IMM). The recurring themes about meaning-making through translanguaging and trans-semiotizing in the mathematics education presentation were identified and explicated through detailed examples. A fine-grained analysis of the speaker's PowerPoint slides and the audio recording as well as the iterative coding and comparison of the visual and oral presentation repertoires provided a multimodal lens to observe how translanguaging and trans-semiotizing interplayed to facilitate communication at the intercultural, bi/multilingual multimodal tertiary mathematics seminar.

To ensure trustworthiness of data analysis, the different types of research data were carefully compared and mutually verified at each PowerPoint slide. Thick descriptions (i.e. all PowerPoint slides were analyzed) and direct quotations (i.e. original texts except for the speaker's private information were presented) of the data were applied to illustrate the translanguaging and trans-semiotizing strategies utilized during the presentation. All raw data were kept for audit trail (Yin, 2009), and the multiple communicative resources employed in Professor Liu's visual and oral presentations were summarized and illustrated in this chapter to allow for dependability and transferability of the research (Lincoln & Guba, 1985). Peer reviews (Ary et al., 2002) were conducted among the three authors after each data analysis and negotiations were made to reach consensus on the interpretation of the data. All three authors are bi-literate (i.e. Chinese and English) and trilingual (i.e. Cantonese, English and Putonghua) and are familiar with both the educational background of Mainland China (where Professor Liu conducted his research) and the language policy in Hong Kong (where Professor Liu's seminar was held). The first draft of the article was emailed to the speaker of the presentation (i.e. Professor Liu) both for publication approval and for member check (Ary et al., 2002). In addition, the international student whose feeling about Professor Liu's presentation was quoted in this study and three Mathematics Education PhD students who attended the seminar were also invited to double check the credibility and confirmability (Lincoln & Guba, 1985) of the data analysis in the present study.

Translanguaging and Trans-Semiotizing in an Intercultural Bi/multilingual Multimodal Tertiary Mathematics Presentation

In Professor Liu's presentation, both translanguaging (between Chinese and English) and trans-semiotizing (between verbal explanations and visual displays, mathematics symbols, images and graphic organizers, etc.)

strategies were adopted to form a unified system to make mathematical meanings. The following analysis of the PowerPoint slides and the presentation transcript offers a glimpse of how these strategies interplay to achieve the goal of intercultural bi/multilingual multimodal tertiary mathematics exchange.

Although the majority of the PowerPoint information was in English, the oral presentation was mainly in Chinese, which, to some extent, facilitated the understanding of the audience members, who were of complex linguistic backgrounds. A dark blue background with contrasting text (a large yellow font for key information such as headings and a smaller white font for details) were utilized in the PowerPoint to foreground and highlight the topic of the presentation (e.g. Slide 1; Figure 6.1). Two main questions were asked to address the mathematical problem-solving steps of 'what, why and how'. Each question was presented at the center of the slide (e.g. Slide 2 [Figure 6.2] and Slide 14 [Figure 6.15]) to attract the audience's attention, with discourse markers ('Part N') indicating the sequence.

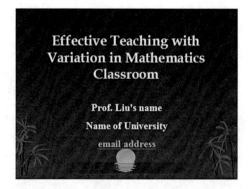

Figure 6.1 Slide 1

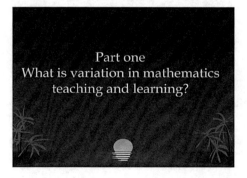

Figure 6.2 Slide 2

To tackle the first question, Professor Liu clarified the key concept 'variation in mathematics' by distinguishing the definition of 'variation' in his research from that in Marton's theory (Gu *et al.*, 2004). Such distinguishing of definitions was essential, because it elucidated the narrow and broad senses of the key mathematics concept employed in his study and in Marton's research, respectively.

As shown in Slide 3 (Figure 6.3), the English mathematics terms 'conceptual variation' and 'procedural variation' were translated into the Chinese terms 概念性变式 and 过程性变式. Thus, Chinese scaffolded English mathematics lexis acquisition, since it acted as a sense-making resource to bridge the epistemological gap resulting from some audience members' developing English. The juxtaposition of Chinese and English on the PowerPoint slide was beneficial for developing the audience's multilingual awareness (García, 2008) and strengthening the associations of their available linguistic repertoire (Carlo *et al.*, 2004), which was important in the intercultural academic exchange. A classifying graphic organizer was used to visually present the logical semantic relations of conceptual variation and procedural variation with their own subcategories. Compared to texts, graphic organizers have an 'enhanced computational power' that accelerates mental processing (Rowley-Jolivet, 2004: 147). As for the multimodal layout (Kress & van Leeuwen, 2006), the heading in Slide 3, 'Different variations in mathematics teaching', was presented as *ideal*, something idealized as the generalized essence of information; and the graphic organizer was presented as *real*, something more specific and detailed. The bilingual enhancement of the two key concepts, 'Conceptual variation (概念性变式)' and 'Procedural variation (过程性变式)', on the left, was presented as *given*, something known and self-evident; and the remaining part of the graphic organizer (categories in English) was presented as *new*, something problematic or unsolved, which the speaker elaborated on in the subsequent slides (Slides 4–13). All of these multimodal elements constructed a coherent

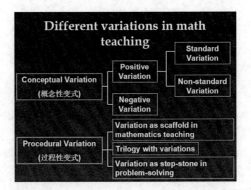

Figure 6.3 Slide 3

visual composition. Translanguaging between Chinese and English and the graphic organizer interplayed in a well-coordinated way.

To facilitate understanding of the complex mathematic discourse, Professor Liu employed oral presentation strategies such as classification, exemplification and contrast. For instance, he introduced the concept 数学的两重性 [duality in mathematics] to classify 'variation' into 'conceptual variation' and 'procedural variation'. The English words 'concept' and 'process' were introduced to elaborate on the dense Chinese noun phrase 数学的两重性. Professor Liu presented a concrete example, 2+3, to illustrate the difference between concept and process. The three parallel concept pairs were placed in contrasting positions in the graphic organizer with examples provided in the oral presentation. To highlight the key concept 'scaffold', Professor Liu provided both its Chinese translation 脚手架 and the English phrase 'step by step' to explain the Chinese concept 铺垫 (*pudian*, which, according to Professor Liu, is the Chinese way of doing scaffolding) and to describe procedural variation as a process. The oral presentation offered further elaboration on the mathematics concepts on the PowerPoint, which, to some extent, facilitated the communication between the speaker and the audience.

In Slide 4 (Figure 6.4), Professor Liu explained conceptual variation by shifting from a linguistic mode to a graphic organizer. This may have helped the audience better comprehend the field-specific knowledge, as the logical relations were expressed visually by the cognitively less-demanding graphic organizer, which is a quicker mode than language (Stöckl, 2004) and allows 'immediacy' and 'transparency' (Bolter & Grusin, 1999) in visual communication. To overcome the hindrance to comprehension caused by the dense English noun phrases, Professor Liu adopted presentation strategies such as classification (i.e. classifying conceptual variation learning methods into 'Sample-based learning' and 'Definition-based learning') and exemplification (i.e. using examples to illustrate the concreteness and

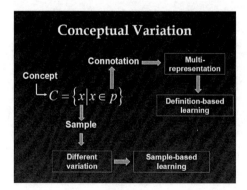

Figure 6.4 Slide 4

abstractness of mathematics concepts). The presentation was conducted in a process of crisscrossing between the PowerPoint information and the speaker's oral elaboration; that is, the speaker tried to quote directly some key words in English from the PowerPoint slides and then exemplified and elaborated on them during oral presentation. As a result, although Putonghua was the main medium of oral presentation, English key concepts such as 'sample', 'element', 'learning by sample', 'learning by element', 'standard' and 'sample-based learning' (provided with the Chinese translation [基于样例学习]) also emerged, occasionally, in the oral presentation. Namely, Professor Liu was translanguaging between the oral presentation and the written presentation, with the oral presentation more Putonghua based and the written presentation more English based, suiting his own repertoire of resources (i.e. he is more adept in written than spoken English). Besides the aforementioned strategies, mathematics symbolism was also employed to guide understanding of the abstract concepts; for instance, both the logical signs { } and the mathematics concept 'set' were used to show the relations between elements in the concept. Number pairs (mathematics symbolisms) such as 0 and 3, and 1 and 4, were listed on the board to facilitate the audience's understanding of the abstractness of -3.

Slide 5 (Figure 6.5) was a concrete example to help the audience consolidate conceptual variation. Professor Liu translanguaged between Chinese and English to introduce the abstract concepts, which, to some extent, eased the cognitive processing load for the audience. For instance, the dense English noun phrases 'infinite non-recurring decimals' and 'infinite recurring decimals' were presented in Chinese, 无限不循环小数 and 无限循环小数, possibly so that the majority of the audience (mostly Chinese) might have more automatic processing of these technical terms in their familiar Chinese than their unfamiliar English. Similarly, the abstract mathematical concept 'irrational number' was translated into Chinese, 无理数, with concrete examples and arrows of logical relations to alleviate

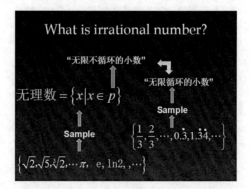

Figure 6.5 Slide 5

the linguistic barrier in the comprehension of the mathematics concept. Such translanguaging and trans-semiotizing scaffolding was a 'functional integration' (Bezemer & Kress, 2008) of the two languages and the logical symbols shared by the professor and the audience. The use of Chinese and the overt contrastive analysis of mathematics terms in Chinese (无理数) and English ('irrational number'), to some extent, deepened the audience's cognitive processing of mathematic concepts (Laupenmuhlen, 2012) and facilitated the internalization of the mathematics register (Tavares, 2015). In this way, mathematical meaning making might have been carried on more smoothly, and the audience's linguistic repertoire might have been activated to facilitate their reasoning and understanding of the mathematics concepts.

Professor Liu's introduction of procedural variation started with Slide 6 (Figure 6.6), a transitional slide that classified the procedural variations he was to explain. In Slide 7 (Figure 6.7), an example of procedural variation was presented – 铺垫: 多位数的加法 [*pudian*: multi-bit addition]. A graphic organizer was used to illuminate the teaching process of multi-bit

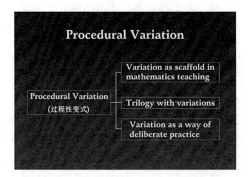

Figure 6.6 Slide 6

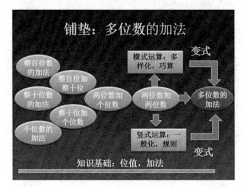

Figure 6.7 Slide 7

addition from left to right and from simple to complex. The PowerPoint animation demonstrated the key variation steps in the teaching procedure: 'Knowledge base: place value, addition' was placed at the bottom with a bold line underneath the words, a metaphor for the solid knowledge base. This line was shown on the slide before any other step of the multi-bit addition process appeared. Arrows of logical relations, ↑, → and ↓, were used to compare two different types of operations in multi-bit addition: 横式运算 [horizontal operation] and 竖式运算 [vertical operation].

Apart from the visual presentation of the graphic organizer in Slide 7, in the oral presentation, Professor Liu also compared the procedural variation in a primary mathematics lesson in Hong Kong with the cases in mainland China. In order to smooth away the linguistic obstacles in his Putonghua-based oral presentation, Professor Liu exploited both the board (another multimodal tool) and the mathematics operations (another essential semiotics in the communicative repertoire) to present and explain the stages of procedural variations (Figure 6.8).

The provision of the vertical operations, which are mathematics symbolisms shared by all mathematics professionals at the seminar, offered useful scaffolding for those in the audience who did not understand the simplified Chinese characters or Putonghua, which was the main medium of the oral presentation. When demonstrating the examples of procedural variation, Professor Liu also emphasized the key concepts by inserting their English translations into his oral presentation, for instance, 'step by step' and 'basic examples'.

In Slide 8 (Figure 6.9), the concept 铺垫 [pudian] introduced in Slide 7 was elaborated on by differentiating the Chinese concept from its English counterpart, scaffolding. This was illustrated by the visual metaphors of *pudian* (the left picture) contrasting the Western metaphor of scaffolding (the right picture), connected by a two-way arrow, ← →, with the characteristics of each scaffolding practice listed in bullet points under the corresponding image. These visual cues might bridge the cognitive gap between the heading at the top and the verbal texts at the bottom, because the topologically oriented visual images and the typologically oriented

$$
\begin{array}{ccccc}
 & & & & 502 \\
235 & 235 & 240 & 262 & 173 \\
+143 & +147 & +180 & +\ \ 93 & +125 \\
\end{array}
$$

$$
\begin{array}{ccc}
235 & 235 & 275 \\
+143 & +147 & +143 \\
\end{array}
$$

Figure 6.8 The mathematics operations on the board

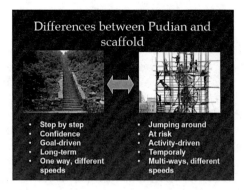

Figure 6.9 Slide 8

verbal texts (Lemke, 2002) complement, coinstantiate and cocontextualize each other. During the oral presentation, Professor Liu explained the English bullet-point notes by providing examples in Putonghua, with the most important concepts either repeated in English (e.g. the phrase 'step by step') or translated into Chinese and written on the blackboard (e.g. 铺垫, in simplified Chinese characters). Thus, translanguaging between Chinese and English, together with intercultural background knowledge (e.g. the comparison between mathematics education in mainland China and in the US), acted as a meaning-negotiation strategy to explain the intercultural differences between the Chinese concept *pudian* and the Western concept of scaffolding. The interplay of diverse semiotic resources of Chinese, English, visual images and verbal texts might have created 'multiplying meanings' and recontextualized mathematics knowledge (Lemke, 1998).

Because of the abstractness of the theme 'trilogy with variations' in the second aspect of procedural variation (Slide 9 [Figure 6.10]), Professor Liu provided its Chinese translation, 变式三部曲, to facilitate the understanding

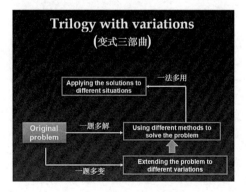

Figure 6.10 Slide 9

of those in the audience who might not be familiar with the discourse of English mathematics. A graphic organizer with arrows formed an animated flowchart indicating the sequence of the procedural variation. This was accompanied by the sequential logical connectors 首先 [first], 然后 [then], 第一步 [Step 1], 第二步 [Step 2] and 最后 [finally], highlighted in the oral presentation to clarify the logical sequence in the 'trilogy with variations'. Although the verbal information in the PowerPoint was basically in English, the speaker tried to label the Chinese phrases in the same four-word pattern, '一…多…', beside the corresponding arrow that indicated the purpose of each step in the graphic organizer. By doing so, the heading 'Trilogy with variations (变式三部曲)' was clarified by the logical relationships between '一题多解 (using different methods to solve the problem)', '一题多变 (extending the problem to different variations)' and '一法多用 (applying the solution to different situations)'. To demonstrate how 'trilogy with variations' operates in practical mathematics teaching, examples of 一题多解, 一题多变, and 一法多用 were also provided. For instance, Slide 10 (Figure 6.11) exemplified how the factorization equation $x^2+2x-3=0$ can be solved in three different ways; namely, 一题多解 [using different methods to solve the problem].

Slides 11–13 were examples that explained the concept 'variation as a way of deliberate practice'. Professor Liu illustrated the requirement of the mathematics problem with both text and drawing (Slide 11 [Figure 6.12]), then demonstrated Solution 1 in a table and Solutions 2 and 3 in two different equations (Slide 12 [Figure 6.13]), '多种解法' [multiple solutions]). Finally, seven different kinds of variations were suggested to solve the mathematics problem (Slide 13 [Figure 6.14]), '多种变式' [multiple variations]).

As shown in the previous examples, Chinese was the main verbal information in these four PowerPoint slides. In Slide 10, abstract mathematics terms such as '因式分解' [factorization] and '二次曲线' [quadratic curve] were all listed in simplified Chinese characters. If presented in English, they might pose linguistic challenges to the mathematics professionals

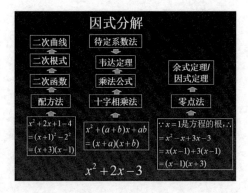

Figure 6.11 Slide 10

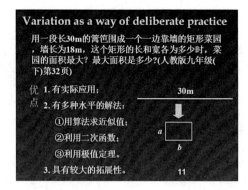

Figure 6.12 Slide 11

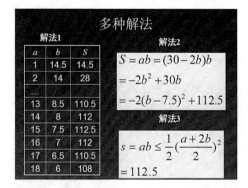

Figure 6.13 Slide 12

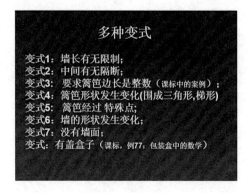

Figure 6.14 Slide 13

whose native language was not English. Similarly, in Slides 11 and 13, the mathematics problems and variation samples were all in Chinese, since they were quoted directly from either the mathematics textbooks or the national mathematics curriculum of mainland China. For those in the audience whose native language was Chinese, the Chinese information in the slides conveyed the mathematics meanings more explicitly, which might have facilitated their understanding of both the science content and the English lexical knowledge (Tian & Macaro, 2012; Turnbull *et al.*, 2011). Professor Liu also provided, in the slides, many mathematics symbols common to all mathematics professionals (e.g. the equations and arrows in Slide 10, the diagram in Slide 11, the table and equations in Slide 12 and the sequential numerals in Slide 13) to facilitate the understanding of those who did not understand Putonghua or simplified Chinese characters.

In the second part of the presentation (transitioned by Slide 14 [Figure 6.15]), Professor Liu answered the research questions from five main perspectives.

First, a network model was demonstrated in Slide 15 (Figure 6.16) to illustrate the necessity of forming a rational cognitive structure in mathematics learning. PowerPoint animation had been designed to portray

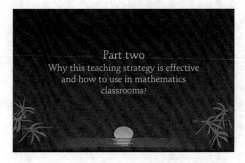

Figure 6.15 Slide 14

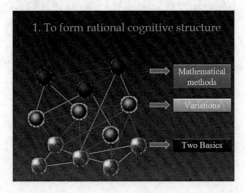

Figure 6.16 Slide 15

the formation of the network step by step, with arrows pointing to the corresponding labels to indicate the meaning of each section of the network: first the 'Two Basics' at the bottom, then the 'Mathematical Methods' at the top and, finally, the different kinds of 'Variations' that link learners' basic mathematics knowledge with the various mathematical methods. Such procedural animation might have helped the audience to grasp the main points of the slide. Professor Liu also introduced the cultural background of mathematics education in mainland China and an example of a successful mathematics teacher to elucidate the importance of forming a rational cognitive structure in mathematics learning. He further accentuated the indispensability of forming the rational cognitive structure by writing the Chinese phrase 搭架子 [to build up a framework] on the blackboard. To help the audience understand the abstract network, Professor Liu made an analogy between a mathematics knowledge framework and a warehouse congested with goods to emphasize the principle that a systematic knowledge framework leads to effective mathematics learning. Although the verbal information in Slide 15 was solely in English, Professor Liu tried to employ an array of visual and oral presentation strategies such as the PowerPoint animation, the cultural background of mathematics education in mainland China, the example of the successful mathematics teacher, the Chinese noun phrase 搭架子 and the analogy between a warehouse and students' cognitive structure. All these strategies integrated to form potentially beneficial resources in the communicative repertoire, which expanded gradually with the efforts of both the speaker and the audience.

When Professor Liu presented his second proposal, 'To work on large cognitive units', in Slide 16 (Figure 6.17), he depicted a mathematics lesson in mainland China to argue for the importance of helping students form large cognitive units in their mathematics learning. Graphic organizers were designed to represent both the original design and the improved new design of the lesson.

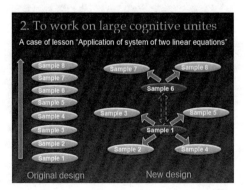

Figure 6.17 Slide 16

Because of the obvious differences between the structures of the two graphic organizers, by comparing their designs, audience members from different language backgrounds might realize the superiority of the interconnected cognitive structure in the new design (on the right) over the linear arrangement of the isolated information units in the original design (on the left). Thus, although the verbal information on the PowerPoint slide was only in English, and the oral presentation was mainly in Putonghua, the visual presentation by the graphic organizers might have facilitated the audience's comprehension. In addition to the visual presentation, Professor Liu also emphasized some key terms; for example, he wrote the Chinese word 启动 [to activate] on the blackboard to underscore the importance of helping students organize their knowledge according to interrelated cognitive units. He tried to impress on the audience the advantages of the interrelated knowledge system using an analogy between mathematics experts and chess masters. Hence, Chinese, English, graphic organizers and presentation strategies became mutually complementary resources in the communicative repertoire shared by the participants in the presentation.

In Slide 17 (Figure 6.18), Professor Liu introduced his third proposal, 'To follow the main line of mathematics knowledge structure', by quoting directly from both the ancient Chinese learning theory 学记 (*Xue Ji*) and the National Research Council document, both of which supported Professor Liu's claim that mathematics education should follow the main line of knowledge structure.

Taking into consideration the complicated linguistic backgrounds of the audience, the theme of the slide was presented in English but was summarized by the Chinese noun phrase 知识主干 [knowledge framework]. The text from the National Research Council was also translated into English, presumably to cater to those in the audience who did not understand Chinese. On the other hand, although the rules from the Chinese ancient learning theory were quoted directly in classical Chinese literary style,

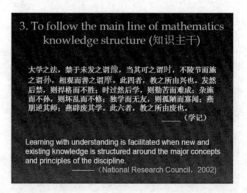

Figure 6.18 Slide 17

Professor Liu summed up the four major principles by highlighting four key characters – 豫 [preventability], 时 [timeliness], 孙 [step by step] and 摩 [collaboration] – in a sharp yellow color and further explained them with a modern Chinese idiom, 万变不离其宗 [remain essentially the same despite all apparent changes], and metaphors of teaching designs like 主线 [main line] and 副线 [subline] at different stages of students' mathematical development.

Professor Liu's fourth suggestion, 'To focus on basic sample problems and reducing strategies', was presented in Slide 18 (Figure 6.19) and Slide 19 (Figure 6.20).

In Slide 18, a flowchart was designed to illustrate the complex logical relations of reducing strategies (化归思维) to model the mathematical thinking process. The flowchart was animated: starting from 'Unknown problem', reduced (shown by the directed arrows) consecutively to 'Variation 2' and 'Variation 1' and then further to the 'Sample problem', which was again deduced (indicated by directed arrows), step by step, back toward

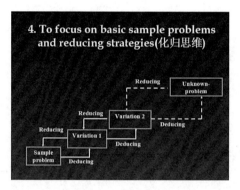

Figure 6.19 Slide 18

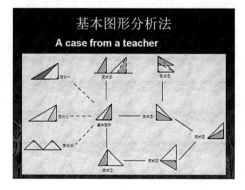

Figure 6.20 Slide 19

the unknown problem itself. Such an abstract model of reducing strategies was exemplified by the基本图形分析法 [basic graphics analysis method] in a teacher's lesson. This was demonstrated by a diagram of various groups of setsquare combinations in Slide 19. Furthermore, the graphs were presented alongside Chinese to complement each other semiotically. The 基本图形 [basic graph] can generate different variations: 变化一 [Variation 1], 变化二 [Variation 2], 变化三 [Variation 3] and so forth. In this way, Chinese, English and diagrams coinstantiated each other to achieve a coherent semiotic whole in the academic mathematics presentation discourse.

Slide 20 (Figure 6.21) demonstrated Professor Liu's last proposal, 举一反三与一以贯之 ['drawing inferences about other cases from one instance' and 'one principle running through it all']. This condensed information conveyed by the two Chinese idioms was represented by a graphic organizer that used English text and was designed in such a way that the basic sample problem was connected to Variations 1 to 3 by double arrows in opposite directions. The graphic organizer thus demonstrated how the basic sample problem can deduce or induce Variations 1, 2 and 3 mutually and why teachers should help learners infer other mathematics problems from one instance. Hence, the English information in the graphic organizer complemented the Chinese in the heading. Again, translanguaging and trans-semiotizing strategies interplayed to exemplify abstract mathematics thinking processes.

The previous analysis of Professor Liu's presentation is summarized in Table 6.1, which provides an overall view of the communicative repertoire employed in Professor Liu's intercultural bi/multilingual multimodal mathematics presentation. The translanguaging and trans-semiotizing strategies adopted in the presentation will be further discussed in the following section.

Figure 6.21 Slide 20

Table 6.1 Summary of multiple communicative resources used in Professor Lui's intercultural bi/multilingual multimodal mathematics-presentation

Structure of presentation	Slide	PowerPoint presentation	Oral presentation
Effective teaching with variation in math classroom	1	English, color, font size	Putonghua
Q1: *What is variation in math teaching and learning?*	2	English, discourse marker (Part one)	Putonghua, concept clarification
Different variations in math teaching	3	English, Chinese, graphic organizer,	Putonghua, English (*concept, process; scaffold, step by step*)
1. Conceptual Variation	4	English, mathematic symbolism, graphic organizer, logical sign (arrows)	Putonghua, English (*sample, element, learning by sample, learning by element, standard, sample-based learning*)
(an example) What is irrational number?	5	English, Chinese, mathematic symbolism, logical sign (arrows)	Putonghua
2. Procedural Variation	6	English, Chinese, graphic organizer	Putonghua
A.捕垫:多位数加法	7	Chinese, graphic organizer, logical sign (arrows), animation	Putonghua, English (*step by step, basic examples*)
Differences between Pudian and scaffold	8	English, images, logical sign (arrow)	Putonghua, English (*step by step*), intercultural comparison
B. Trilogy with variations (变式三部曲)	9	English, Chinese, graphic organizer, logical sign (arrows)	Putonghua, sequential logical connectors
1) 因式分解 (example of "一题多解")	10	Chinese, mathematic symbolism, graphic organizer, logical sign (arrows)	Putonghua
Variation as a way of deliberate practice	11	English, Chinese, mathematic symbolism, diagram	Putonghua
2) 多种解法(example of "一题多变")	12	Chinese, mathematic symbolism, table	Putonghua
3) 多种变式(example of "一法多用")	13	Chinese, sequential numbers	Putonghua
Q2: *Why this teaching strategy is effective and how to use in math classrooms?*	14	English, discourse marker (Part two)	Putonghua
1. To form rational cognitive structure	15	English, diagram, logical sign (arrows, labels), sequential number, animation	Putonghua, intercultural comparison, analogy
2. To work on large cognitive units	16	English, graphic organizers, logical sign (arrows), sequential number	Putonghua, analogy
3. To follow the main line of mathematics knowledge structure (知识主干)	17	English, Chinese, color of words, sequential number	Putonghua
4. To focus on basic sample problems and reducing strategies (化归思维)	18	English, Chinese, graphic organizer, sequential number, animation	Putonghua
(an example) 基本图形分析法	19	English, Chinese, diagram, sequential numbers	Putonghua
5. 举一反三与一以贯之	20	English, Chinese, graphic organizer, logical sign (arrows), sequential number	Putonghua

Discussion

The data analysis summarized in Table 6.1 shows that translanguaging is a naturally occurring phenomenon for multilingual domain-specific communicators (Canagarajah, 2011a, 2011b). The translanguaging approach to the bilingual mathematics presentation not only activates the audience's linguistic repertoire (first language [L1] and second language [L2]) but also 'extends the repertoire of semiotic practices and transforms them into dynamic mobile resources that can adapt to global and local sociolinguistic situations' (García & Li, 2014: 18). Grounded in Lin (2012), both translanguaging (between everyday oral language, academic oral language and academic written language in L1 and L2) and trans-semiotizing (between languages and other multimodalities) are essential meaning-making strategies that contribute to effective communication, especially for linguistically disadvantaged communicators. The strategic use of the shared linguistic repertoire (L1 and L2), complemented by semiotic resources such as pictures, graphic organizers, sound and gestures, facilitates efficient communication and expands the common semiotic repertoire of the communicators (see Figure 6.22).

Along with Lin's (2012) framework, Lim's (2004) integrative multi-semiotic model (IMM) provides an approach for analyzing multisemiotic texts from three codeploying strata: context plane (register, genre, culture and ideology), content plane (verbal and visual grammar and discourse systems) and expression plane (linguistic and visual systems).

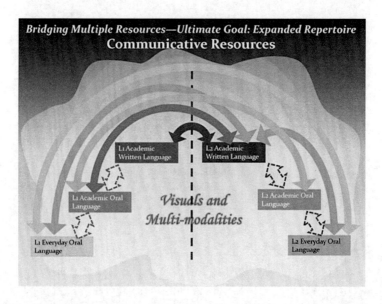

Figure 6.22 Bridging multiple resources – ultimate goal: Expanded repertoire (Source: Lin, 2012: 93)

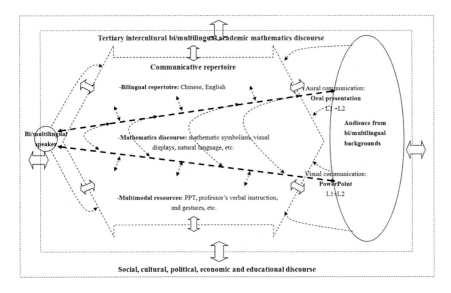

Figure 6.23 A framework of intercultural bi/multilingual multimodal mathematics presentation discourse

Drawing on both Lin (2012) and Lim (2004), a framework of intercultural bi/multilingual multimodal mathematics-presentation discourse (Figure 6.23) is developed to map out, topologically and typologically, the complex nature of meaning making in Professor Liu's bi/multilingual and multimodal mathematics presentation.

This framework comprises three discourse layers: First, the social, cultural, political, economic and educational discourse continuously structures the social ideology, language status, bi/multilingual identities and intercultural differences. Second, this first-layer discourse constantly shapes the tertiary intercultural bi/multilingual academic mathematics discourse (the second layer), since university mathematics discourses are directly fashioned by international education development and social expectations. Third, the discourse of communicative repertoire is co-constructed and mutually shared by both the speaker and the audience from bi/multilingual backgrounds. This third layer consists of the bilingual repertoire (e.g. Chinese and English), mathematics discourse (mathematics symbols, visual displays, natural language, etc.) and multimodal resources (PowerPoint, graphic organizers, verbal instructions and gestures, etc.). This communicative repertoire (the third layer) is continuously influenced by the intercultural bi/multilingual academic mathematics discourse (the second layer); for example, the languages, multimodalities and speaker–audience interactions in Professor Liu's presentation were all affected by the international and institutional norms of academic seminars. These three discourse layers interact ecologically in the bi/multilingual multimodal mathematics presentation. The communicative repertoire, in turn, affects the transformation of the academic mathematics discourse, which further influences the development of both the academia and the institution.

Based on this framework, Professor Liu's presentation can be interpreted as a communication process between the speaker (who speaks Putonghua and has access to English) and the audience (who are from bi/multilingual backgrounds and may speak Cantonese, Putonghua, English or other languages) via two main channels: visual communication by the PowerPoint slides and aural communication by the oral presentation. Language was the basic semiotic resource in both aural communication (mainly in Chinese and, occasionally, in English) and visual communication (mainly in English, complemented by Chinese). Translanguaging between Chinese and English occurred flexibly and dynamically, either within the same communication channel (e.g. juxtaposing '变式三部曲' and 'trilogy with variations' on the PowerPoint) or between the two channels (e.g. bridging the linguistic gap between 'scaffold' in the PowerPoint and '铺垫' in the oral presentation) to facilitate the meaning making of the bi/multilingual audience. Such translanguaging arising from the bilingual repertoire was further complemented by the trans-semiotizing among the three semiotic systems in the shared communicative repertoire; namely, the bilingual repertoire (Chinese and English), the mathematics discourse including mathematics symbolisms (e.g. equations, formulas and mathematics terms) and visual displays (e.g. graphic organizers, tables and arrows) and the multimodal resources (e.g. PowerPoint, animation, blackboard layout and gestures). As illustrated by Lemke (1998, 2003), language is a typological semiotic system for making categorical distinctions that functions to describe and contextualize mathematical problems (O'Halloran, 2005), whereas mathematics symbols and visual displays are topological semiotic systems for constructing continuous patterns of covariation and creating connection between physiological perceptions and the physical world. In Professor Liu's presentation, the three semiotic systems in the communicative repertoire were integrated to make meaning by translanguaging and trans-semiotizing from one mode to another in order to facilitate the audience's comprehension of the academic presentation (Figure 6.24).

It should be noted that the translanguaging and trans-semiotizing strategies adopted by both the speaker and the audience were not isolated or static but were integrated and dynamic, with ongoing selecting and mapping. As shown in Figure 6.24, Professor Liu's presentation was full of dynamic interactions between the speaker and the audience (e.g. presenting information and seeking feedback vs. obtaining and interpreting information), visual and aural communications (e.g. translanguaging between the Chinese in oral presentation and the English information in PowerPoint slides), the speaker's selection of resources from the

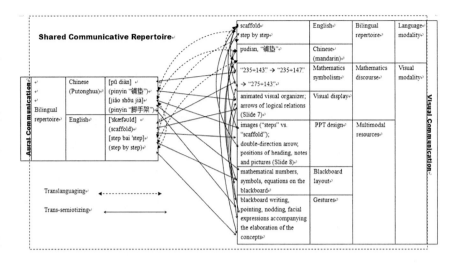

Figure 6.24 Meaning making by translanguaging and trans-semiotizing via (partially) shared communicative repertoire

(partially) shared communicative repertoire and the audience's search for corresponding resources from the (partially) shared repertoire to overcome barriers to comprehension. It is worth noting that communication success does not require a fully shared communicative repertoire. The searching and selecting of available communicative resources might lead to further expansion of each participant's own communicative repertoire; for example, after each time a translanguaging or trans-semiotizing strategy was used, that strategy might become the acquired knowledge of both the speaker and the audience. When processing new information, they might have retrieved the previous strategy more quickly from the communicative repertoire and integrated it with other strategies to overcome the new obstacles. Take *pudian* versus scaffolding as an example: The term *pudian* (i.e. the Chinese version of scaffolding) was first introduced in English as 'scaffold', then translated into 脚手架, next paraphrased as the English phrase 'step by step' (in both the oral presentation and the PowerPoint slide), then further coupled with the Chinese characters 铺垫 and, finally, associated with the picture (of stone steps) in Slide 8 (Figure 6.9) to contrast with the Western concept of scaffolding. Thus, within the communicative repertoire, the resources related to *pudian* grew gradually. It was through one instance after another of translanguaging and trans-semiotizing strategies applied crisscrossingly between the aural and visual communication processes that the bi/multilingual and multimodal resources for the concept *pudian* increased, and the communicative repertoire cobuilt and (partially) shared by both the speaker and the audience expanded. As a result, the hindrances to communication in intercultural bi/multilingual contexts were gradually reduced, while the means of assistance kept growing in the common communicative repertoire.

Judging by the audience's responses (e.g. their occasional laughter and their questions during the question-and-answer section), the majority of the members (including students from mainland China, local professors and students from Hong Kong) could understand the presentation. Even the international students (who knew very little, if any, Chinese) seemed to 'have a feeling' (i.e. grasp the general ideas) of the presentation:

Professor Liu: Are you understand what I...

International student: Uh... because as for mathematics, *I can have a feeling, I could get a feeling because there's a mathematical language which is universal*. With that language, so that's why in that *example, I can understand what you are talking*, two types of variations.

Professor Liu: Are you agree?

International student: Sorry?

Professor Liu: Are you agree with me?

International student: I, I, I *did not get fully understood*, but I *just had a feeling of* what you are talking about...

(Excerpt from transcript of Professor Liu's oral presentation 46:29)

It can be seen that communication effects varied according to the different access that members of the audience had to the three semiotic systems in the communicative repertoire. The more communicative resources that were employed by the communicating participants, the better the communication effects would be achieved. As shown in Figure 6.23, language being the basic means of both the aural and visual communication in Professor Liu's presentation, translanguaging served as an essential strategy to facilitate the multilingual audience's comprehension. The members of the audience who were from mainland China and shared similar cultural and linguistic backgrounds with the speaker would have no difficulty understanding the presentation, and the translanguaging strategy assisted them in consolidating their English vocabulary of the mathematical terminology. For the Hong Kong professionals who did not understand much Putonghua, translanguaging (between Putonghua and English in the oral presentation and between Mandarin and English in the PowerPoint) was crucial for their meaning making during the presentation. Nevertheless, although the non-Chinese audience members did not understand Chinese (either Putonghua or Mandarin) and could not rely much on translanguaging (e.g. between Putonghua and English) to understand the presentation, they could have resorted to trans-semiotizing between the other semiotic resources (e.g. the mathematics symbols and the visual displays) in Professor Liu's multimodal presentation. As the international student in the audience emphasized, 'I could get a feeling because there's a mathematical language which is universal'; namely, the audience could still make use of trans-semiotizing, drawing on resources in the mutually constructed communicative repertoire. According to Lim (2004), meaning making is achieved based on the 'cocontextualizing relations' between the language and the visual displays in a multisemiotic text. The interaction between language and visual resources mutually contextualizes at every instantiation. On one hand, those in the audience (e.g. mainlanders and Hong Kongers) who were able to employ both translanguaging and trans-semiotizing strategies had more resources at their disposal to allow the meaning of signs in one modality to 'reflect' that of the other, which shares cocontextualizing relations. On the other hand, those who could not rely much on translanguaging in this context (e.g. the international students who did not know Chinese) may have encountered more 'recontextualizing relations'; specifically, the meanings of the two modalities were 'at odds with' or 'unrelated to' each other (Lim, 2004: 239). Under such circumstances, trans-semiotizing functioned by coordinating the diverse semiotic resources in the partially shared communicative repertoire to help these members of the audience tackle the comprehension barriers.

Conclusion

To sum up, this study examines a bi/multilingual mathematics presentation from sociocultural, multilingual and multimodal perspectives. Translanguaging and trans-semiotizing interplay to integrate intercultural semiotic resources such as Chinese, English, pictures, mathematics symbols and graphic organizers in a mathematics presentation discourse.

The findings of this research echo translanguaging practices in previous literature; namely, translanguaging is 'the ability of multilingual speakers to shuttle between languages, treating the diverse languages that form their repertoire as an integrated system' (Canagarajah, 2011a: 401). The analysis of Professor Liu's presentation shows that strategic use of bi/multilingual resources and multimodalities in the intercultural and bi/multilingual context may facilitate intercultural communication and the academic language development of emergent bilinguals. This sheds light on bilingual education especially in content and language integrated learning (CLIL) contexts. It may also empower teachers and learners at bilingual education schools, where 'dominant language ideologies often prevent even well-meaning bilingual teachers from embracing translanguaging to teach and assess' (García & Li, 2014: 135). It is essential that translanguaging in education practices avoids the view of education as an autonomous concept of literacy that is detached from cultural and ideological contexts. Rather, it would be more enlightening if translanguaging and trans-semiotizing are viewed through the lens of 'continua of biliteracy' (Hornberger & Link, 2012: 274) as bi/multilingual practices that value and incorporate students' dynamic multilingual and multimodal communicative repertoires as resources for learning and intercultural communication.

Notes

(1) To protect the speaker's privacy, a pseudonym, 'Professor Liu', is used in this chapter. The speaker's personal details in the PowerPoint (Figure 6.1) have also been changed to 'Professor Liu's name', 'Name of University' and 'email address,' accordingly.

References

Ary, D., Jacobs, L. and Razavieh, A. (2002) *Introduction to Research in Education*. Belmont, CA: Wadsworth Group.

August, D. and Shanahan, T. (2008) Introduction and methodology. In D. August and T. Shanahan (eds) *Developing Reading and Writing in Second-Language Learners: Lessons from the Report of the National Literacy Panel on Language-Minority Children and Youth* (pp. 1–18). New York: Routledge.

Bezemer, J. and Kress, G. (2008) Writing in multimodal texts: A social semiotic account of designs for learning. *Written Communication* 25, 166–195.

Bolter, J.D. and Grusin, R. (1999) *Remediation: Understanding New Media*. Cambridge, MA: The MIT Press.

Canagarajah, S. (2011a) Codemeshing in academic writing: Identifying teachable strategies of translanguaging. *The Modern Language Journal* 95 (3), 401–417.

Canagarajah, S. (2011b) Translanguaging in the classroom: Emerging issues for research and pedagogy. *Applied Linguistics Review* 2, 1–28.

Carlo, M.S., August, D., McLaughlin, B., Snow, C.E., Dressler, C., Lippman, D.N., Liverly, T.J. and White, C.E. (2004) Closing the gap: Addressing the vocabulary needs of English-language learners in bilingual and mainstream classrooms. *Reading Research Quarterly* 39, 188–215.

Chapman, A. and Lee, A. (1990) Rethinking literacy and numeracy. *Australian Journal of Education* 34 (3), 277–289.

Djonov, E. and van Leeuwen, T. (2013) Between the grid and composition: Layout in PowerPoint's design and use. *Semiotica* 197, 1–34.

García, O. (2008) Multilingual language awareness and teacher education. In J. Cenoz and N.H. Hornberger (eds) *Encyclopedia of Language and Education* (2nd edn, Vol. 6: Knowledge about Language, pp. 385–400). Berlin: Springer.

García, O. (2009) *Bilingual Education in the 21st Century: A Global Perspective*. Oxford: Wiley-Blackwell.

García, O. (2011) Theorizing translanguaging for educators. In C. Celic and K. Seltzer (eds) *Translanguaging: A CUNY-NYSIEB Guide for Educators* (pp. 1–6). http://www.nysieb.ws.gc.cuny.edu/files/2012/06/FINAL-Translanguaging-Guide-With-Cover-1.pdf (accessed 7 July 2015).

García, O. and Li, W. (2014) *Translanguaging: Language, Bilingualism and Education*. Basingstoke: Palgrave Macmillan.

Gu, L., Huang, R. and Marton, F. (2004). Teaching with variation: A Chinese way of promoting effective mathematics learning. In L. Fan, N.Y. Wong, J. Cai and S. Li (eds)

How Chinese Learn Mathematics: Perspectives From Insiders (pp. 309–347). Singapore: World Scientific Publishing.

Halliday, M.A.K. (1994) *An Introduction to Functional Grammar.* London: Edward Arnold.

Halliday, M.A.K. (2013) Languages, and language, in today's changing world. Research seminar given at the University of Hong Kong, 23 October 2013.

Hornberger, N. and Link, H. (2012) Translanguaging and transnational literacies in multilingual classrooms: A biliteracy lens. *International Journal of Bilingual Education and Bilingualism* 15 (3), 261–278.

Kress, G. and van Leeuwen, T. (2001) *Multimodal Discourse: The Modes and Media of Contemporary Communication.* Oxford: Oxford University Press.

Kress, G. and van Leeuwen, T. (2006) *Reading Images: The Grammar of Visual Design* (2nd edn). London: Arnold.

Laupenmuhlen, J. (2012) Making the most of L1 in CLIL. In D. Marsh and O. Meyer (eds) *Quality Interfaces: Examining Evidence and Exploring Solutions in CLIL* (pp. 237–251). Eichstaett: Eichstaett Academic Press.

Lemke, J.L. (1998) Multiplying meaning: Visual and verbal semiotics in scientific text. In J.R. Martin and R. Veel (eds) *Reading Science: Critical and Functional Perspectives on Discourses of Science* (pp. 87–113). London: Routledge.

Lemke, J.L. (2002) Language development and identity: Multiple timescales in the school ecology of learning. In C. Kramsch (ed.) *Language Acquisition and Language Socialization* (pp. 68–87). London: Continuum.

Lemke, J.L. (2003) Mathematics in the middle: Measure, picture, gesture, sign, and word. In M. Anderson, A. Sáenz-Ludlow, S. Zellweger and V.V. Cifarelli (eds) *Educational Perspectives on Mathematics as Semiosis: From Thinking to Interpreting to Knowing* (pp. 215–234). Brooklyn, NY: Legas.

Lincoln, Y. and Guba, E. (1985) *Naturalistic Inquiry. Thousand Oaks,* CA: Sage Publications.

Li, W. (2011) Moment analysis and trans-languaging space. *Journal of Pragmatics* 43, 1222–1235.

Li, W. and Zhu, H. (2013) Translanguaging identities and ideologies: Creating transnational space through flexible multilingual practices amongst Chinese university students in the UK. *Applied Linguistics* 34 (5), 516–535.

Lim, F.V. (2004) Developing an integrative multi-semiotic model. In K.L. O'Halloran (ed.) *Multimodal Discourse Analysis: Systemic-Functional Perspectives* (pp. 220–240). London: Continuum.

Lin, A.M.Y. (2012) Multilingual and multimodal resources in L2 English content classrooms. In C. Leung and B. Street (eds) *English: A Changing Medium for Education* (pp. 79–103). Bristol: Multilingual Matters.

Lin, A.M.Y. (2015) Egalitarian bi/multilingualism and trans-semiotizing in a global world. In W.E. Wright, S. Boun and O. García (eds) *Handbook of Bilingual and Multilingual Education* (pp. 19–37). Hoboken, NJ: Wiley-Blackwell.

Martin, J.R. (1992) Genre and literacy-modeling context in educational linguistics. *Annual Review of Applied Linguistics* 13, 141–172.

Merriam, S.B. (2002) *Qualitative Research in Practice: Examples for Discussion and Analysis.* San Francisco, CA: Jossey-Bass.

Marshall, C. and Rossman, G.B. (2006) *Designing Qualitative Research.* Thousand Oaks, CA: Sage Publications.

Mazak, C.M. and Herbas-Donoso, C. (2014) Translanguaging practices and language ideologies in Puerto Rican University science education. *Critical Inquiry in Language Studies* 11 (1), 27–49.

Moschkovich, J. (2010) *Language and Mathematics Education: Multiple Perspectives and Directions for Research.* Charlotte, NC: Information Age Publishing.

O'Halloran, K.L. (2005) *Mathematical Discourse: Language, Symbolism and Visual Images.* London: Continuum.

Rowley-Jolivet, E. (2004) Different visions, different visuals: A social semiotic analysis of field-specific visual composition in scientific conference presentations. *Visual Communication* 3 (2), 145–175.

Rubinstein-Avila, E., Sox, A., Kaplan, S. and McGraw, R. (2014) Does biliteracy+mathematical discourse=binumerate development? Language use in a middle school dual language mathematics classroom. *Urban Education* 1–39.

Schleppegrell, M.J. (2007) The linguistic challenges of mathematics teaching and learning: A research perspective. *Reading and Writing Quarterly* 23 (2), 139–159.

Stöckl, H. (2004) In between modes: Language and image in printed media. In E. Ventola, C. Charles and M. Kaltenbacher (eds) *Perspectives on Multimodality* (pp. 9–29). Amsterdam: John Benjamins.

Tavares, N.J. (2015) How strategic use of L1 in an L2-medium mathematics classroom facilitates L2 interaction and comprehension. *International Journal of Bilingual Education and Bilingualism* 18 (3), 319–335.

Thompson, D.R. and Rubenstein, R.N. (2000) Learning mathematics vocabulary: Potential pitfalls and instructional strategies. *Mathematics Teacher* 93 (7), 568–574.

Tian, L. and Macaro, E. (2012) Comparing the effect of teacher code-switching with English-only explanations on the vocabulary acquisition of Chinese university students: A lexical focus-on-form study. *Language Teaching Research* 16 (3), 367–391.

Turnbull, M., Cormier, M. and Bourque, J. (2011) The first language in science class: A quasi-experimental study in late French immersion. *The Modern Language Journal* 95, 182–198.

Yin, R.K. (2009) *Case Study Research: Design and Methods* (Vol. 5). Thousand Oaks, CA: Sage Publications.

7 Multilingual Policies and Practices in Indian Higher Education

Cynthia Groff

Introduction

Linguistic diversity abounds in India, with its complex history of rulers and empires, and with its diverse people groups divided by geography, culture, religion, race, caste, class and gender. And yet the nation, at least in rhetoric, celebrates this variety, embracing the motto 'Unity in diversity'. During my ethnographic fieldwork in the Kumaun region of North India, I noticed the value placed on linguistic diversity and the acceptance of mixed language use: 'Speak however you like!' Multiple linguistic identities can be embraced in a context in which Kumauni, Hindi and Sanskrit are all considered 'ours', and multiple linguistic resources are used in educational contexts (Groff, 2010, 2013).

A language ideology that values multilingualism and diversity is also reflected in the common expression, 'Every mile the water changes, every four miles the speech'.[1] Just as the water from each village and spring is unique, linguistic features vary – and are expected to vary – from place to place. Speakers can make use of their multiple linguistic resources in creative ways. However, multilingual language practices, though extremely common, are sometimes frowned upon. The discourse of unity comes into tension with the discourse of diversity. Does India have 122 languages, as shown in the 2001 census, or more than 780 languages, as described in the ongoing People's Linguistic Survey of India (see Anand, 2013)? Twenty-two of these languages are recognized in the constitution. Sometimes smoothing over the differences is considered most prudent for national interests as well as for standardized education.

Within the context of Indian linguistic diversity, I focus on the situations faced by linguistic minorities, particularly in educational contexts where minorities are often disadvantaged (Jhingran, 2005; Mohanty, 2005). My approach values linguistic diversity and diverse language practices as resources (Cummins, 2007; García, 2007; Hornberger,

2002; Ruiz, 1984) while acknowledging the artificial nature of linguistic categories (Makoni & Pennycook, 2007). The various terms and definitions associated with translanguaging have been addressed elsewhere in this volume. For this chapter, my goal, in simplest terms, is to describe multilingual language policies and practices in India within their historical and ideological context, showing that the use of multiple languages within one institution, within one classroom and within one speech event is quite common in higher education in India. The first section addresses the history of language policy in India, particularly in relation to language use in higher education institutions, highlighting the ongoing tensions surrounding the medium of instruction in India. Here, higher education refers to post-secondary education leading to bachelor's and professional degrees and beyond. English has been portrayed as a superior language, as a link language and as a language of empowerment, but its role is contested in relation to Hindi and the other regional languages. The second section addresses language practices in Indian higher education, providing examples from my own fieldwork and from a small survey of university faculty. Without providing definitive answers, I raise the questions of what can be learned regarding translanguaging from the Indian context, how strategic the use of translanguaging is or should be and to what extent the term translanguaging provides a euphemism for a common practice that has previously been frowned upon as substandard in educational contexts.

Language Policy and Higher Education in India

As in all formerly colonized nations, higher-education language policies in India have been greatly influenced by the nation's colonial past. Through 150 years of British rule, traditional educational systems were replaced by a British system of education. The default language of higher education was (and remains) English. Still, the question of medium of instruction not only in primary and secondary school but also in higher education was a matter of debate in colonial times and remains controversial today.

Colonial language-in-education debates: English as superior, developed language?

Education in ancient India has been described as localized, with language choice reflecting the student's role in society and following hierarchical roles prescribed at birth (Annamalai, 2005). In contrast, the colonial education policy of the British was centralized, standardized and state controlled. The language of instruction was chosen for political reasons: for usefulness to the British administration and for instruction in European values. English was an obvious language choice, given the colonialist belief that 'education should impart to the colonial subjects the European values and knowledge, scientific and social, of that time' (Annamalai, 2005: 21). The English language was considered by the British rulers to be a superior language, the language best suited for conveying advanced education in India. Claims that regional languages were not developed enough linguistically to fill the role of media of instruction in higher education and that they would need to be further developed before taking such a role have continued into postcolonial times, unfounded as such claims may be (Annamalai, 2005; Khubchandani, 2008; Krishnamurti, 1990; Mahmood, 1974).

In 1835, the chairman of the General Committee on Public Instruction, T.B. Macaulay, made his infamous statement proclaiming the superiority of English for educating an Indian elite, justified by the supposed underdevelopment of the Indian languages:

> We have to educate a people who cannot at present be educated by means of their mother-tongue. We must teach them some foreign language. The claims of our own language it is hardly necessary to recapitulate. It stands preeminent even amongst the languages of the West. (Sharma, 1985: 2)

That same year a resolution was passed approving Macaulay's recommendations.

Yet, opinions about which language(s) to use as media of instruction at all levels of education were not without nuance, and the question sparked numerous debates in colonial India. Krishnamurti (1990) calls this a 100-year debate, with conflicting opinions characterized as orientalist, Anglicist, and vernacularist. Annamalai (2005) describes the strategic implications of these three positions: (1) The orientalist position promoted the use of classical Indian languages in education, thus making use of the traditional Indian elite and translating European knowledge and values into classical Indian languages. (2) The Anglicist position promoted the use of the English medium for educating a small portion of the population, who would then teach their own people, the goal being assimilation. This position became policy in 1835 after Macaulay's recommendation. (3) The vernacularist position promoted the teaching of European knowledge and values directly to the majority through regional languages or vernaculars. This strategy was considered 'expensive and impractical' (Annamalai, 2005: 22) by most colonial policymakers. Annamalai describes this final position as the foundation of postcolonial policy, with the promotion of 'European' knowledge being replaced by the promotion of 'modern' knowledge. However, the Anglicist position remains present in essence in current Indian education, including the cultivation of an English-educated elite (Annamalai, 2005), as seen in Table 7.1.

While primary and secondary education were increasingly offered in Indian languages throughout the colonial era (see Krishnamurti, 1990),

Table 7.1 Colonial decisions relevant to language in higher education

1835	Macaulay's Minute	Recommended English education for an Indian elite
1854	Wood's Dispatch	Reaffirmed the importance of English in education but promoted vernacular languages at the school level
1882	Hunter Commission	Promoted vernacular languages in primary education for subjects not leading to university study
1904, 1913	Resolutions on Educational Policy	Recommended that the switch from vernacular languages to English take place at the age of 13 and that English skills be improved at the secondary level
1915	Proposal in Parliament	Sparked debates regarding the use of vernaculars as languages of instruction in secondary schools
1924	1st Conference of Indian Universities	Discussed the question of medium of instruction and of examination but established no policy
1937	Abbott-Wood Report	Recommended the use of vernacular languages in secondary school, with English as compulsory subject

English remained the medium of instruction and examination in colleges and universities. The emphasis in higher education was thus on learning English, which promoted rote memorization rather than inquisitiveness in education (Jayaram, 1993). For more on colonial and postcolonial language-in-education policies, see Daswani (2001), Dua (1986), Ekbote (1984), Ramanathan (2005), Khubchandani (1981, 2001) and Sharma (1985).

Uniting academics, uniting India: English as link language

Beyond the question of language development, the English language has maintained its role in India and in Indian higher education because of its role as a link language – a common language intended both for national solidarity and for use as a lingua franca (Krishnamurti, 1990). On the academic level, the importance of having a common language for Indian scholarship has promoted the continued use of English and sparked debate over the potential role of Hindi as opposed to other regional languages in higher education. English also provides a link to international scholarship and has been seen, at the very least, as an important library language. Politically, the question of a common language for multilingual India has sparked fierce controversy. No universally accepted national language existed for the diverse subcontinent, and language was a central issue in the struggle to unite the diverse Indian states.

At independence, the problem of a common language was addressed in the constitution by naming Hindi, the language of the northern majority, as the official language but keeping English as an auxiliary official language. The intention was to keep English in place for a temporary period during which governmental operations could be transitioned to Hindi or another regional language. The status of English was to be reconsidered in 15 years, but 65 years later, English remains a *de facto* co-official language alongside Hindi. Besides the practicality of using English, which is the common language of the elite throughout India, Hindi has never been a common language for all Indians.[2] Southern states expressed, sometimes violently, their concern that Hindi would become the language of power at their expense. In response, the Official Language Act of 1963 (as amended, 1967) provided for the continuation of the status of English as an associate language for as long as desired by non-Hindi states.

Separate decisions were made regarding the official languages of the Indian states and union territories (which today number 36). Following the States Reorganisation Act of 1956, the borders of the Indian states were redrawn based on language, allowing each state to promote its own regional language as the language of the majority of its population. However, Jayaram and Rajyashree (2000: 26) point out that 'in almost all the states, initial enthusiasm died and indifference prevailed soon which led to amendments in the Official Language Act providing continuance of English for most of the official purposes'.

Similarly, in higher education, rhetoric has been strong for the switch to Indian languages as media of instruction. However, actual implementation has been slow. The following description of language-in-education decisions in independent India follows the struggle among English, Hindi and the regional languages both as languages to be taught and languages of instruction.

Post-independence language-in-education planning in India

The distinction between languages to be taught and media of instruction has not always been clear in debates about language in education. In both cases, decisions are often made for political rather than educational reasons. Also important to keep in mind regarding the following national-level educational recommendations and decisions are the roles of the states and the individual universities in the interpretation and implementation of policies. Regarding the question of language, India's University Education Commission of 1948–1949 stated that 'no other problem has caused greater controversy among educationalists and evoked more contradictory views from our witnesses' (Ministry of Education, 1962). A series of policies and recommendations have supported the use of Indian languages in higher education since independence (see Table 7.2). When the major recommendations were being made in the 1960s, 35 universities were allowing regional language for examinations, and in 15 universities, students were able to choose a regional language as the medium of instruction (Dasgupta, 1970). However, in addition to a lack of consensus, the lack of a specific time frame for the transition from English as medium of instruction has slowed or completely stalled implementation.

Establishing the permanent hegemony of the colonial language in government and in universities seemed inappropriate to policymakers in a newly independent India with numerous powerful languages of its own. However, the linguistic diversity of India itself promoted the retention of English because of resistance to the domination of one Indian language over the others. Although English has been the preferred mediator, especially among the elite, political rejection of Hindi also promoted the development of the other regional languages. The educational motivation for promoting regional languages involves equalizing access to education for speakers of those regional languages. And yet, current educational practices reflect an opposite trend, with a move toward more English in education.

Table 7.2 Post-independence decisions relevant to language in higher education

1948	National Planning Committee on General Education	Reported that English diverted students' time and energy and recommended use of the mother tongue for secondary school
1949	University Education Commission	Recommended that English be replaced by Indian languages as soon as possible, particularly regional languages, though optionally the federal language
1955	The Kanzru Committee of the University Grants Commission	Recommended a transition from English to Indian languages in the university, though gradual, along with the continued study of English by all university students
1956	Official Language Commission	Echoed a statement from the 1949 commission that only modern literary languages were fit for instruction
1961	Chief Ministers' Conference	Focused on language issues for national integration; reached no agreement on the appropriate language for higher education, though assumed an eventual switch from English to Hindi or regional languages

Table 7.2 (Continued)

1962	National Integration Council	Endorsed the recommendations of the 1949 commission
1966	Report of the Education Commission of 1964–1966	Urged education in mother tongue or regional languages for increased creativity and to reduce social gaps; made recommendations for the teaching of English, bilingual proficiency, the development of Indian languages and the establishment of all-India English-language universities
1967	Statement to Parliament by Minister of Education Triguna Sen	Announced the government of India's support of a transition to regional languages for education in all stages and subjects, though recognizing that the pace of the changeover would vary between and within universities
1967	Conference of Vice-Chancellors	Recommended a switch to regional languages at the undergraduate level within 5–10 years and the continuation of English in postgraduate and research levels because of a dependence on English literature
1968	The Three Language Formula of the Ministry of Education	Adopted as national education policy, following 1956 and 1966 proposals; recommended the consecutive introduction of three languages through primary and secondary education

Current trends in education: English for empowerment?

India currently has the third-largest higher education sector in the world, after China and the US, with English remaining the primary language for tertiary education (Altback, 2005). Enrollment in India's 700 degree-awarding institutions has increased significantly, especially within the past 15 years (University Grants Commission, 2013). Comprehensive statistics on current media of instruction at Indian universities are difficult to find. One survey of 108 universities reported that 80% of programs offer instruction and examinations in English and 20% offer these in another language. Non-English programs, two-thirds of which are in Hindi, tend to be in the arts and humanities (Gargesh, 2006). The Hindi language is still being promoted in tertiary education through awareness-raising events such as essay and typing competitions, workshops, celebrations and debates, and through the translation of documents into Hindi (University Grants Commission, 2010). Although many institutions offer courses both in English and in one or more of the regional languages, Indian-medium options are stigmatized and class distinctions prevail between the two tracks (Annamalai, 2005).

While Indian universities have been moving toward using more regional languages for instruction since independence, this trend has been met by another international trend: that of introducing English as the medium of instruction at the university level (and lower) in non-English-speaking countries. The demand for English as the medium of instruction at all levels of education has been increasing in India. Although this demand reflects international trends toward English, the importance of English in earlier stages of education in India also reflects the continued dominance of English at the university level in a system that favors students taught through English throughout their educational careers. Indian scholars throughout the past decades have noted the increasing 'enthusiasm for English education' (Dasgupta, 1970). Jayaram (1993) noted that more Indians want to learn English than ever before. English continues to be dominant in higher education, especially in the sciences, and is increasingly moving into primary and secondary schools as well (Meganathan, 2011). No longer associated with colonial domination, English is being embraced as an important international language and as a means for upward social mobility, economic opportunity and empowerment.

High-quality English-medium instruction at the primary and secondary levels is available only through expensive private schools in India, a fact that perpetuates a class-based divide, with unequal access to English implying unequal access to education at all levels (Ramanathan, 2005). Current practices at the university level keep English out of reach of lower-income and lower-caste groups, as observed by Ramanathan (1999) in the Gujarati context. Such practices include (a) the use of tracking streams at the college level, barring some students from English-medium instruction; (b) the teaching of English literature rather than English language; and (c) extensive use of grammar-translation methods (Ramanathan, 1999). Jayaram (1993) also noted that language study in Indian universities has focused on literary and cultural appreciation of the language rather than on its functional purposes or on developing the ability to express oneself in that language. 'Thus, the inability of the students to use languages effectively as a means of communication is a major problem and the prime failing of university education' (Jayaram, 1993: 97). This was despite the fact that the heavy language load in the Indian curriculum up to the undergraduate level resulted in about 50% of students' study time being devoted to language (Jayaram, 1993).

Because of the concrete advantages associated with better English education, state governments have been under pressure to introduce English earlier and earlier in government schools. Reflecting debates about the medium of instruction in colonial times, Annamalai (2005) describes the tensions as follows:

> The conflict between the goal of mass education through native languages and elitist education through English creates a tension between the policy of the government and the demands of the people, between government schools that implement the policy and the private schools that fulfill popular demands. The tension leads to divergence between policy and practice with regard to the medium of education. (Annamalai, 2005: 22)

Such divergences between policy and practice reflect spaces for the implementation of diverse practices in education. Although English has been present in Indian education for generations as the 'superior' language, as the link language and as the language of empowerment, Indian languages have also been present, whether explicitly promoted in policies or not. The following section moves beyond policy questions to address multilingual language practices evident in higher education in India.

Language Practices and Higher Education in India

Diverse multilingual language practices abound in India. A dialect continuum stretches from east to west across the northern Hindi belt, representing numerous linguistic varieties, and the use of Hinglish is also common in urban areas. Speakers of smaller languages or 'dialects' in the north also claim Hindi as their own and freely mix and switch languages, depending on context (Groff, 2010). Hindi messages are typed into cell phones in Roman script, with the frequent addition of English terms, while English words appear on many signs in Hindi's Devanagari script. In the southern and northeastern states also, many languages come into contact.

Multilingual norms extend into education as well, regardless of official policy. In the Kumaun region of Uttarakhand where I conducted my ethnographic fieldwork, Hindi is the official medium of instruction at all state-run government schools, but many children come to school speaking only their home language, Kumauni. Joining the many linguistic minorities around the world, they could find themselves submerged in a context that hinders their understanding and communication. However, most teachers in the Kumaun nowadays are themselves speakers of Kumauni. Although the use of mother tongue support in a language such as Kumauni, often minimized as a backward dialect, is usually considered 'low standard', some teachers and administrators admitted their practice of using Kumauni in the classroom. As one Kumauni teacher explained, 'Whatever it takes to explain it to the children is used. But Hindi is the reading/studying medium. We use Kumauni to help the little children understand, but we don't use it all of the time' (H; PQ:08March27[3]). Similarly, the use of Hindi is common in rural English-medium schools and in English classes (Groff, 2010, 2013).

This section provides glimpses of multilingual language practices, and perspectives on such practices, in higher education. Examples are drawn from my fieldwork in North India and from recent survey responses from university faculty. Rather than providing comprehensive evidence of language practices, these examples shed light on the fact that translanguaging practices do occur, and encourage further research into current practices on university campuses and in university classrooms in India, as well as research on the effectiveness of such practices.

Research methods

My ethnographic research was based in the village of Kausani in the Kumaun region of North India and included nine months of primary fieldwork in 2007–2008. Through observations and interviews, I explored themes relevant to language and education, especially as experienced and expressed by Kumauni young women and educators. My research also extended beyond the school and village setting to such sites as the Kumaun University campuses in Almora and Nainital. One such visit included an opportunity to lead a discussion about language attitudes and teaching methods in a bachelor's-level course for future English teachers, as described below. I documented the events with detailed field notes immediately after they occurred and took into account contextual factors in the inductive analysis process. Names have been excluded or changed to protect privacy. The example from the University of Delhi was drawn from a questionnaire addressing language use in the university classroom, which was distributed digitally to several faculty members in mid-2014.

The analysis of data was iterative and inductive, involving repeated reading and coding of the data based on themes that emerged throughout the research, including the theme of mixed language use. Through triangulation, data from multiple sources were used to provide alternative perspectives on a situation or additional support for a hypothesis. The examples in this section offer a hint of what is happening in terms of language use in some university classrooms in India within the language policy context described above.

Resorting to Hindi at Kumaun University

Kumaun University was established in 1973 and received full recognition from the University Grants Commission in 1984. The university website explains, 'The university being located in the upland hilly area of new state of Uttarakhand has made all out efforts to serve the educational needs of the socially and economically weak region' (Kumaun University, 2014). As this statement implies, this university is not attracting students from the top English-medium schools of the country but is catering primarily to the needs of local students, many educated at rural Hindi-medium government schools: 'The main focus of the University has been to include the courses which are relevant and facilitate the learners in developing skills for easy job access' (Kumaun University, 2014).

Multilingual language practices at Kumaun University are reflected in the admissions handbook and on the website. The handbook is bilingual but not through the translation of content. Rather, some content is presented in Hindi and some in English. The surface links and texts of the university website are in English, except for the name and address header in Devanagari script, parallel to the English. However, many of the information links lead to documents that are entirely in Hindi (Kumaun University, 2014). My conversations with professors and teachers in training at Kumaun University drew my attention to the multilingual nature of classroom interaction common at the university as well as the strong social implications of knowing more English.

An English professor at the Nainital branch of Kumaun University explained to me that all of their BA students were required to take a language course in their first year of study, either English or Hindi. She said that the English department gets the smartest students: the 'smarter set'. The introductory class is a foundational course, focusing on grammar, whereas the other English courses focus on literature. When I asked about the English proficiency of the students and how she teaches them, she said that the professors need to 'resort to Hindi' in their classes in order to help the students understand.

> When we look out and see blank faces, we know that we need to use Hindi. The students are also multilevel. Some have gone to English-medium schools, others think that the past tense of 'think' is 'thank'. I need to deal with a constant balance in teaching English. It is difficult to teach Shakespearean English, etc. to students who don't even know the basics of English. (E; PQ:07Aug22)

This professor also describes English as important for students' job prospects and, quite honestly in the case of girls, for the 'marriage market'. The students, especially in rural areas, she said, perceive English as a tool for empowerment.

A Hindi professor at the Almora branch of Kumaun University talked with me about the economic, social and academic reasons for students' growing demand for English. From an academic perspective, accessing and disseminating literature becomes a linguistic challenge. According to this professor, the English textbooks are often superior in content compared with the Hindi textbooks, which are sometimes translations. She also cites her own struggle with disseminating her work, which is published primarily in Hindi. Our conversation switched freely between Hindi and English. I paraphrase her words in the following quote:

> I write in Kumauni and in Hindi. I am not practiced in English. That English base was not formed. It was very weak. For myself, I have no financial problem. I have a good job and a salary. However, I face difficulties in interacting with others and when I want to show my work – my literature, my academic writing. When it comes to the English-only medium, I am bound. I can't go ahead without English.
> (E/H; PQ: 08Feb25)

The national question of providing a link language for India and for Indian academia remains an issue on the ground and has clearly not been resolved in favor of Hindi, even in a Hindi-dominant region. Although the use of Hindi is common, even the default, at Kumaun University, the pressure to use English is felt in the classroom as well as in publishing. At the same time, faculty members express the importance of mother tongue support in higher education.

English teachers in training at Kumaun University: 'Please use mother tongue'

Dr Barman is the instructor for a course on English teaching in the Education Department at the Almora branch of Kumaun University. The class has about 59 students, with 35–40 of them 'present' or attending class. The students in this class are in a one-year BEd program, having completed a minimum of a BA. When she first started teaching this class, Dr Barman said that she was using only English. One afternoon, when she came to class, she found a clear message written for her on the chalkboard in English: 'Please use mother tongue'. From that day, she also started to use Hindi in her classroom instruction. When I visited the class, students were submitting lesson plans handwritten in English. Because they will be teaching English, Dr Barman explained, they needed to write their lesson plans in English. Dr Barman talks about the challenges of teaching English in this environment, where the students have not been exposed to much English: 'This makes it difficult for them to learn. The language teaching is totally based on the teacher' (E; PQ:08Feb25).

While some of Dr Barman's students had attended English-medium schools, the majority had come through the Hindi-medium government school system. During the discussion that I led with this class, the distinction between these two groups was clearly evident in student participation and social interaction. First, I needed to make some adjustments in my own language use. I started out in English, acknowledging that my American accent might sound different to them. When I asked the class if everything was clear in my introduction, Dr Barman suggested that I talk very slowly. She also followed up my English instructions with Hindi explanations, knowing the needs of her students. My field notes describe my partial adaptation:

> In retrospect, I wish I would have used more Hindi or encouraged discussion in Hindi since only those who were most fluent in English had the courage to join the discussion. ... At some point in the discussion, I started using some Hindi – summarizing and asking questions in Hindi – sometimes partially repeating myself in Hindi and English.   (FN:08Feb25)

As we discussed useful language-learning strategies, some students mentioned the importance of using Hindi as a tool in English-language teaching. This issue sparked debate among the students, highlighting the differences in their educational backgrounds and the context-dependence of language choices: In some English-medium schools Hindi is completely prohibited, but in the government schools English-only would not be appropriate even for English class. They also debated the importance of family background and support versus motivation and eagerness to learn in determining English abilities. I noticed social tensions under the surface in the class and coming out in the discussion, highlighting differences in social status and in opinion between the 'English-medium' and 'Hindi-medium' students.

In closing the discussion with these future English teachers, I transitioned to the question of what methods they would use to teach English, keeping in mind their own language-learning experiences, and asked for their responses in writing. One girl spoke up: 'I would teach with the help of the local dialects'. I asked her to say more. She would teach English using Kumauni and Hindi. 'So many can't even understand Hindi', she said, so she would use their dialects as a tool. She later clarified that she would still use English texts but would allow spoken support in Kumauni or Hindi. Some negative reactions came from other students, especially from a talkative girl who had clearly come from an English-medium school. One student said that this would not work. 'If you instill the local dialect in the students, they can't learn English'. Another argued that English should be taught in English. But another student responded, 'English to English is not possible in the rural context' (E; PQ:08Feb25). Regardless of opinions on the use of more stigmatized linguistic varieties like Kumauni, there seemed to be some consensus that English would need to be taught through Hindi in the government schools. Dr Barman's example of being asked to 'use mother tongue' in that same class substantiated the point.

In writing about their preferred teaching methods, many of Dr Barman's students agreed that the support of a known language would be important in teaching English:

So to teach English, help of Hindi must be taken. Otherwise, they won't be able to understand.

We would teach English in local dialects. English to English is not possible with the students of rural areas. In government school even English is taught in Hindi. We should use both Hindi and English while teaching English.

I think that we learn English by oral communication. ... When we teach English, we should use their common language so that they understand the meaning of lesson. (E; Student essays:08Feb25)

These future English teachers were grappling with the tension between providing their students with sufficient exposure to oral English and providing them with sufficient comprehensible instruction. Both are complicated by a rural context in which very little English support is available outside the classroom. While the demand for English is strong, the need for mother tongue support is strong as well. Multilingual practices are clearly needed and are noticeably present. Regarding whether her students need to know English to prepare for university, one Kumauni high school teacher explained linguistic practices at the university in this way: 'They are talking in Hindi, but some words they talk in English. Not all Hindi, not all English – mixed!' (E; DQ: 07Aug7).

Natural use of multiple languages at the University of Delhi

The University of Delhi was established in 1922, although some of its branches have a much longer history. Zakir Husain Delhi College, for example, has roots in the 17th century, has used Persian, Arabic, Sanskrit and later Urdu or Hindustani as media of instruction and became one of the first colleges to provide English education, with separate oriental and English sections. Currently ranked one of India's top universities, the University of Delhi is also one of the country's largest universities, with 132,435 regular students and 261,169 students in non-formal education programs, which include correspondence courses and continuing education (University of Delhi, 2014). The admissions handbook and website are entirely in English, except for the name of the university, written in Devanagari script in the header. As far as admissions requirements, an English exam is obligatory for admission to science courses, while for some other courses an exam in another language is sufficient. Regarding reservations for traditionally oppressed groups, the handbook states,

The Colleges shall not refuse admission to any SC/ST candidate on the basis of medium of instruction. Any deficiency in the knowledge of any particular language should be removed, remedial classes for which may be arranged by utilizing grants that are available from University Grants Commission. (University of Delhi, 2014)

While English dominates at the University of Delhi, the university still has a Directorate of Hindi Medium Implementation, which is involved in translating and publishing books and materials in Hindi to encourage the use of Hindi as the medium of instruction in various subjects (University of Delhi, 2014).

Several faculty members at the University of Delhi generously shared with me their experiences and perspectives on language use in the university classroom through a questionnaire distributed in 2014.[4] The three respondents are language instructors in the Department of Slavonic and Finno-Ugrian Studies and are native speakers of Indian languages. As they explained in their responses, multiple languages naturally come into their classroom practice, which includes the use of both Hindi and English 'as and when required'. The languages of informal conversation with and among the students are both English and Hindi. The instructors have received no specific directives from the university regarding language policy or language use in the classroom. Switching between languages in the classroom comes naturally for them and requires little explanation. One instructor states simply that she explains situations in 'Hindi/ English/Bulgarian'. A Russian-language instructor explains her approach in beginners' classes as follows:

> Commands like 'Please read, let us read' are given sometimes in English, sometimes in Hindi (later in Russian). Explanation of phonetic and grammar rules is done in Hindi and English. When some students don't understand the explanation in English, I immediately shift to Hindi. If I am short of words in Hindi the students pitch in and try to find analogies.

For more advanced classes, all three languages are used. During discussions of Russian culture with the students, for example, 'there is free flow of English, Hindi, and Russian'. Regarding a choice for Hindi over English, she says, 'Sometimes I use Hindi specifically when I know that an example from Hindi will be better understood than in English. I also see in what language the majority of the students will grasp the particular idea I want to put across'.

These instructors describe the use of multiple languages in the same event as 'very useful and pragmatic'. Linguistic diversity 'adds pep to the classroom teaching' and is dealt with 'most naturally. It comes automatically'. For students, they say, the use of multiple languages 'saves time and cuts across cultural barriers'. Students 'don't question this at all. It is taken for granted'. The multilingual environment of India, of Delhi and of the university is reflected in the classroom with the natural use of multiple languages, as one instructor explained: 'In our environment it is the most natural course to follow. For me it is necessary that the students understand what they are reading and learning so I don't hold any bars against translanguaging'.

Conclusions: Translanguaging and the Indian Context

In light of the multilingual practices already present in Indian higher education, I conclude by raising the questions of what can be learned regarding translanguaging from the Indian context, how strategic the use of translanguaging is or should be and to what extent the term translanguaging provides a euphemism for a common practice that has previously been frowned upon as substandard in educational contexts.

What can be learned regarding translanguaging from the Indian context? Compared with most formerly colonized nations, Indian languages have made significant headway in the higher education system. India also models an atmosphere in which diversity is, to a great extent, expected and valued. The fluidity of linguistic forms (Makoni & Pennycook, 2007) is acknowledged with terms like *boli*, which describes a spoken variety and does not fit the concrete countability of *bhasha* or language (Groff, 2013). This fluidity extends to the natural use of multiple languages within the same speech event.

Some Indian scholars have recognized the multilingual language practices common in Indian education and have presented recommendations in support of linguistic diversity. Khubchandani describes common multilingual practices as follows:

> [S]tudents listen to one language and write answers in another; formal teaching in the classroom is conducted in one language but informal explanations are provided in another. This milieu promotes a good deal of code-switching and hybridization of two or more contact languages.
> (Khubchandani, 2008: 374)

He emphasizes the importance of respecting and building on this natural multilingualism, although such 'grassroots folk multilingualism' has usually been undervalued (Khubchandani, 1992: 102). Mohanty *et al.* (2010: 214) make a similar observation, noting that the diverse on-the-ground realities differ from official policy in India: 'it is not uncommon for classroom activities to be informally transacted in different languages, particularly when the officially prescribed language of teaching is not the home language for some or most of the students'. Agnihotri (2007: 197) also states that 'any classroom in India is in general multilingual' and calls for language practices that acknowledge the natural multilingual practices common in society, respect the linguistic knowledge of students and treat multilingualism 'as a resource, strategy and a goal'. Turning to higher education, Mahmood (1974: 286) concludes, 'Whatever be the medium of instruction, every university should be multilingual'. Krishnamurti (1990) presents his vision for what should have happened after independence in Indian higher education:

> Teachers ... could have used the syntax of the regional language with a free admixture of English/international terminology. They would have thereby developed styles suitable to teach different subjects. ... The preparation of textbooks and standardization of terms should have followed in due course after employing styles involving free code switching in the classroom for at least one decade. (Krishnamurti, 1990: 22)

His recommendation for reversing the current situation involves the use of regional media of instruction at all levels, promoting the development of the language through use and 'Allowing teachers and students to freely use their variety/style for acquiring modern knowledge through the mother tongue/regional language' (Krishnamurti, 1990: 23). These descriptions and recommendations acknowledge the linguistic diversity that exists in Indian classrooms and the potential for using that diversity in instruction.

If the multilingual language practices in Indian classrooms can be termed translanguaging, how strategic should such translanguaging be? Although the practice of switching back and forth between languages in the classroom may come naturally to teachers, the question remains as to how effective this practice is for students. In particular, the habit of translating directly from one language to another may do more harm than good. A *de facto* result of the lack of planning for the transitions in media of instruction throughout the Indian education system is what Annamalai (2001) terms 'unplanned simultaneous bilingual education'. While acknowledging the importance of multilingual practices, Khubchandani (2001) calls for better planning for the transition in media of education in higher education, as well as the development of 'positive attitudes to speech variation in multilingual repertoires' (Khubchandani, 2008: 376).

More systematic research is needed to understand current practices of language use in Indian higher education and to determine which practices are most effective. At the school level, Mohanty et al. (2010: 211) report poor implementation of policies and a wide range of practices 'where multilingual diversity seems to have yielded to chaos', but they also provide positive examples of 'code-mixing for effective communication in the classroom' (Mohanty et al., 2010: 224). They conclude from their observations at schools for tribal children in Odisa that 'translanguaging classroom practices are often used strategically for effective communication' (Mohanty et al., 2010: 224), with classroom practices that are 'noticeably multilingual and multicultural' (Mohanty et al., 2010: 225).

Finally, does the term translanguaging provide a euphemism for a common practice that has previously been frowned upon as substandard in educational contexts? Although India's 'unity in diversity' values multilingualism, the pressure for unity sometimes obscures diversity. Similarly, multilingual languaging practices face conflicting ideologies and are often stigmatized as substandard, especially in educational contexts. As I reflect on Annamalai's (1990) observation that bilingual education faces less resistance in India when not centrally planned, I wonder about the extent to which translanguaging practices are present, though unacknowledged and unproblematized, in Indian university classrooms. These and other questions remain to be addressed in the Indian context.

In summary, language-in-education policies have been debated in India for generations. During colonial times, English was promoted as the superior, developed language. In post-independence India, policies and recommendations promoted a transition toward Indian languages in higher education. English remained significant, however, as a link language, uniting diverse regions and diverse scholars, and as a tool for economic advancement. Turning from policy to language practices in education, a multilingual ideology is demonstrated in the natural use of multiple languages at Kumaun University and the University of Delhi.

Notes

(1) In Hindi: *'Kos kos par badle paani, chaar kos par baani'*.
(2) Also worth noting is the lack of homogeneity in the so-called Hindi-speaking regions and the debates surrounding the artificial separation of Muslim-affiliated Urdu from Hindi in newly independent India.
(3) In citing notes and transcripts, I identify the language being used as Hindi (H) or English (E). I also differentiate between field notes (FN); paraphrased quotes (PQ) written, as I remembered them, in the voice of the speaker; and direct quotes (DQ).
(4) Special thanks to Dr Neelakshi Suryanarayan for her help with data collection at the University of Delhi.

References

Agnihotri, R.K. (2007) Identity and multilinguality: The case of India. In A.B.M. Tsui and J.W. Tollefson (eds) *Language Policy, Culture and Identity in Asian Contexts* (pp. 185–204). Mahwah, NJ: Lawrence Erlbaum.
Altback, P.G. (2005) Higher education in India. In S. Tiwari (ed.) *Education in India* (Vol. 1; pp. 244–252). New Delhi: Atlantic.
Anand, K. (2013) India speaks ... 780 ways. *The Indian Express.* 11 August 2013. See http://archive.indianexpress.com/news/india-speaks...780-ways/1153717/ (accessed 17 June 2015).
Annamalai, E. (1990) Dimensions of bilingual education in India. *New Language Planning Newsletter* 4 (4), 1–3.
Annamalai, E. (2001) *Managing Multilingualism in India: Political and Linguistic Manifestation* (Vol. 8). New Delhi: Sage.

Annamalai, E. (2005) Nation building in a globalized world: Language choice and education in India. In A. Lin and P. Martin (eds) *Decolonisation, Globalisation: Language-in-Education Policy and Practice* (pp. 21–38). Clevedon: Multilingual Matters.

Cummins, J. (2007, November) Pedagogies of Choice in Educating Bilingual Students. Paper presented at the Second International Conference on Language, Education and Diversity, Hamilton, New Zealand.

Dasgupta, J. (1970) *Language Conflict and National Development: Group Politics and National Language Policy in India.* Oakland, CA: University of California Press.

Daswani, C.J. (ed.) (2001) *Language Education in Multilingual India.* New Delhi: UNESCO.

Dua, H.R. (1986) Language planning and linguistic minorities. In E. Annamalai, B. Jernudd and J. Rubin (eds) *Language Planning: Proceedings of an Institute* (pp. 43–72). Mysore: Central Institute of Indian Languages.

Ekbote, G. (1984) *A Nation without a National Language.* Hyderabad: Hindi Prachar Sabha.

García, O. (2007, November) Contesting and Constructing Plural Language Practices and Identities of US Latinos. Paper presented at the 2nd International Conference on Language, Education, and Diversity, Hamilton, New Zealand.

Gargesh, R. (2006, June 8) Languages Issues in the Context of Higher Education in India. Paper presented at Language Issues in English-Medium Universities across Asia. University of Hong Kong. See www.fe.hku.hk/clear/highlights.html (accessed 22 September 2014).

Groff, C. (2010) Language, education, and empowerment: Voices of Kumauni young women in multilingual India. PhD thesis, University of Pennsylvania. See http://repository.upenn.edu/edissertations/115 (accessed 27 June 2015).

Groff, C. (2013) Multilingual discourses and pedagogy in North India. In J.A. Shoba and F. Chimbutane (eds) *Bilingual Education and Language Policy in the Global South* (pp. 190–206). London: Routledge.

Hornberger, N.H. (2002) Multilingual language policies and the continua of biliteracy: An ecological approach. *Language Policy* 1 (1), 27–51.

Jayaram, N. (1993) The language question in higher education: Trends and issues. *Higher Education* 26 (1), 93–114.

Jayaram, B.D. and Rajyashree, K.S. (2000) State official language policy implementation: A geolinguistic profile in sociolinguistic perspective. Mysore: Central Institute of Indian Languages.

Jhingran, D. (2005) *Language Disadvantage: The Learning Challenge in Primary Education.* New Delhi: APH Publishing.

Khubchandani, L.M. (1981) *Multilingual Education in India.* Pune: Center for Communication Studies.

Khubchandani, L.M. (1992) *Tribal Identity: A Language and Communication Perspective.* New Delhi: Indian Institute of Advanced Study.

Khubchandani, L.M. (2001) Language demography and language education. In C.J. Daswani (ed.) *Language Education in Multilingual India* (pp. 3–47). New Delhi: UNESCO.

Khubchandani, L.M. (2008) Language policy and education in the Indian subcontinent. In S. May and N.H. Hornberger (eds) *Encyclopedia of Language and Education* (2nd edn; pp. 369–381). New York: Springer.

Krishnamurti, B.H. (1990) The regional language *vis-à-vis* English as the medium of instruction in higher education: The Indian dilemma. In D.P. Pattanayak (ed.) *Multilingualism in India* (pp. 15–24). Hyderabad: Orient Longman.

Kumaun University (2014) University website. See http://kuexam.ac.in/ and http://www.kunainital.ac.in/ (accessed 28 June 2015).

Mahmood, M. (1974) Language politics and higher education in India. *The Indian Journal of Political Science* 35 (3), 277–286.

Makoni, S. and Pennycook, A. (eds) (2007) *Disinventing and Reconstituting Languages.* Clevedon: Multilingual Matters.

Meganathan, R. (2011) Language policy in education and the role of English in India: From library language to language of empowerment. In H. Coleman (ed.) *Dreams and Realities: Developing Countries and the English Language* (pp. 57–86). London: British Council.

Ministry of Education (1962) The Report of the University Education Commission (December 1948–August 1949) Vol. 1. Government of India Press.

Mohanty, A. (2005, October) Perpetuating Inequality: Language Disadvantage and Capability Deprivation of Tribal Mother Tongue Speakers in India. Paper presented at the Cornell Conference on Language and Poverty, Ithaca, NY.

Mohanty, A., Panda, M. and Pal, R. (2010) Language policy in education and classroom practices in India: Is the teacher a cog in the policy wheel? In K. Menken and O. García (eds) *Negotiating Language Policies in Schools: Educators as Policymakers* (pp. 211–231). New York: Routledge.

Ramanathan, V. (1999) 'English is here to stay': A critical look at institutional and educational practices in India. *TESOL Quarterly* 33 (2), 211–231.

Ramanathan, V. (2005) *The English-Vernacular Divide: Postcolonial Language Politics and Practice.* Clevedon: Multilingual Matters.

Ruiz, R. (1984) Orientations in language planning. *NABE Journal* 8 (2), 15–34.

Sharma, B.N. (1985) *Medium of Instruction in India: A Backgrounder Based on Official Documents of the Government of India.* New Delhi: Central Secretariat Library, Dept. of Culture.

University Grants Commission (2010) Annual Report 2009–2010. New Delhi: University Grants Commission. See http://www.ugc.ac.in (accessed 22 September 2014).

University Grants Commission (2013) Higher education in India at a glance. New Delhi: University Grants Commission. See www.ugc.ac.in/pdfnews/6805988_HEglance2013.pdf (accessed 27 June 2014).

University of Delhi (2014) University website. See http://www.du.ac.in/du/ (accessed 27 June 2015).

8 Translanguaging within Higher Education in the United Arab Emirates

Kevin S. Carroll and Melanie van den Hoven

Introduction

As other chapters in this volume have documented, the face of higher education and the languages used have changed with increased internationalization (Altbach *et al.*, 2009). As access to tertiary education becomes more widespread, debates concerning the balance between national languages and English as an international language used by faculty, students and administrators have become more openly discussed (Doiz *et al.*, 2013). Such has not been the case in the Gulf Cooperation Council (GCC) countries of Saudi Arabia, Kuwait, Bahrain, Qatar, Oman and the United Arab Emirates (UAE), where English is used largely as the medium of instruction at the tertiary level (Weber, 2011). Within this region, institutions for higher education have been erected in rapidly growing cities, which just four to five decades ago were undeveloped desert lands with a scarce local population (Kirk, 2010). Oil revenues within the GCC have resulted in intense investment within all sectors of society and have prompted a large migration of expatriates to all GCC countries (Dresch & Piscatori, 2005). Furthermore, excess oil revenues have allowed local governments to invest in education with the goal of building a strong local workforce to replace, or at least work alongside, expatriate workers. In this chapter, we will present data from interviews with six knowledgeable and experienced professors and administrators regarding the place of Arabic and English in the system of higher education within the UAE. We will argue that influential monolingual ideologies in favor of English have contributed to a regional context prohibitive of open research on documenting translanguaging practices in the classroom.

Multilingualism in Higher Education

Historically, the academy and other educational institutions have largely mirrored the monolingual ideologies of European and North American universities, where the use of code-switching or translanguaging practices has been viewed as an impure or illegitimate means of teaching and disseminating knowledge (Creese & Blackledge, 2010). However, more recently, multilingualism in higher education has become more obvious where the internationalization of higher education has forced universities to rethink how they balance attracting tuition from high-paying foreigners with maintaining local linguistic traditions that benefit a local or national student population (Phillipson, 2015). Whether it is Europe's Erasmus Mundus project, with the goal of increasing enrollment in European institutions from students from Africa, Asia and the Americas (Coleman, 2006), or the use of study materials developed in local languages such as Afrikaans, Sotho, Xhosa and Zulu (van der Walt, 2013), multilingual efforts in higher education are complex and multilayered (Ricento & Hornberger, 1996). Similarly, 'The problem with identifying one language as a LoLT [language of learning and teaching] in a particular country or institution in Africa is that official policy seldom reflects the reality of teaching and learning' (van der Walt, 2013: 53). When policies do not align with what teachers believe to be the most effective mode of teaching or with teachers' own linguistic competencies, then higher educational contexts become ripe for bilingual and potentially even multilingual exchanges as the teaching and learning of content is brokered through complex, bi- and multidirectional exchanges between the learner, his or her classmates, the textbooks they are using, and the instructor.

The market-driven forces of higher education are undeniable as businesses and well-known universities look to cash in on their global name recognition (Phillipson, 2015). The wealth of GCC nations and their goals of becoming the next intellectual hubs, at least in Qatar and the UAE, have facilitated partnerships throughout the region with these well-known institutions (Ibnouf et al., 2014; Karram, 2014; Knight, 2011; Lane 2011). Internationally recognized institutions have opened campuses in the gulf, such as New York University and Paris's Sorbonne in Abu Dhabi, Wollongong's Dubai Campus, and Carnegie Mellon, Georgetown, Northwestern and University College London in Qatar. The presence of such internationally recognized institutions has attracted the attention of local Arabs as well as other degree-seekers from around the region. What is interesting is that with few exceptions, the language of instruction in all of these institutions is almost exclusively English, not Arabic or French. (The majority of the undergraduate courses at Paris Sorbonne–Abu Dhabi are given in French, but all the graduate programs are offered in English.) Thus, the mere presence of these prestigious institutions serves as a symbol of what constitutes knowledge and the vehicle through which knowledge is disseminated: English.

While English is now the medium through which the majority of tertiary education is transmitted, this has not always been the case within the UAE. Formally established in 1971 as an independent country, the UAE comprises seven different semi-autonomous emirates: Abu Dhabi, Dubai, Sharjah, Ajman, Fujairah, Umm al Quwain and Ras al-Khaimah. Higher education in the UAE formally started in 1976 with the founding of UAE University (UAEU) in Al Ain, Abu Dhabi, as the flagship institution within the seven emirates (Findlow, 2005). Originally founded as a college focusing on Sharia law and Islamic studies, UAEU has since moved to offer:

A full range of accredited, high-quality graduate and undergraduate programs through nine Colleges: Business and Economics; Education; Engineering; Food and Agriculture; Humanities and Social Sciences; IT; Law; Medicine and Health Sciences; and Science. With a distinguished international faculty, state-of-the art new campus, and full range of student support services, UAEU offers a living-learning environment that is unmatched in the UAE. (United Arab Emirates University, 2015)

According to Findlow (2005), the early faculty at UAEU, similar to teachers within the primary and secondary schools, were largely Egyptian and from other Arabic-speaking countries; however, as the university worked to gain more international prestige with the addition of programs in engineering, medicine, science and economics, there was a shift in hiring practices to bring in English-speaking faculty who, with their research, would raise the recognition of the institution. After having been open for less than 40 years, the university claims to be 'ranked as the number one research university in the GCC, number two in the Arab World, and #385 globally' (UAE University Website, 2015). This is a remarkable achievement for such a young institution in a region where the majority of students are the first in their families to attend tertiary education (Clarke, 2007).

Through interviews and our lived experience in the UAE, it became obvious that language use within the country has varied widely in the country's brief history. After the unification of the seven emirates, there was an initial push toward uniting them under one national identity, which, similar to the other GCC countries, was couched within their devotion to Islam and common understanding of Arabic. This push was also tied to Gamal Abdel Nasser's call in the 1950s and 1960s for Pan-Arabism and solidarity with Palestine (Findlow, 2000). Such political movements meant the opening of schools and the creation of institutions of higher education where the language of instruction was largely Arabic. As oil wealth has continued to grow, the move toward diversifying the local economy has called on the increased involvement of Emiratis through Emiratization

(Godwin, 2006). However, such diversification has hinged largely on the Emiratis becoming more educated in employable sectors of the expanding economy, such as oil and gas, which has been a major adjustment from their nomadic Bedouin life of just two generations ago. Such a change in expectations and lifestyle has posed real challenges for Emiratis without specialized technical training to compete on a global platform or even in their own country, considering the prevalence of imported labor and highly qualified expatriates working in the areas of science, medicine and engineering (Davidson, 2009).

Shortly after the creation of the UAE, major investments were made in the expansion of public education along with a system of higher education, which started with the opening of UAEU (Kirk, 2015). While these investments were building in prestige and numbers over the years, Emirati children, primarily males, who showed promise and had good marks in their secondary schools were (and still are, albeit with less frequency) sent to the United States, Australia and the United Kingdom for their tertiary education (Ministry of Higher Education & Scientific Research, 2014: 94). The government-funded scholarships for these students paid for their travel, housing and tuition, all with the understanding that they would come back and work in the country (Al-Zubaidi, 2010). Such scholarship programs were, and still are, taken advantage of by many Emirati men and some women, though this is in decline in the post-9/11 era (Ministry of Higher Education & Scientific Research, 2014). Nevertheless, those who have taken advantage of these scholarships in English-speaking countries have often returned to ascend to the highest positions in various government organizations (Salem, 2014a). Therefore, it is understandable that the experiences of these Emirati men will influence policies throughout the country. One particular way in which these experiences manifest themselves into policies is through the language of instruction in schools. While an important goal of the Emirati government is to 'Emiratize', or to get more locals involved in decisions at all levels of education (Davidson, 2009), other stated goals, such as enhancing the civic engagement of Emiratis and preserving national identity, seem to be in conflict with English-medium policies for higher education.

Similar to other GCC nations, the UAE has been aggressive in creating a bilingual environment both in their educational sector and the general public space. While Arabic is the only official language (The Federal National Council, 2010: 7), the legacy of the former British protectorate and the use of English around the world explains the high status awarded to the language in curricular matters. From the perspective of expatriates living in the UAE, it is remarkably easy to function in English with minimal knowledge of local Arabic. With the exception of the call to prayer five times per day, which is performed in Classical Arabic, the linguistic backdrop of the country features both English and Arabic at almost all times. Most government websites and even text messages sent from the government are in Arabic, but they are often accompanied by English translations, and public signage is often bilingual. In addition, price tags in shopping malls are in Arabic and English, as are menus in restaurants in most cities. Furthermore, while students acknowledge the primary use of Arabic and English, their linguistic realities include a host of other languages (van den Hoven & Carroll, forthcoming). The use of Arabic and English has been evident within the last decade as the country has worked aggressively to position itself as the go-to country in the Middle East for foreign business and tourists (Government of Abu Dhabi, 2008).

As has been documented through the various chapters in this volume, there are a plethora of contexts where translanguaging practices happen organically. However, all of these contexts are similar in that the language policies allow for multiple languages in content-area classrooms, whether officially or unofficially. In this chapter, we will argue that while Arabic and English bilingualism is increasingly the stated goal of the educational systems within the UAE (Fox, 2008), this bilingualism is couched within a monolingual ideology widely adopted in Western countries, namely the UK, the US and, more recently Australia, that has profoundly influenced policymakers in the UAE. Furthermore, the adoption of a rentier economy, where a country essentially 'rents' out the rights of their natural resources to outside entities (Anderson, 1987; Smith, 2004), has resulted in the need for an expatriate workforce that, within the UAE, largely use English as a lingua franca.

Research Questions

The original purpose of this chapter was to document translanguaging practices in content-area classrooms within the country. However, it was clear quickly after we started inquiring into the topic that there were very real barriers preventing access to classrooms where translanguaging practices could be observed as well as potential risks to researchers and research participants. After discussing different research methodologies with members of two different institutional review boards for ethics, we decided not to attempt to document such language practices out of fear that said documentation could have a negative impact on participants' job security. Through continued discussions with faculty from various institutions and content areas, it was obvious that the use of English as the medium of instruction (EMI) generated strong reactions from bilingual Arabic–English professors as well as non-Arabic-speaking professors. Given that conducting a semester-long ethnography of a classroom was deemed unethical by one of the institutional review boards for human subjects, our focus shifted to documenting and better understanding language policies within the UAE as reported by experienced professors and administrators within the country. The participants ranged from high-ranking administrators in top-level universities to professors and other mid-ranking administrators who were interested in the topic of language policy. Thus, the main objective of this chapter is to better understand how faculty members within the UAE community view translanguaging practices.

Methodology

With the help of our bilingual colleagues, six participants were recruited through a snowball sampling strategy (Biernacki & Waldorf, 1981). The snowball sampling was used because of the often sensitive nature of using Arabic in classes that are understood to be English medium. Each participant engaged in a face-to-face interview, lasting approximately one hour, with the English-speaking male researcher. To protect the anonymity of the participants, no names or identifying details are shared in this report. The interviews were conducted in or around the institution where each participant worked, primarily in one of the seven emirates. Five of the six interviews were digitally recorded and later transcribed; one of the participants did not allow digital recording of the interview, but notes were taken throughout the interview and later transcribed and analyzed, albeit without a verbatim script. After transcription, TAMS Analyzer was used to identify reoccurring themes throughout the various interviews and enable triangulation of the findings with relevant research on EMI in the UAE and the gulf in general.

Participants

All participants in this study were employees of institutions of higher education throughout the UAE. One participant was an adjunct faculty and had worked at various institutions within the country while two others were full-time teaching faculty, and all three had worked at different postsecondary institutions in the country. The other three participants held primarily administrative positions. Two of these participants held the highest administrative positions within their respective institutions and the third worked in the student services arm of his institution. Five participants were male and one female, and all had doctoral degrees from Western universities. Similar to the diversity on many college campuses in the UAE, the participants had diverse nationalities: two were British, one was American, one Australian, one French and one Emirati. All but one of the participants spoke both English and Arabic fluently. Among the five Arabic–English bilingual participants, four could be characterized as relatively balanced bilinguals, having grown up using both Arabic and English, while one Emirati male participant reported using English as his second language.

As a condition of participating in the research, the participants had been living and working in the UAE for more than 10 years, though one exception was made for a high-ranking university official (Participant 4) who had spent less time in the UAE. It was important that the participants had a decade of experience so that their firsthand reports would enrich our understanding of the ways that different administrations had interpreted or implemented different language policies. While we had access to many non-Arabic-speaking colleagues who were willing to participate, it was important to interview only bilingual Arabic and English-speaking faculty, with the exception of the high-ranking participant, because they would be able to offer greater insight, based on firsthand experience, into how Arabic is used in content-area courses. Furthermore, as Arabic–English bilinguals, they would have had the opportunity to use translanguaging practices in their own teaching or administration, which was of particular interest to our study.

Findings

Throughout this section, we will discuss the most salient themes that emerged from our interviews. The two themes that were repeated throughout our coding were the ambiguity in language policies and the need for simplified instruction in and use of Arabic. In the following sections, we will focus on our participants' views on these themes and how they relate to the literature and our own lived experience within the country.

Ambiguous language policies

In the UAE, the Ministry of Higher Education & Scientific Research (MOHESR) and its compliance arm, the Commission for Academic Accreditation (CAA), oversee tertiary education in the country. Decisions made within the MOHESR trickle down into policy via CAA's strict requirements regarding languages of instruction, syllabi, assessment and evaluation measures. Thus, the impact and influence of CAA's policies have great influence on the delivery of content within all institutions within the country. This power was described when Participant 3, an administrator from a small college within the UAE, said, 'CAA makes the requirements and we fall under CAA, so we do not need specific language policies in our policy documents because it is understood that our instruction will be in English, because that is what CAA requires'. The policy that requires English to be used as the medium of instruction in tertiary programs in the country, with the exception of Islamic Studies and Law, was one of the recurring themes that emerged from the review of literature and the six interviews. While Participant 3 stated that the English-medium requirement is an understood component of CAA approval, our detailed analysis of the

CAA and MOHESR websites yielded no clear language policy. In fact, little to no mention of the language of instruction, Arabic or English, was made throughout the policy documents published on both websites.

Regarding the shift in the emphasis on courses offered in English, Participant 1, a professor at UAEU for over eight years, discussed how the move to EMI, along with high wages and excellent living stipends, had attracted faculty members from all over the world, and great emphasis was put on English-medium teaching policies. While the initial language policies were the vision of a former vice chancellor, Participant 1 attested to the fact that the pendulum has swung away from strict language policies to a more laissez-faire orientation where professors are expected to teach in English but are rarely monitored for their daily teaching practices.

Similarly, Participant 2, an administrator and professor at UAEU, reported that many bilingual professors commonly use Arabic in their teaching, thus echoing Participant 1's assertion that Arabic is indeed used in the content classroom. Participant 2 reported that the use of Arabic was largely tied to the fact that 'Once students pass the Foundations Program [the remedial-level program that focuses primarily on English] they do not use English again because their professors are largely Arabic speakers and teach in Arabic'. When asked why the professors teach in Arabic when they know the course is supposed to be English medium, he responded that there is a lot of pressure for students to pass and for professors to receive good evaluations. 'One way to make sure that students do well and that they understand is by teaching in Arabic. No one has ever been fired for teaching in Arabic'.

While Participant 1 and Participant 2 agreed that content was indeed being taught in Arabic, they had differing opinions on the inherent risk involved. Participant 1 was a professor but taught primarily remedial-level courses with the occasional first-year content-area course, whereas Participant 2 worked in student services and had taught in both foundational and content-area courses. Participant 2's position in the administration gave him a unique perspective, and his lack of concern for those using Arabic was interesting. Nevertheless, all the participants in the study reported that as a researcher it would not advisable to document where Arabic was being used in what were supposed to be English-medium classrooms because doing so would highlight linguistic realities within the institution that were best left unreported.

The taboo nature of using Arabic in the English-medium classroom emerged frequently when talking with content-area teachers. All professors understand firsthand the difficulties that many Emirati students, particularly those from government schools, have in learning material in their second language (Troudi & Jendli, 2011). Participant 6 discussed in detail the anxiety and potential for contractual repercussions resulting from disobeying the tacit language policies associated with EMI in the UAE:

It's being used as a threat, as a tool, but I mean because perhaps the teacher is doing something else, isn't sufficiently ... I don't know ... submissive or ... and so, yes, you've been speaking Arabic and we're going to have to let you go, but I don't believe I've ever actually seen it happen but I have seen bilingual teachers getting very anxious and getting very upset because they've been accused. Because it's a horrible accusation to make [being accused of speaking Arabic in an English-medium class] and you can just see the look of shame and anxiety on their faces when they're being told that they have been committing this heinous sin, speaking Arabic in an English-language classroom, but has anybody lost their job? Not that I can recall. It might have been used as a pretext, but not 'You've taught Arabic, I'm sorry ... Clear your desk,' has never happened.

While participants agreed that instructors are traditionally not fired for their use of Arabic in EMI classes, bilingual instructors indicated that they themselves grappled with this ever-present dilemma. Participant 5, who is an adjunct professor and teaches students in the equivalent of an associate's degree program, was very open about her use of Arabic in English-medium courses. She reported that she openly confessed to her supervisor that she uses Arabic in the classroom. However, she also recognized that her program does not offer bachelor's degrees and therefore there seemed to be more flexibility to work around the English-only mandate. Furthermore, she acknowledged that her students were nontraditional and often had families and worked during the day and oftentimes did not want to be bothered with learning material solely in English.

As an explanation for why instructors use Arabic for instruction, Participant 2 reported that they do so because 'They want to keep their students happy. Teaching in Arabic or using a lot of Arabic in your English-medium class allows students to understand. If students understand they will give you high marks on your evaluation. This facilitates job security'. Keeping students happy is particularly important in GCC nations because the concept of tenure is nonexistent. The contracts that professors sign are tax-free and often much more lucrative than in their home countries and also include housing benefits, stipends for children's schooling and airfare for returning home to their countries of origin each summer (Davidson, 2009). Thus, as part of the rentier economy, where foreign labor is deemed replaceable, it makes sense that professors prioritize job security by making efforts to maintain high student evaluations. For some instructors of content-area classes, this has entailed using Arabic to teach their content area efficiently so that students will 'learn the material quicker' (Participant 5). However, for others it also means limiting their use of Arabic out of fear that administrators will disapprove of such practices.

Simplifying instruction and using Arabic

Our interview with Participant 3, an Emirati male who has served in a number of top administrative positions in various local institutions, sheds light on his own English-language acquisition processes and how it has shaped his beliefs about how Emirati students will learn English. He said:

> I am from the camp of camping, meaning I believe that if you are going to learn a second language you need to be immersed in it. When I was in the UK, I lived with a family who did not speak Arabic. They only spoke to me in English and I was forced to use the language. The same happened when I was in the United States; no one spoke to me in Arabic. Students need to be exposed to the language; if they are not, they will not learn it.

Through reflecting on his immersion experience in the United Kingdom, Participant 3 highlights the necessity for students to be sufficiently exposed to the target language. He also expresses how he was forced to speak English because accommodations in Arabic were not made for him. This 'tough love' attitude has been a pervasive theme among many of the Emirati administrators we have met over the course of our combined seven years working in the country. Furthermore, increased English education is the overriding theme of private school education throughout the country and in the newly adopted New School Model for students in the Abu Dhabi emirate, which features English-medium instruction throughout primary and secondary schooling (Abu Dhabi Education Council, 2014). The remaining six emirates all use Arabic as the language of instruction and follow the Ministry of Education curriculum in publicly funded schools.

Unfortunately, the publicly funded primary and secondary schools within the country have historically underperformed when compared to their private school counterparts. For the educated elite, enrollment in the best English-medium private schools in the country and frequent use of tutors enhance academic readiness for studies abroad. Unfortunately, such access to English is by and large not the case for the average student graduating from publicly funded schools in the UAE today (Godwin, 2006). Although access to private schools allows many Emirati students to learn in an English-medium environment, the majority of currently enrolled higher-education students completed their primary and secondary schooling (Cycle 1, Cycle 2 and Cycle 3) largely in Arabic, with English offered as a foreign language several times per week. Despite relatively limited experiences with English, students continue to enroll in programs of higher education where the curriculum requires English-medium instruction (Belhiah & Elhami, 2015; Fox, 2008).

All of the participants interviewed, with the exception of Participant 3, conceded that students do benefit from first language (L1) support. Participant 1 discussed this targeted use of Arabic and how important he felt it was for college-level learners:

When I first arrived, I thought because I'm bilingual, I would have an edge on everyone else, but at the beginning that wasn't the case. But as time went on, I saw myself using Arabic in class in targeted ways, because it was easier for me and was easier for students. Especially for students at the lower levels who were using Arabic or wanting Arabic because it was part of their scaffold, whereas the higher-level students didn't need it.

Participant 1's targeted use of Arabic in his English courses worked to make his teaching more comprehensible and was more indicative of authentic language environments in which bilinguals use their rich linguistic repertoires to communicate. Similar to Participant 1's targeted use of Arabic, Participant 5, who teaches mathematics at an Emirati institution for higher education, reported using Arabic with great frequency. In describing a mathematics lesson, she argued that her targeted use of Arabic made learning more efficient and effective:

When I put the title as a fraction on the board and I put the translation of the Arabic on top of it, then they have a primary idea about what the topic is going to be about. When I come and go deeper into the topic and I start saying, the top number is the numerator and the bottom number is the denominator, they still look at me with puzzled faces. When I put the translation on [the board], I'd write it in Arabic and write the numerator, then they start. Next lesson, they are aware; I don't need to rewrite this, they are aware of what the topic is going to be about.

The generally low level of English proficiency among students requires teaching personnel to do what they can to make their teaching comprehensible and reduce the cognitive load. The students' limited English-language proficiency also has ramifications for course assessments. Participant 1 discussed this issue when he said, 'I try to minimize the writing exam questions and make them all multiple choice or matching because I know they all have problems with grammar'. As a professor of English, Participant 1 makes the conscious decision to put his students in an environment where they will succeed, knowing that in his English course a focus on form is inherently part of the grading. However, when discussing assessments and classroom teaching at his institution, Participant 4 described how the majority of the content area professors 'use Arabic when needed; there is a degree of dualities. The first year of BA, professors concentrate on knowledge; if we focused on language they would fail. The second and third years are transition years and we go hard on them'. Here, Participant 4 discussed the importance of focusing on function or communication over form. Such focus on function buys time for students to build a foundation in the content area that will serve them well in Years 2 and 3, when they transition into a curriculum that is more focused on form. The insistence of Participant 4's institution on focusing on form in Year 1 is obviously linked to maintaining student enrollment, but it is also a basic principle of bilingual education that works to shelter students' instruction by building background that will be necessary in their future courses.

Why not accept translanguaging?

Given the *de facto* use of English-medium courses throughout tertiary education within the UAE, coupled with the presence of many bilingual professors, the context is ripe for translanguaging practices in content classrooms. Furthermore, the low English-proficiency requirements for students to study in content areas associated with science, technology, engineering and mathematics (STEM) fields further open the door for a scenario in which bilingual instructors can use their understanding of students' L1 to make their teaching comprehensible, regardless of the broader national mandates for EMI. However, just because translanguaging practices undoubtedly occur does not mean that it is easy or even ethical to document them. Because the language policy of the MOHESR states that instruction will be in English, documenting such translanguaging practices would be evidence of a professor breaking the rules. Whether or not the institutions' administration would look the other way or reprimand the professor depends largely on the particular context. Thus, documenting such practices inherently involves undue risks for participants and the researcher.

The emergence of the UAE as an international hub for business and tourism increased the importance of English in the nation (Davidson, 2005; Lane, 2011). Therefore, while there are persistent rumblings about increasing the importance of Arabic in formal education (Pennington, 2014; Salem, 2014b), few advocate a complete return to Arabic as the medium of instruction despite the legacy of Arabic as a great language of learning. Nevertheless, recent literature within the field of bilingual education points to the usefulness of Arabic in some content areas, including the return of Qatar to Arabic-medium practices in higher education (Belhiah & Elhami, 2015). The importance of English within the region, as described in Findlow (2006), was reiterated by Participant 3, who argued, 'English is the language of science and technology, and if the UAE wants to improve and grow and have a future as a global country we need to improve our English'. Such feelings about English are common in the UAE, where the lingua franca of higher education between the majority of foreign-born professors and local Emiratis is English and where the power and ideologies inculcated in the language are often unquestioned (Karmani & Pennycook, 2005; Troudi & Jendli, 2011).

From a language policy standpoint, while Arabic holds official status within the UAE and other GCC nations, the *de facto* policies are more emblematic of an environment where acquiring English or transitioning to English within the domain of education is the primary goal (Coleman, 2006; Fishman, 1991). While Arabic obviously holds high prestige and is a marker of local identity, it plays a minimal role in the curriculum of the five institutions where the participants worked. Furthermore, the use of Modern Standard Arabic had almost no official role in the studying of math, science, business or medicine (Troudi & Jendli, 2011). According to Al-Issa and Dahan (2011), such actions present a legitimate threat to local Arabic within this educational context, and the commitment to the exclusive use of English for the teaching of content areas should be re-examined.

Despite recent research advocating for the increased use of Arabic in English-medium courses (Belhiah & Elhami, 2015), the stigmatized nature of translanguaging practices has conditioned professors to feel that they are breaking the rules when using Arabic in the classroom. Furthermore, with little job security and no existence of a tenure system, few professors admit to using Arabic in what are supposed to be English-medium classrooms.

Conclusions

Like many nations around the world, the UAE has been influenced by the internationalization of higher education in featuring EMI (Doiz *et al.*, 2013; Troudi & Jendli, 2011). The formative relationship between the UAE and the United Kingdom in the years before the formation of the UAE federation is a significant influence on English-medium policies in higher education (Karmani, 2005), but so are the experiences of the educated elite, who almost exclusively studied in British or American systems where monolingual ideologies and approaches to language maintenance are commonplace. Furthermore, the region's reliance on a rentier economy requires the abundant use of foreign labor because locals either do not yet have the required skills to run the country on their own or the desire to take low-skilled, low-paying jobs. Such reliance on foreign labor has not only positioned English as the lingua franca within the multilingual nation (Boyle, 2011; Randall & Samimi, 2010) but has also highlighted the positive regard attributed to English-medium higher education. These are all important factors that have influenced the language ideologies that currently place high status and prestige on English, especially as a medium of instruction at the tertiary level.

Unfortunately, while the bilingual context of the UAE is ripe for translanguaging practices, their use is often stigmatized and not openly discussed. While many bilingual Arabic and English instructors report that they indeed use students' L1 in the content classroom along with Arabic, the overt and public use of Arabic is taboo. Such *de facto* policies, while not officially documented on university websites, appear to dissuade bilingual teaching personnel from teaching in Arabic. Nevertheless, these bilingual instructors understand that incorporating students' L1 can and does facilitate understanding of content and thus they undoubtedly use Arabic. Such practices in this context are unethical to document because so doing could jeopardize the positions of both the teaching personnel and the researchers. While this volume has gone to great lengths to document translanguaging practices in higher education around the world, it is important to convey that there are still contexts where such practices are held with such low prestige that they cannot be ethically documented in a systematic manner, unlike in many other contexts with more inclusive language ideologies.

References

Abu Dhabi Education Council (2014) *Policy Manual 2014*. See www.adec.ac.ae/en/MediaCenter/Publications/p-12%20Policy%20manual%202014-15%20-%20ENG/HTML/files/assets/basic-html/page115.html (accessed 18 June 2015).

Al-Issa, A. and Dahan, L.S. (2011) Global English and endangered Arabic in the United Arab Emirates. In A. Al-Issa and L.S. Dahan (eds) *Global English and Arabic: Issues of Language, Culture and Identity* (pp. 1–22). Bruxelles: Peter Lang AG.

Altbach, P.G., Reisberg, L. and Rumbley, L.E. (2009) *Trends in Global Higher Education: Tracking an Academic Revolution*. Paris: UNESCO.

Al-Zubaidi, O. (2010) Arab postgraduate students in Malaysia: Identifying and overcoming the cultural and language barriers. *Arab World English Journal* 1 (1), 107–129.

Anderson, L. (1987) The state in the Middle East and North Africa. *Comparative Politics* 20 (1), 1–18.

Belhiah, H. and Elhami, M. (2015) English as a medium of instruction in the Gulf: When students and teachers speak. *Language Policy* 14 (1), 3–23.

Biernacki, P. and Waldorf, D. (1981) Snowball sampling: Problems and techniques of chain referral sampling. *Sociological Methods & Research* 10 (2), 141–163.

Boyle, R. (2011) Patterns of change in English as a lingua franca in the UAE. *International Journal of Applied Linguistics* 21 (2), 143–161.

Clarke, M. (2007) Language policy and language teacher education in the United Arab Emirates. *TESOL Quarterly* 41 (3), 583–591.

Coleman, J.A. (2006) English-medium teaching in European higher education. *Language Teaching* 39 (1), 1–14.

Creese, A. and Blackledge, A. (2010) Translanguaging in the bilingual classroom: A pedagogy for learning and teaching? *The Modern Language Journal* 94 (1), 103–115.

Davidson, C. (2005) *The United Arab Emirates: A Study in Survival*. Boulder, CO: Lynne Rienner Publishers.

Davidson, C. (2009) *Abu Dhabi: Oil and Beyond*. London: C. Hurst.

Doiz, A., Lasagabaster, D. and Sierra, J.M. (2013) Future challenges for English-medium instruction at the tertiary level. In A. Doiz, D. Lasagabaster and J.M. Sierra (eds)

English-Medium Instruction at Universities: Global Challenges (pp. 213–221). Bristol: Multilingual Matters.

Dresch, P. and Piscatori, J.P. (2005) *Monarchies and Nations: Globalization and Identity in the Arab States of the Gulf*. London: I.B. Tauris.

Findlow, S. (2000) *The United Arab Emirates: Nationalism and Arab-Islamic Identity*. Abu Dhabi: Emirates Center for Strategic Studies and Research.

Findlow, S. (2005) International networking in the United Arab Emirates higher education system: Global–local tensions. *Compare* 35 (3), 285–302.

Findlow, S. (2006) Higher education and linguistic dualism in the Arab Gulf. *British Journal of Sociology of Education* 27 (1), 19–36.

Fishman, J.A. (1991) *Reversing Language Shift: Theoretical and Empirical Foundations of Assistance to Threatened Languages*. Clevedon: Multilingual Matters.

Fox, J. (2008) The United Arab Emirates and policy priorities for higher education. In C. Davidson and P. Mackenzie-Smith (eds), *Higher Education in the Gulf States: Shaping Economies, Politics and Culture* (pp. 110–125). London: Saqi.

Godwin, S.M. (2006) Globalization, education and Emiratization: A case study of the United Arab Emirates. *The Electronic Journal of Information Systems in Developing Countries* 27, 1–14.

Government of Abu Dhabi (2008) *Abu Dhabi Economic Vision 2030*. See www.ecouncil.ae/PublicationsEn/economic-vision-2030-full-versionEn.pdf (accessed 29 June 2015).

Ibnouf, A., Dou, L. and Knight, J. (2014) The evolution of Qatar as an education hub: Moving to a knowledge-based economy. In J. Knight (ed.) *International Education Hubs: Student, Talent, Knowledge-Innovation Models* (pp. 43–61). Dordrecht: Springer.

Karmani, S. (2005) Petro-linguistics: The emerging nexus between oil, English, and Islam. *Journal of Language, Identity, and Education* 4 (2), 87–102.

Karmani, S. and Pennycook, A. (2005) Islam, English, and 9/11. *Journal of Language, Identity, and Education* 4 (2), 157–172.

Karram, G. (2014) A futile search for values and pedagogy? A discursive analysis of the marketing messages of branch-campuses in higher education hubs. *Compare: A Journal of Comparative and International Education* 44 (2), 274–296.

Kirk, D. (2010) *The Development of Higher Education in the UAE*. Abu Dhabi: Emirates Center for Strategic Studies and Research.

Kirk, D. (2015) Innovate or replicate? Education reform initiatives in the Gulf Cooperation Council states. *The Muslim World* 105 (1), 78–92.

Knight, J. (2011) Education hubs: A fad, a brand, an innovation? *Journal of Studies in International Education* 15 (3), 221–240.

Lane, J.E. (2011) Importing private higher education: International branch campuses. *Journal of Comparative Policy Analysis: Research and Practice* 13 (4), 367–381.

Ministry of Higher Education & Scientific Research (2014) *The UAE Educational Fact Book 2013/2014*. See www.mohesr.gov.ae/EN/SERVICESINDEX/Documents/UAE-factbook18Feb-English%20-%20Approved%20copy.pdf (accessed 18 June 2015).

Pennington, R. (2014, December 8) English language 'seducing' UAE pupils. *The National*. See www.thenational.ae/uae/english-language-seducing-uae-pupils (accessed 18 June 2015).

Phillipson, R. (2015) English as threat or opportunity in European higher education. In S. Dimova, A.K. Hultgren and C. Jensen (eds) *English-Medium Instruction in Higher Education in Europe* (pp. 19–42). Berlin: Mouton de Gruyter.

Randall, M. and Samimi, M. (2010) The status of English in Dubai. *English Today* 26 (1), 43–50.

Ricento, T.K. and Hornberger, N.H. (1996) Unpeeling the onion: Language planning and policy and the ELT professional. *TESOL Quarterly* 30 (3), 401–427.

Salem, O. (2014a, November 24) Arabic must be the main language in UAE education, FNC hears. *The National*. See www.thenational.ae/uae/government/

arabic-must-be-the-main-language-in-uae-education-fnc-hears (accessed 18 June 2015).

Salem, O. (2014b, November 25) Question of cancelled scholarships. *The National.* See www.thenational.ae/uae/education/question-of-cancelled-scholarships (accessed 18 June 2015).

Smith, B. (2004) Oil wealth and regime survival in the developing world, 1960–1999. *American Journal of Political Science* 48 (2), 232–246.

Troudi, S. and Jendli, A. (2011) Emirati students' experiences of English as a medium of instruction. In A. Al-Issa and L.S. Dahan (ed.) *Global English and Arabic: Issues of Language, Culture, and Identity* (pp. 23–48). Bruxelles: Peter Lang AG.

The Federal National Council (2010) United Arab Emirates Constitution: By-Law of the Federal National Council. See www.almajles.gov.ae:85/uploads/files/2011/06/20/15206.pdf (accessed 18 June 2015).

United Arab Emirates University (2015) *About UAEU.* See www.uaeu.ac.ae/en/about/ (accessed 29 June 2015).

van der Walt, C. (2013) *Multilingual Higher Education: Beyond English Medium Orientations.* Bristol: Multilingual Matters.

van den Hoven, M. and Carroll, K.S. (2017) Emirati pre-service teachers' perspectives of Abu Dhabi's rich linguistic context. In L. Buckingham (ed.) *Language, Identity and Education on the Arabian Peninsula* (pp. 39–58). Bristol: Multilingual Matters.

Weber, A.S. (2011) Politics of English in the Arabian Gulf. Presented at the 1st International Conference on Foreign Language Teaching and Applied Linguistics (FLTAL'11), Sarajevo (pp. 60–66). See http://eprints.ibu.edu.ba/13/ (accessed 18 June 2015).

9 Teachers' Beliefs about Translanguaging Practices

Aintzane Doiz and David Lasagabaster

Introduction

One of the main consequences of internationalization processes at the university level is the implementation of English-medium instruction, or EMI (Doiz *et al.*, 2013; Smit & Dafouz, 2012). The European University Association (2013) surveyed more than 170 European higher education institutions about their internationalization process, and two out of three universities have reported increasing their offerings of EMI courses. This trend is also observable on other continents such as Asia (Kirkpatrick, 2011) and Africa (van der Walt, 2013), and it is bound to take on a more prominent role in higher education institutions' agendas the world over as they attempt to foster international connections. The implementation of EMI courses has taken place in such a short span of time that research is clearly lagging behind; the little we know about the use of students' and teachers' linguistic repertoires in EMI classes being a very good case in point. In this chapter, we will focus on this under-researched area.

Since the grammar-translation method (in which students apply the grammatical rules they have learned to the translation between the mother tongue and the target language) fell into disuse, and with the current popularity of communicative language teaching – also known as the communicative approach – the use of the first language (L1) in the foreign language classroom has become a controversial issue. In general, it is believed that there is no space for the students' L1 because of the need to use the second language (L2) as much as possible to improve students' language proficiency. This is mainly for two reasons. First, the spread of a monolingual ideology that stands for the idea that only the target language should be used in the foreign language classroom. And second, the publishing houses' preference to publish all their materials in the target language.

The influence of the Canadian immersion programs (Cummins, 2014; Turnbull & Dailey-O'Cain, 2009) has also boosted the exclusive use of the L2 in other teaching contexts, such as EMI and content and language integrated learning (CLIL), the main difference between the two being that the former focuses on content learning only (Smit & Dafouz, 2012), while the latter is a dual-focused approach that has explicit and integrated content and language aims (Coyle *et al.*, 2010). In both approaches, the presence of the L1 is believed to be detrimental because it entails less exposure to the target language. As a result, many university stakeholders, especially those who make decisions, harbor a reluctant attitude toward the use of the L1 because they regard it as indicative of some kind of deficient bilingualism. This negative idea of code-switching is underpinned by the belief that mixing two languages is an easier or lazier way of speaking, and therefore, code-switching:

> Is seen as an easy way out when people cannot be bothered to search for the words they need in a single language. As laziness is not generally considered a virtue, this interpretation obviously depends on believing that it is in some way 'wrong' to mix languages. (Gardner-Chloros, 2009: 14–15)

In addition, even regular code-switchers disapprove of the practice and experience a sense of guilt when specifically asked about its use (Barnard & McLellan, 2014; Gardner-Chloros, 2009). Despite bad press, Macaro (2014: 10) underscores that classroom code-switching 'has figured predominantly in numerous SLA [second language acquisition] and bilingualism journals and it is for this reason that so many doctoral dissertations continue to appear in the topic'. In fact, Gardner-Chloros (2009) notes that over the last four decades there has been an explosion of interest in the subject, which is why it is very difficult to do justice to the profusion of work that has been done on the topic. With this in mind, and despite the growing presence of English as the medium of instruction for content subjects, it is surprising that little has been written about the use that the teaching staff makes of their students' linguistic repertoire at the university level.

Although the administration and education authorities tend to advise an English-only approach, different studies highlight that the use of the L1 is commonplace. In fact, in a recent volume edited by Barnard and McLellan (2014), the contributors demonstrated that in diverse Asian contexts the teaching staff recurrently falls back on the students' L1. Table 9.1 shows the percentages of L1 and L2 use in different countries in both EMI and English as a foreign language (EFL) classes.

The data obtained from these four different university contexts reveal that code-switching is commonplace in all classes, although it may show considerable interteacher (Thailand) or even intrateacher (Taiwan and Vietnam) variation. In any case, Table 9.1 demonstrates that the students' L1 is present in class despite the 'English only' official language policy in all of these Asian countries in both the EFL and EMI classrooms (Wang & Kirkpatrick, 2013). One of the main conclusions to be drawn from the essays in

Table 9.1 Use of the L1 in different Asian contexts at the university level

Country	Teaching context	Use of the L1	Use of the L2
Taiwan	EMI	Week 1: 6.2%	Week 1: 93.8%
		Week 2: 14.5%	Week 2: 85.5%
		Week 3: 30.8%	Week 3: 69.2%
China (Beijing)	EFL	Teacher 1: 9.5%	Teacher 1: 90.5%
		Teacher 2: 11.1%	Teacher 2: 88.9%
Thailand	EFL	Teacher 1: 80.3%	Teacher 1: 19.7%
		Teacher 2: 32.6%	Teacher 2: 67.3 %
Vietnam	EFL	Lesson 1: 23%	Lesson 1: 77%
		Lesson 2: 30.3%	Lesson 2: 69.7%
		Lesson 3: 14.6%	Lesson 3: 85.4%
		Lesson 4: 31.7%	Lesson 4: 68.3%

Source: A summary from different contributors in the volume edited by Barnard and McLellan (2014).

Barnard and McLellan is that code-switching is used to very different degrees and for very different reasons by teachers from diverse Asian countries, a conclusion that could also be applied to other contexts. In fact, Macaro (2009: 35–36), after surveying and interviewing teachers regarding the use of the L1, concluded that teachers usually hold three quite distinct theories:

(1) The 'virtual position': This position is represented by teachers who believe that they have to use only the target language in their classes to mirror the environment of the L1 learner and the target language country.
(2) The 'maximal position': This encompasses teachers who believe that exclusive use of the L2 is not attainable because in L2 classes the perfect conditions do not exist, and therefore, these teachers are flexible about using some L1, albeit with a sense of guilt.
(3) The 'optimal position': Some teachers believe that at certain moments the judicious use of the stakeholders' different languages can enhance learning more than if they stick to the target language. The use of the students' whole linguistic repertoire paves the way for translanguaging, and teachers who support the optimal position will be willing to embrace translanguaging.

Macaro (2014), however, reports that teachers who adopt the optimal position and who deem a multilingual pedagogy to be beneficial are in the minority. The spread of the English-only language policy, the subsequent pressure on both English teachers and teachers who teach content subjects through the medium of English and multilingual language teachers' sense of guilt about using their own and their students' linguistic resources led Swain et al. (2011) to produce a handbook with the following telling title:

How to Have a Guilt-Free Life Using Cantonese in the English Class. The main goal of this guide was to rid teachers of English of their sense of guilt when using the students' L1, since if the L1 is used judiciously, it can help to scaffold English-language learning. Although research shows that 'What emerges is an increasing possibility that banning the first language from the communicative second language classroom may in fact be reducing the cognitive and metacognitive opportunities available to learners' (Macaro, 2009: 49), the idea that instruction should be carried out exclusively in the target language without recourse to students' L1 is still very much entrenched. It is in this context where translanguaging, that is to say, 'the multiple discursive practices in which bilinguals engage in order to make sense of their bilingual worlds' (García, 2009: 45), comes to the fore. Translanguaging is becoming a debatable issue, especially in contexts where the foreign language teaching tradition fosters the exclusion of the L1 in the English-medium class. Translanguaging runs counter to the rigid separation of languages in teaching contexts that habitually include 'the association of one teacher with one language, the use of a specific classroom for a specific language, and syllabi and curricula for the different languages' (Menken, 2013: 448). The monoglossic view of bilingualism held by those against translanguaging puts forward the idea that only monolingual pedagogical practices will serve bilingual learners, a perspective adamantly contested by advocates of translanguaging and by the long-established tradition of challenging monolingual bias (Cook, 2012).

Although translanguaging and code-switching are closely related, the former goes beyond the latter because it does not simply represent the alternation of two languages or the use of two languages as two separate monolingual systems by the bilingual teacher and student. Translanguaging (or Macaro's 'optimal position') is a more systematic and strategic process that allows the speaker to make meaning and to foster the affective side of language use in such a way that bilinguals use the whole linguistic and semiotic repertoire at their disposal to shape their experiences and create meaning. Consequently, translanguaging becomes a pedagogical practice accepted by teachers as legitimate in bilingual classrooms in which both languages are used for all purposes and in all domains (García, 2009; García & Li, 2014). Research has shown that multilingual discursive practices make students more academically successful by 'promoting a deeper and fuller understanding of the subject matter' (Lewis *et al.*, 2012) and more at home when they have the opportunity to resort to the different languages that make up their linguistic repertoire (García, 2009; García & Li, 2014). In addition, research has demonstrated that students' linguistic repertoires offer a wealth of resources from which multilingual speakers can draw (Cummins, 2014; Turnbull & Dailey-O'Cain, 2009). Translanguaging thus becomes the natural result of languages coming into contact both inside and outside the classroom setting. For example, translanguaging or hybrid language practices, as well as the consideration of students' sociohistorical lives, are found among the promoters of a collective Third Space in bilingual classrooms in the US, 'in which traditional conceptions of academic literacy and instruction for students from non-dominant communities are contested and replaced with forms of literacy that privilege and are contingent upon students' sociohistorical lives, both proximally and distally' (Gutiérrez, 2008: 148).

With this in mind, in this chapter we intend to analyze the beliefs of teachers involved in EMI courses at the tertiary level, since most of the research on translanguaging has been carried out in secondary education and in EFL contexts, whereas research studies specifically focused on EMI university courses are rather scant. 'Beliefs', which can be defined as 'propositions individuals consider to be true and which are often tacit, have a strong evaluative and affective component, provide a basis for action, and are resistant to change' (Borg, 2011: 370–371), thus becomes a key word in our study.

Although teachers' beliefs and their teaching practices do not always match and their relationship is understood to be a complex one (Basturkmen, 2012), research on teachers reveals that the former often have a strong effect on the latter (Zhang & Liu, 2014). As Kubanyiova (2014) points out, teachers' practices are closely related to how they believe teaching should be carried out and to the teaching methods they have internalized throughout their careers. Since research on teachers' beliefs has been conducted mainly among native speakers (Borg, 2009) in preservice contexts (Borg, 2011), the analysis of in-service non-native English-speaking teachers' beliefs on translanguaging is of the utmost importance because their beliefs may have a strong impact on their use of or lack of translanguaging teaching practices and, eventually, on their students' learning process.

Last but not least, it needs to be noted that most of the research carried out on teachers' language-related beliefs has been undertaken among language specialists. Since the vast majority of EMI teachers at the university level are specialists in different areas (geography, economics, history, biology, etc.) but not in language teaching and learning (they are neither language teachers nor applied linguists), the analysis of their beliefs on the applicability and usefulness of translanguaging is worthy of researchers' attention, since the need to use a foreign language as the means of instruction determines the teachers' classroom practices.

The Study

Research questions

Since the review of the literature above leads us to conclude that the examination of EMI teachers' beliefs on translanguaging needs to be addressed, in this chapter we put forward the following two research questions:

(1) What are the *beliefs* of teachers regarding the use of the L1 in EMI?
(2) What are teachers' self-reported *practices* regarding the use of the L1 in EMI?

Research context

This study was carried out in the Basque Autonomous Community (BAC) in the north of Spain. This is an officially bilingual community, Basque and Spanish, where since the early 1980s there has been a revitalization process to bolster the learning of the minority language, Basque. According to the latest sociolinguistic map (Basque Government, 2013), 56% of the population speaks Basque to some extent, whereas 30 years ago this percentage was much lower at only 30%.

The University of the Basque Country (UBC) is the only public and by far the largest university in the BAC (it has over 5,300 teaching staff, approximately 45,000 students and 1,700 administration personnel). Since its inception in 1980, it has been officially bilingual in Basque and Spanish, and the implementation across the board of classes in Basque alongside classes in Spanish has been a clear goal within the bilingual policy adopted by the institution. However, the UBC's authorities were not impervious to the spread of EMI in Europe and in response they created the multilingualism program (MP) in 2005. In the MP, students can choose to join optional or compulsory subjects delivered in a foreign language. According to Doiz *et al.* (2011: 349), the official documents state that the goals of the program are (i) to continue the experimental trilingual program introduced by the Basque government in primary and secondary schools at the tertiary level; (ii) to improve local students' proficiency in a foreign language and provide them with specialized language and access to references in the foreign language; (iii) to improve students' work and career prospects; (iv) to facilitate the pursuit of postgraduate degrees abroad; and (v) to attract international students and teachers. No language proficiency level in a foreign language (mainly English) is required for students to enroll in the courses, but teachers who want to participate in the program need to show proof of their language competence in a foreign language at the C1 level (Common European Framework of Reference for Languages).

Since its inception, the MP has grown at an exponential rate, and although its scope was at first rather limited in origin, there are currently more than 140 subjects (i.e. around 7% of all courses on offer) taught through the medium of English, French being the only other foreign language with just eight subjects. In the academic year 2013–2014, 2,829 students enrolled in the program and 162 teachers participated in it.

It is important to note that in our review of the official documents dealing with the MP, we did not encounter any reference to the use of students' and teachers' L1s in the English-medium classes. Hence, it may be concluded that there is no official language policy concerning translanguaging or code-switching practices at the UBC. In addition, to our knowledge no study has examined the use of Spanish in Basque classes at the university level, and consequently, no comparison between translanguaging in the two official languages and in EMI contexts can be made.

The participants

In this chapter, we will examine the opinions put forward by teachers from different fields of study who participated in three discussion groups. The use of discussion groups helps to capture and analyze ideological discourses and elicit different viewpoints in the form of spontaneous expressions and contradictions (Iglesias-Álvarez & Ramallo, 2002). It also produces data and provides insights that are less likely to emerge in one-on-one discussions but which are prone to be found in a group setting. Furthermore, the interaction and discussion that take place in discussion groups encourages the sharing of memories, ideas and experiences and allow the participants to learn about other participants' experiences and to talk about their own. In the present case, we intended to gather firsthand information about our participants' beliefs and practices regarding the role of the L1 in the EMI courses running at the UBC since the 2005–2006 academic year. Table 9.2 provides a description of the participants.

After checking the list of teachers participating in the MP, we emailed a pool of teachers randomly chosen from the three faculties with the largest offerings in the MP: Faculty of Engineering, Faculty of Social and Communication Sciences and Faculty of Economics and Business Studies. There were five female and eight male teachers, and except for two bilingual teachers in Spanish and English, all participants were multilingual. They had been teaching at the UBC for an average of 17.8 years, so they were highly experienced. Their EMI teaching experience was more limited, with a mean of 4.6 years. Eight of the participants had taken EMI-related courses (focused on methodology, pronunciation, etc.) provided by the UBC.

All the participants delivered their courses in English and fulfilled the requirement of showing English proficiency at the C1 level as required by the MP. In addition, a few had some knowledge of other languages such as German, Portuguese or French. The majority of the teachers had taught in the MP for three years when the discussion group took place, with the exception of five who had participated in the program for five or more years. The majority of the participants (9 out of 13) had received some training in teaching in English in courses organized by the university for the teachers in the MP, such as 'teaching your subject in English', 'classroom pedagogy' and 'English pronunciation'.

Since the teachers' participation in the MP is voluntary, the reasons that motivated our teachers to take part in the program differed. Some

Table 9.2 Description of the participants

	Faculty	Gender	Languages*	Teaching experience (years)	EMI experience (years)	In-house training courses
Teacher 1	Economics	Female	Sp. and En.	14	8	No
Teacher 2	Economics	Female	Sp., Ba. and En.	21	5	Yes
Teacher 3	Economics	Male	Sp., Ba. and En.	24	3	Yes
Teacher 4	Economics	Male	Sp., some Ba. and En.	20	6	No
Teacher 5	Economics	Male	Sp., Ba., En. and Po.	22	3	Yes
Teacher 6	Engineering	Female	Sp. some Ba., Fr. and En.	27	4	Yes
Teacher 7	Engineering	Male	Sp. and En.	16	3	No
Teacher 8	Engineering	Male	Sp., Ba. and En.	16	12	Yes
Teacher 9	Communication	Male	Sp., Ba., En., Ge., some Fr. and Po.	15	3	Yes
Teacher 10	Communication	Male	Sp., Ba. and En.	7	3	Yes
Teacher 11	Communication	Female	Sp., Ba., En. and Fr.	8	3	Yes
Teacher 12	Communication	Female	Sp., Ba. and En.	16	3	No
Teacher 13	Communication	Male	Sp., Ba. and En.	25	4	Yes

*Sp.=Spanish; Ba.=Basque; En.=English; Fr.=French; Ge.=German; Po.=Portuguese.

mentioned the incentive of having a reduction in their teaching load during the first two years of their participation in the program, as granted by university policy. Others noted the advantage of having a smaller pool of students and increasing the possibility of working with researchers from other countries. The majority, however, provided the personal reasons of practicing their English, losing the fear of speaking English in public and a desire to face a challenging situation. In fact, their willingness and commitment to improve their English went beyond the time dedicated to the actual teaching, since many dedicated part of their free time outside academia to listening to English-language podcasts, movies and reading, among other activities.

Questions prepared beforehand were used as prompts to engage the group in the discussion, which was led by an assigned researcher from a group of three, which included the two authors of this chapter. Our participation was kept to a minimum because our role was mainly to bring up issues for discussion. The group discussions were recorded, transcribed and analyzed individually by the two authors of this chapter. The validity of the description and interpretation of the data was achieved by agreement between the two authors of this chapter. First, the researchers analyzed the data individually and focused on the participants' beliefs and practices, the latter being delved into regarding L1 use in the university setting and with materials and assessments. Next, they shared their interpretations and worked on them until they reached an agreement, which is summarized in Table 9.3. The consensual interpretation of the data is provided in the following section. The discussion groups took place in Spanish, but the participants' selected contributions have been translated into English here for ease of reference.

Results and Discussion

RQ1: What are the beliefs of teachers regarding the use of the L1 in EMI?

Generally speaking, there seems to be no doubt in the teachers' minds that English should be the main language in the EMI classroom. However, there are some subtle differences among the participants that may be couched within Macaro's framework discussed previously, as we will see.

The majority of the participants (Teachers 1, 3, 5, 6, 8, 9, 10 and 13) subscribe to Macaro's virtual position, according to which all interactions are exclusively in English. This view is attributable to the beliefs held for many decades in foreign-language teaching that the use of the students' L1 is detrimental to learning the target language and that an increase in the exposure to the target language is instrumental in its acquisition (Lasagabaster, 2013: 2). Consequently, the teachers in this group believe

Table 9.3 Summary of the participants' beliefs and practices

Spk	Beliefs			Practices			
	Virtual	Maximal	Optimal	Inside the class	Outside the class	Materials	Exams
1	X		(X)	L2 Voc: L1	L1	L2	L2
2		X		L2 Voc: L1	L2	L2	L2 (words L1)
3	X			L2 Voc: L1	L2	L2	L2
5	X			L2	L1	L2	L2
6	X			L2 Voc: L1	L1	L2	L2 (L1)*
7	No opinion			L2 Voc: L1	L1	L2	Any language
8	X			L2 Voc: L1	L2	L2	L2
9	X			L2 Voc: L1	L1	L2	L2
10	X			L2 Voc: L1	L1	L2	L2
11			X	L2 Voc: L1	L1	L2/L1	L2
12			X	L2 Voc: L1	L1	L2/L1	L2 (L1)*
13	X			L2 Voc: L1	L2	L2	L2

*In line with the institutional policy, the use of the students' L1 is allowed, but this is not the preferred choice.

that their role is to mirror the environment of the students' L1 in English by the creation of an English-only context. Three main ideas stand out in the participants' comments. First, the immersion effect is underscored: For them the ideal teaching context is one where English is the only language used (Teachers 9 and 3). Second, there is an explicit recognition of the artificiality of the use of the foreign language by and among non-native speakers (Teacher 5). Third, the L1 is detrimental to the goals of EMI and should be avoided (Teacher 10):

> If the subject is in English, it is in English, even though it would be easier for me to use my L1 as well sometimes. (Teacher 9)
>
> When the students use their L1 outside class with me, the dynamics of what you are trying to achieve – speaking in English – suffers, the immersion effect is partially lost, or at least the immersion effect that can be achieved here is somewhat lost. (Teacher 3)
>
> We are trying to generate a microcosmos where there is some immersion, even though it may be a bit artificial. (Teacher 5)
>
> The use of the L1 is detrimental to what we are trying to do here. (Teacher 10)

Obviously, they are aware that speaking and functioning in English constitutes an immense challenge for many of the students, but the teachers believe that this difficulty is an inherent part of EMI and learning an L2. That is the reason why the students' effort and their linguistic limitations are counterbalanced by a leniency with regard to their linguistic inaccuracies (e.g. ungrammatical sentences, lack of fluency, mispronunciations). The teachers argue that what matters is that students make the effort to use English and communicate the main ideas they want to convey, despite the mistakes (Teacher 5). Against this backdrop, it is their responsibility to encourage students to participate in English and to make them feel comfortable:

> The important thing is for the students to be understood. It does not matter if they make mistakes. We have our limitations in English, but I will not tolerate disrespect or a student being mocked because of his poor English. We'll try to do our best and we'll see as we go along. (Teacher 5)

Two teachers provided additional reasons in support of the all-in-English view. First, it is considered an ethical matter:

> When a student takes a course in English, their transcript will reflect that. Moreover, having taken courses in English may be important for job applications, et cetera, so we must be honest ... One has to bear in mind that it is the students' choice to take this course in English. (Teacher 2)

Second, one participant fears that the use of the L1 (in our case, Spanish or Basque) may lead to a practical problem in line with Swain and Lapkin's (2000) concern regarding the eventual replacement of the L2 by the L1 if the use of the L1 is encouraged:

> The problem I see with using Spanish or Basque to resolve a comprehension problem is that once you do that, they are going to do the same thing and it is hard to maintain the use of their L1. (Teacher 9)

While the majority of the teachers support the virtual position, only two, Teachers 11 and 12, take the optimal position that lies at the other end of the continuum proposed by Macaro (2009). These two participants believe that being flexible is of the utmost importance when it comes to the use of languages. For them, languages should not be compartmentalized, and linguistic flexibility should be the guiding principle. This idea is very nicely captured in the following statements:

> I live multilingualism in a very natural way. (Speaker 12)
> Using the students' L1 is not great, but it is not the end of the world when it happens. If you can lean on the languages you speak,

just like you would lean on a crutch to help you, why shouldn't you use them? (Teacher 11)

For Teachers 11 and 12, it is important not to put too much pressure on students and teachers regarding the use of English. In fact, they believe that both students and teachers should not feel guilty whenever they use their L1s. Thus, they propose that the students' linguistic repertoire should be used in class, although its use should not be generalized.

As for the maximal view, this position is represented by one teacher, Teacher 2. According to this view, while the use of English at all times is desirable, the occasional use of the L1 is inevitable because of the circumstances and the context:

> Students need to get accustomed to being in a class where English is used as much as possible, which is not 100% of the time, of course. (Teacher 2)

Finally, two special cases are worth mentioning: a teacher who does not have a clear opinion on this matter and another who admits to being open to a change of point of view. Teacher 7 admits to not having an opinion regarding the use of the L1 in EMI, although his practice is consistent with the virtual position, as we shall see below. The reasons for his indetermination may be attributable to two facts. First, teachers in the EMI program do not receive much specific training, which may lead to reflection on EMI practices and other matters. Second, since EMI at the UBC is a top-down initiative, the teachers did not take any part in its development and implementation. In the second case, Teacher 1 (an advocate of the virtual position) believes that changing her position is a possibility. Teacher 1 questions the need to be strict about the use of the L1 and hypothetically considers the possibility of applying EMI to small groups of students whose level of English is low and who would not be expected to actively participate in English. She views this situation as a means of providing confidence to the students, who will eventually feel ready to speak in English. Teacher 1 also reflects on what it means for her to be bilingual, one of the ultimate aims of EMI. For her, a genuinely bilingual society is a society where teachers use the language they want and students participate in the language they prefer.

RQ2: What are teachers' self-reported practices regarding the use of the L1 in EMI?

There are three main components of the self-reported practices regarding the use of the L1 in EMI: (i) inside and outside the classroom (e.g. office hours), (ii) the materials (e.g. references, handouts, videos) and

(iii) the assessment tasks. We analyze each of these components in turn in the following paragraphs.

(i) The self-reported use of the L1 inside and outside the classroom

With the exception of two teachers (Teachers 5 and 13) who claimed that they never used the L1, all the participants admitted to using the students' L1 occasionally. Two issues account for the use of the L1: what the L1 is used for and the place where the interaction with the student takes place.

The L1 is introduced in the EFL and CLIL settings to fulfill different functions (see Lasagabaster [2013] for a summary of this issue): to help students understand content, to make them feel comfortable in class, to promote debate and to deal with disciplinary issues and class organizational issues (Turnbull & Arnett, 2002). In the EMI context under scrutiny, the all-in-English policy is relaxed when it is clear to the teachers that students are having trouble. The L1 is then used to help students understand an idea, to clarify a term, to provide the translation of specialized vocabulary or to clear up false cognates that may be misinterpreted. All teachers, regardless of their beliefs with respect to EMI, do this. In addition, some teachers (Teachers 7, 9 and 10) use the L1 to talk about organizational matters such as deadlines for class assignments or general announcements:

> I don't use the L1 to teach but I do it if I have to make an announcement, for example. (Teacher 7)

Hence, the teachers' beliefs and their actual practices differ slightly.

Outside the classroom, the L1 is also present, counter to the teachers' beliefs that the L2 should be used at all times. Thus, the majority of the teachers, with the exception of Teachers 2, 3, 8 and 13, accept the use of the L1 during their office hours and in one-on-one interactions with students. The main reason provided for this behavior is that the students tend to use the L1 much more in these contexts, and the teachers follow this tendency. In addition, the teachers are a bit more permissive with the students' use of their L1 in these contexts because they want their students to feel comfortable, especially in the one-on-one interactions:

> I don't want to discourage students from coming to my office hours because they might feel uncomfortable speaking in English. I want to create a relaxed atmosphere and I want students to feel free to ask. So it is important to find the right balance among the use of the various languages. (Teacher 2)

Despite the acceptance by most of the teachers of the use of the L1 in these contexts, the teachers clearly state that the students need to make the effort to speak in English, as one of the participants pointed out:

I don't want to be the only one speaking in English. I don't want to be speaking in English while the student is speaking in Basque or Spanish to me. (Teacher 1)

(ii) The use of the L1 in the materials

The teachers' beliefs are consistent with their use of the L1 in the class materials. On the one hand, the teachers who support the virtual and the maximal positions utilize materials in English alone. On the other hand, the teachers who are closer to the optimal position allow students to work with references in their L1 and use videos or visual materials in the L1, although they use materials primarily in English.

The teachers' commitment to the all-in-English position involves, in many cases, a great effort because it means undertaking the translation into English of class materials (e.g. texts, handouts, power-point presentations, exercises, references) by the teachers themselves. For some of the teachers, the translation of the materials into the L2 was a daunting task, since in some cases they did not get any help from their departments (Teacher 6).

I had to translate everything into English on my own. It was enormous work, terrible. (Teacher 6)

Only one of the teachers did get help for the translation from his department, and another teacher stated that it was easier to get the materials in English than in Basque. All in all, the teachers spare no efforts to implement their belief in the all-in-English approach.

(iii) The use of the L1 in the assessment tasks

As far as assessment measures are concerned, the statutes of the UBC (Estatutos de la Universidad del País Vasco, 2011) establish in Article 17.1b that students should be assessed in the language the course is officially offered in, either Basque or Spanish. In the case of subjects taught in English, while there is no specific language policy on this matter, since the inception of the program the university authorities have encouraged flexibility. In line with the institutional stance, some of the teachers accommodate students' individual requests or allow students to write exams in their L1 (Teachers 6 and 12). Yet, the analysis of the speakers' discourses reveals that all the teachers, including the ones that defend the optimal and the maximal positions, are quite adamant about the use of English and do not agree with the students' use of the L1 in the assessment tasks:

If the subject is in English, the exam should be in English … and the student should use English. (Teacher 9)

If a student asked me to do the exam in Spanish, I would say, 'No, you have to do it in English. I am not going to grade your English'. (Teacher 5)

Teacher 11, whose teaching was characteristic of the optimal position, expressed her misgivings about letting students use their L1 on an individual basis, since for her, doing so would inevitably put them at an advantage compared to the students who, despite their limitations in English, had decided to make the effort to write the exam in English. In fact, all the teachers are aware of students' linguistic limitations and take different measures to help students overcome them. Teacher 9, for instance, adapts his exams (e.g. he includes some questions in his exams that do not require lengthy or elaborate answers), Teacher 2 accepts the occasional use of words in Spanish or Basque and all the teachers, with the exception of Teacher 8, make concessions to their students' use of English and do not penalize inadequate choice of words or ungrammaticalities (Teacher 1):

> I don't want them to get stuck because they cannot find the right word in English. But I don't want them to waste time or interrupt their train of thought because they need to look a word up in the dictionary. So it is okay to provide the word in Spanish or Basque. (Teacher 2)
> Sometimes they use words that don't exist in English. They make them up. But this is also true for Spanish: I have become more permissive with their writing in Spanish as well. (Teacher 1)

There are two main reasons for the teachers' leniency regarding the grammaticality of the language used in the exams. First, they do not see themselves as English teachers, a fact that has also been observed elsewhere (Airey, 2012; Dafouz, 2011). Second, their main concern is the subject matter, the content. This position is taken to an extreme by Teacher 7, who, despite taking the virtual position, states:

> I don't care whether they write the exam in Esperanto. I'll find myself a way to understand what they are saying, as long as they can show that they know physics. (Teacher 7)

As stated before, Teacher 8 represents one exception to the teachers' leniency about the formal aspects of the students' written production and claims to have no qualms about failing students whose expression in English is not adequate.

Table 9.3 summarizes the main findings presented in this chapter. Teacher 4 is not included in the table because he left the discussion group early.

All in all, the following are our main findings. (i) The majority of the teachers advocate the virtual position, with the exception of Teachers 11 and 12, who prefer the optimal position, and Teacher 2, who takes the maximal position. (ii) For the most part, the teachers' beliefs regarding the use of the L1 seem to be consistent with their self-reported practices. However, there are some small discrepancies between the teachers' practices and their beliefs. In the case of the teachers who support the virtual position, all but two participants allow the occasional use of the L1 under certain circumstances despite their belief that it is their responsibility to immerse the students in the L2. The two representatives of the optimal position, in conflict with their own beliefs, support the students' use of the L2 instead of the L1 in exams. (iii) It is hard for some teachers to have a clear-cut opinion on the use of the L1 in EMI: Teacher 7 does not have a clear opinion on the matter, while Teacher 1 admits to being persuadable to take the optimal position (marked with an X in parentheses in Table 9.3), despite her initial support of the use of the L2 at all times.

Conclusions

The UBC has a flexible language policy (there is no top-down language policy fostering an English-only perspective), which is in line with the disparity in the *teachers' beliefs* described in this chapter: Such disparity ranges from non-acceptance to acceptance of the use of the L1 (e.g. immersion or virtual position vs. translanguaging or optimal position). However, in their everyday *teaching practices* most of the participants are prone to exclude the L1. These practices are undeniably influenced by a number of factors. We believe that a pivotal factor is the general trend in the BAC to keep the languages in separate compartments at both preuniversity and university levels, excluding the use of the L1 when learning either the L2 or the foreign language. This compartmentalization has been influenced by the Canadian immersion programs in their equivalent Basque programs, the cornerstones of the revitalization of Basque. A second factor is the widespread belief that the more exposure to and use of the L2, the better students' English proficiency will be.

However, despite their stated beliefs, all but two of the teachers admit to resorting to the L1 in some circumstances (which adds to the credibility of their report, since many of them believed that this should not be done), leading us to conclude that we need to observe EMI classes to delve into this mismatch between beliefs and practices. Observational studies need to be conducted, since this triangulation would allow us to draw more definitive conclusions based on deeper analysis. Our study relies on teachers' self-reported practices, which may differ from what is actually going on in EMI classes. A follow-up study should therefore be based on classroom observation, which will allow us to pinpoint to what extent self-reported practices match the teachers' actual practices.

Yet, there seems to be some evidence suggesting that our results are in line with common practices in EMI in other contexts. For example, in one of the studies compiled by Barnard and McLellan (2014), Stroupe (2014) observed that EMI teachers at a Japanese university were less likely to code-switch than their EFL colleagues, results that match those obtained by Lee and Macaro (2013) in the Korean context. These results seem to point to the fact that the teaching approach, whether EMI or EFL, may also play an important role in the use of the L1 in class, since less code-switching is observed in the former. However, more research is needed to draw more robust conclusions on this matter.

Our study reveals that EMI teachers tend to rely on the L1 mainly when a breach in comprehension is feared or has already occurred (e.g. unfamiliar technical words and difficult concepts or ideas to grasp). Teachers and students resort to the L1 when an explanation or a translation of a word or whole expressions is required (Costa, 2012: 35). However, as we have seen, translanguaging is not habitual in classroom practices, as evidenced by the fact that it is not generally accepted in classroom interactions and assessment tasks. In fact, all but one of the teachers in our study believe that students should make an effort to write assessment-related tasks (essays, exams, etc.) only in English. Translanguaging is nevertheless quite common outside the class context, especially during office hours and one-on-one interactions. The divide between inside and outside class seems to play a role in our participants' translanguaging practices.

The fact that many of the participants have not even considered translanguaging can be attributed to their lack of reflection on this issue and the fact that they are not language experts. In this vein, reflection could help teachers draw conclusions about their current use of the L1 in their EMI classes. A compelling case for the importance of teacher reflection is made by Tien (2014). In her double role as teacher and researcher, she describes her inner conflict when it comes to finding a balance between the official English-only language policy and her attempts to help her students in the learning process in an EMI context:

> The more I looked at the data, the more I reflected on the importance of how much I should use the languages (English and Mandarin) in a more systematic way, not only to deliver the lecture 'optimally' (Macaro, 2009) but also to pay more attention to the students' use of the target language. I reflected that I should be in a position to help them both to understand the lecture and to enhance their target language and communicative competence. (Tien, 2014: 32)

Furthermore, as Basturkmen (2012: 289) underscores, more experienced teachers are prone 'to have more experientially informed beliefs' than those less experienced, which may lead to a tighter correspondence between beliefs and teaching practices. In our sample the participants had on average an EMI teaching experience of 4.5 years.

In our opinion, two main pedagogical implications based on our data can be drawn. The first has to do with the compelling need to integrate form-focused and content-based instruction with literacy-based approaches and language across the curriculum (Lyster, 2007). Our participants do not seek a balance between language and content, however, as the latter is clearly the EMI teachers' main focus of attention. It is thus essential that our participants are made aware of this counterbalanced approach and the need to focus not only on content but also on language forms, since this approach will help students make the most of EMI.

The second implication is that EMI teachers may need training on how to break away from the monolingual view of language codes (Cook, 2012), since research indicates that multilingual language practices help students gain a better understanding of the subject matter (Lewis *et al.*, 2012). Teacher 1 is a good case in point as she moves from the virtual position to the optimal position throughout the discussion while she reflects on her everyday teaching practices. Seminars focused on the benefits of translanguaging (see García & Li, 2014) could help teachers overcome prejudices and the monolingual ideology.

Acknowledgments

The results presented in this chapter are part of the following research projects: FFI2012-34214 (Spanish Ministry of Economy and Competitiveness) and IT311-10 (Department of Education, University and Research of the Basque Government. We would also like to wholeheartedly thank the teaching staff for their willingness and generosity to participate in this study. Similarly, we would like to express our gratitude to the two anonymous reviewers for their insightful comments on a previous version of this chapter.

References

Airey, J. (2012) 'I don't teach language': The linguistic attitudes of physics lecturers in Sweden. *AILA Review* 25, 64–79.
Barnard, R. and McLellan, J. (eds) (2014) *Codeswitching in University English-Medium Classes: Asian Perspectives*. Bristol: Multilingual Matters.
Basque Government (2013) *V encuesta sociolingüística*. Vitoria-Gasteiz: Gobierno Vasco/ Eusko Jaurlaritza.
Basturkmen, H. (2012) Review of research into the correspondence between language teachers' stated beliefs and practices. *System* 40, 282–295.
Borg, S. (2009) Language teacher cognition. In A. Burns and J.C. Richards (eds) *The Cambridge Guide to Second Language Teacher Education* (pp. 163–171). Cambridge: Cambridge University Press.
Borg, S. (2011) The impact of in-service teacher education on language teachers' beliefs. *System* 39, 370–380.
Cook V. (2012) Multicompetence. In C. Chapelle (ed.) *The Encyclopedia of Applied Linguistics* (pp. 3768–3774). Oxford: Wiley-Blackwell.
Costa, F. (2012) Focus on form in ICLHE lectures in Italy. *AILA Review* 25, 30–47.
Coyle, D., Hood, P., and Marsh, D. (2010) *CLIL: Content and Language Integrated Learning*. Cambridge: Cambridge University Press.
Cummins, J. (2014) Rethinking pedagogical assumptions in Canadian French immersion programs. *Journal of Immersion and Content-Based Language Education* 2, 3–22.

Dafouz, E. (2011) English as a medium of instruction in Spanish contexts. In Y. Ruiz de Zarobe, J.M. Sierra and F. Gallardo del Puerto (eds) *Content and Foreign Language Integrated Learning* (pp. 189–209). Bern: Peter Lang.

Doiz, A., Lasagabaster, D. and Sierra, J.M. (2011) Internationalisation, multilingualism and English-medium instruction: The teachers' perspective. *World Englishes* 30, 345–359.

Doiz, A., Lasagabaster, D. and Sierra, J.M. (eds) (2013) *English-Medium Instruction at Universities: Global Challenges*. Bristol: Multilingual Matters.

Estatutos de la Universidad del País Vasco [Statutes of the University of the Basque Country] (2011) BOPV [Official Bulletin of the Basque Country], 38, 24 February 2011.

European University Association (2013) *Internationalisation in European Higher Education: European Policies, Institutional Strategies and EUA Support*. Brussels: European University Association.

García, O. (2009) *Bilingual Education in the 21st Century: A Global Perspective*. Malden, MA: Wiley/Blackwell.

García, O. and Li, W. (2014) *Translanguaging: Language, Bilingualism and Education*. London: Palgrave Macmillan.

Gardner-Chloros, P. (2009) *Code-Switching*. Cambridge: Cambridge University Press.

Gutiérrez, K. (2008) Developing a sociocritical literacy in the third space. *Reading Research Quarterly* 43, 148–164.

Iglesias-Álvarez, A. and Ramallo, F. (2002) Language as a diacritical in terms of cultural and resistance identities in Galicia. *Studies in Sociolinguistics/Estudios de Sociolingüística* 3, 255–287.

Kirkpatrick, A. (2011) English as a medium of instruction in Asian education (from primary to tertiary): Implications for local languages and local scholarship. *Applied Linguistics Review* 2, 99–120.

Kubanyiova, M. (2014) Motivating language teachers: Inspiring vision. In D. Lasagabaster, A. Doiz and J.M. Sierra (eds) *Motivation and Foreign Language Learning: From Theory to Practice* (pp. 71–89). Amsterdam/Philadelphia, PA: John Benjamins.

Lasagabaster, D. (2013) The use of the L1 in CLIL classes: The teachers' perspective. *Latin American Journal of Content and Language Integrated Learning* 6, 1–21.

Lee, J.H. and Macaro, E. (2013) Investigating age in the use of L1 or English-only instruction: Vocabulary acquisition by Korean EFL learners. *The Modern Language Journal* 97, 887–901.

Lewis, G., Jones, B. and Baker, C. (2012) Translanguaging: origins and development from school to street and beyond. *Educational Research and Evaluation: An International Journal on Theory and Practice* 18 (7), 641–654.

Lyster, R. (2007) *Learning and Teaching Languages through Content: A Counterbalanced Approach*. Amsterdam/Philadelphia, PA: John Benjamins.

Macaro, E. (2009) Teacher use of codeswitching in the second language classroom: Exploring 'optimal' use. In M. Turnbull and J. Dailey-O'Cain (eds) *First Language Use in Second and Foreign Language Learning* (pp. 35–49). Bristol: Multilingual Matters.

Macaro, E. (2014) Overview: Where should we be going with classroom codeswitching research? In R. Barnard and J. McLellan (eds) *Codeswitching in University English-Medium Classes: Asian Perspectives* (pp. 10–23). Bristol: Multilingual Matters.

Menken, K. (2013) Emergent bilingual students in secondary school: Along the academic language and literacy continuum. *Language Teaching* 46, 438–476.

Smit, U. and Dafouz, E. (2012) Integrating content and language in higher education: An introduction to English-medium policies, conceptual issues and research practices across Europe. *AILA Review* 25, 1–12.

Stroupe, R. (2014) Commentary on codeswitching in two Japanese contexts. In R. Barnard and J. McLellan (eds) *Codeswitching in University English-Medium Classes: Asian Perspectives* (pp. 76–90). Bristol: Multilingual Matters.

Swain, M. and Lapkin, S. (2000) Task-based second language learning: the uses of the first language. *Language Teaching Research* 4, 251–274.

Swain, M., Kirkpatrick, A. and Cummins, J. (2011) *How to Have a Guilt-Free Life Using Cantonese in the English Class: A Handbook for the English Language Teacher in Hong Kong.* Hong Kong: Research Centre into Language Acquisition and Education in Multilingual Societies, Hong Kong Institute of Education. See www.ied.edu.hk/rcleams/handbook/handbook.pdf (accessed 20 June 2015).

Tien, C.-Y. (2014) Codeswitching in a university in Taiwan. In R. Barnard and J. McLellan (eds) *Codeswitching in University English-Medium Classes: Asian Perspectives* (pp. 24–32). Bristol: Multilingual Matters.

Turnbull, M. and Arnett, K. (2002) Teachers' uses of the target and first languages in second and foreign language classrooms. *Annual Review of Applied Linguistics* 22, 204–218.

Turnbull, M. and Dailey-O'Cain, J. (eds) (2009) *First Language Use in Second and Foreign Language Learning.* Bristol: Multilingual Matters.

van der Walt, C. (2013) *Multilingual Higher Education: Beyond English Medium Orientations.* Bristol: Multilingual Matters.

Wang, L.X. and Kirkpatrick, A. (2013) Trilingual education in Hong Kong primary schools: A case study. *International Journal of Bilingual Education and Bilingualism* 16, 100–116.

Zhang, F. and Liu, Y. (2014) A study of secondary school English teachers' beliefs in the context of curriculum reform in China. *Language Teaching Research* 18, 187–204.

10 Concluding Remarks: Prestige Planning and Translanguaging in Higher Education

Kevin S. Carroll

Historically, institutions of higher education have worked to unify nations and build the prestige of the languages in which they operate. The first modern-day universities of Europe used Latin as the primary medium of instruction, which promulgated scientific publications in the language and led to the general perception that those who were able to use Latin were intelligent and purposeful. While institutions of higher education have not always used the language of the local masses, the language chosen as the medium of instruction has had great symbolic and practical implications. For example, the use of English in the first universities of India awarded high status to the language of the colonizer and immediately positioned it as a gatekeeper for upward mobility and access to higher education (Annamaliai, 2004). In India and other countries around the world, tertiary language policies have had an impact on the goals of primary and secondary schools. As a result, schools with teaching personnel able to work in the language of the tertiary level have been seen as the most prestigious. Schools that teach in languages or varieties that are not used at the tertiary level are often deemed to be antiquated or inferior.

In this chapter, I will argue that one of the fundamental necessities in increasing access and equity in higher education is prestige planning among non-dominant languages. I use the term *non-dominant languages* in line with Benson and Kosonen's (2013: 1) definition, where it 'refers to the languages or language varieties spoken in a given state that are not considered the most prominent in terms of number, prestige or official use by the government and/or the education system'. Building the prestige of non-dominant languages by using translanguaging practices in higher education would ultimately raise the status of such languages and potentially have a trickle-down effect on primary and secondary schools. Using the research published throughout this volume, I will present how the use of translanguaging practices can act as a prestige planning mechanism that can impact linguistic minorities' success in higher education.

While understanding students' linguistic needs is imperative for their success in higher education, the use of translanguaging as an ideology is not a panacea for all of the ills of access and equity. While most of the chapters in this volume praise and document the usefulness and authentic nature of translanguaging practices, a critique of the term and its implications is necessary. Through providing a preliminary critique of the use of translanguaging, it is my hope that further discussion and scholarship will be dedicated to unpacking the term and its influence on formal, tertiary education. The chapter will conclude with suggestions for the future of translanguaging as it relates to language policy and prestige planning along with some points of action for language planners and policy actors.

Prestige Planning and Higher Education

The field of language planning is often divided into three areas. The first two, proposed by Kloss (1969) and reframed and defined by Haugen (1983), are corpus planning, which is concerned with the codification and dissemination of a language, and status planning, which discusses the official and *de facto* rules regarding when and how languages are used. The third, coined by Cooper (1989), is acquisition planning, which examines language in education and how systems of education address language. Compared to these three pillars of language planning, prestige planning, or attitude planning as it is sometimes referred to, is a more recent term used to describe the attitude that users of language have toward their languages and those around them (Haarmann, 1990).

Consequently, prestige planning has everything to do with users' attitudes toward language and can have very little to do with a language's official or unofficial status. Movements to revitalize languages have often been successful in changing the status of non-dominant languages through policy initiatives. However, changing the official status of a language does not necessarily mean that the speakers of the affected language will change their beliefs and attitudes toward the usefulness of the language in question. Bamgboşe (2000: 54–55) discusses how language planners and policy experts have faced resistance toward instituted mother tongue instruction programs because students and parents alike see little value in the formal use of their non-dominant language. Such feelings of low prestige toward non-dominant languages are a result of decades and even centuries of colonization (Benson & Kosonen, 2013; Smith, 1999), and it is in these colonized contexts where prestige-planning efforts are most needed (Baldauf, 2004; Zhao & Liu, 2010).

One example of how the prestige of language factors into higher education is exemplified on the Caribbean island of Aruba, where Papiamento holds joint official status with Dutch and high prestige in communication among locals and serves as an identity marker of who is Aruban (Carroll, 2010). However, despite the high prestige of Papiamento in social domains, Dutch holds much higher prestige in formal academic settings. As a product of Dutch colonization, in Aruban academic contexts the ability to move from grade to grade hinges on students' ability to proficiently use Dutch. Similarly, the institutions of higher education that most islanders attend are Dutch medium, and thus the importance and prestige of Dutch is reinforced. This context has led to the lower prestige of Papiamento for the purposes of formal schooling, making it difficult for educational reformers to increase the amount of Papiamento-medium instruction in local schools (Dijkhoff & Pereira, 2010).

Similar to what was discussed in Chapter 8, Carroll and van den Hoven described the context of the United Arab Emirates (UAE), where locals use Emirati Arabic in verbal exchanges with one another, yet Standard Arabic, which is markedly different, holds higher prestige in schools and in formal and written domains of language use. Similar to Papiamento in Aruba, within the UAE Emirati Arabic has high prestige because it serves as a marker of local identity and works to distinguish locals from expatriated speakers of Arabic, yet the requirement of English-medium instruction (EMI) in tertiary institutions raises the prestige of English in formal academic settings. Such decisions have prompted revisions to the primary and secondary schools within the country, where English plays an increasingly important role.

Historically, multilingual nations have struggled with an unbalanced prestige of languages used within their borders. Groff (Chapter 7) describes the historical context of language in tertiary education in northern India and explains how 'Although India's "unity in diversity" values multilingualism, the pressure for unity sometimes obscures diversity. Similarly, multilingual languaging practices face conflicting ideologies and are often stigmatized as substandard, especially in educational contexts' (p. 136). Thus, while at a national level the language policies of India have attempted to allow for the inclusion of some non-dominant languages, the prestige of such languages is not high enough that they are used alongside Hindi or English in formal schooling without fear of stigmatization. In contexts where deep-rooted beliefs equate the use of a dominant language to superior intelligence, prestige-planning efforts are of the utmost importance.

Translanguaging in Higher Education

The purpose of the explosion of research regarding the theorizing of translanguaging and its potential in classrooms has overwhelmingly been to disrupt monolingual ideologies and provide more meaningful and inclusive instruction to linguistic minorities around the world. Celic and Seltzer

(2011) along with García and her colleagues at the City University of New York have gone to great lengths to document translanguaging as it happens and provide practical suggestions and advice on how such practices can be adopted in formal teaching environments. Nevertheless, the brunt of research regarding translanguaging practices has been focused on primary and secondary environments, much of which has been in after-school programs or complimentary schools (Creese & Blackledge, 2010). On the fringe of this inspiring research has been a small proportion of studies that take place in traditionally multilingual countries. Throughout this volume, we have gone to great lengths to extend the discussion of translanguaging practices to parts of the world where higher education has predominately catered to bilingual students.

The recent popularity of the term *translanguaging* opens the door for academics and policymakers to go beyond the monolingual ideologies that have historically characterized tertiary education. As Makelela presented in Chapter 2, such adoption of *ubuntu* translanguaging pedagogies (UTP) promotes an inclusive perspective of language using what Ruiz (1984) termed a language-as-resource orientation. The use of UTP in preservice teacher preparation courses builds the prestige of local non-dominant languages, but it also provides teachers in training with the tools to use such practices in their future work.

Permitting language policies that promote translanguaging practices at all levels of an institution would inevitably raise the prestige of local languages and send a message to students that their linguistic resources are accepted (Carroll & Mazak, forthcoming 2017). This was the case in Mazak *et al.* (Chapter 5), which described how three instructors of different content areas used a variety of translanguaging techniques to make their content comprehensible to students while simultaneously countering what Phillipson (2003) describes as the hegemonic tendencies of English in higher education.

As translanguaging practices were used in various ways to convey content to students in Puerto Rico, He *et al.* (Chapter 6) described another aspect of experience in higher education: attending a talk from a renowned guest speaker. As He and her colleagues described, the linguistic complexities of a university audience in Hong Kong provided a venue where Professor Liu had to vary his linguistic approach to accommodate the linguistic needs of the audience. Understanding that his audience would have varying degrees of fluency in Chinese, Professor Liu used what He *et al.* refer to as both translanguaging and trans-semiotizing in his talk and PowerPoint presentation. In so doing, he incorporated Putonghua, English and simplified Chinese characters to make his presentation understood by those in the audience with shared communicative repertoires in these languages. Professor Liu's linguistic practices and his stature as an invited speaker legitimized these practices as worthy of use in a formal lecture. Such practices work to further blur the monolingual ideologies once pervasive in tertiary education.

The breaking down of monolingual ideologies was also a theme of Daryai-Hansen *et al.*'s chapter, which described how students in the German language profile at Roskilde University in Denmark were specifically encouraged to translanguage. Doing so made their experience more meaningful and emblematic of an authentic multilingual environment where users of language are able to pull from their diverse linguistic repertoires to make sense of their education and the world around them. Despite the success of such translanguaging practices in legitimizing the fluid use of language in formal instruction, the widespread use of translanguaging in higher education still faces many challenges.

As Mazak pointed out in the introduction, translanguaging is many things. First and foremost, it is a language ideology or a bilingual lens through which citizens view the world. In taking bilingualism as the norm, this ideology runs counter to monolingual language ideologies that have dominated the rhetoric around nation building and institutions of higher education. She also pointed out that it is a lived theory of how authentic language actually plays out in the lives of those who use more than one language. This lived theory exists in both formal and informal education in contexts worldwide. Furthermore, as has been illustrated in the majority of the chapters in this volume, educators can take a pedagogical stance to allow, advocate and implement translanguaging in their own classrooms. Thus, it is through such implementation that translanguaging becomes a set of practices whereby educators build on and use their students' linguistic resources and background knowledge to convey meaningful content. These pedagogical practices are not limited to code-switching as was demonstrated in He *et al.* (Chapter 6), among many of the other chapters. Finally, the term *translanguaging* is transformational in nature as it attests to the constant evolution of language practices and sees these practices as normal and natural.

Challenges and Criticisms for the Increased Use of Translanguaging

The stigmatized nature of mixing languages in formal instructional settings is obviously the largest obstacle that proponents of translanguaging practices have to overcome. However, those who promote translanguaging must also understand that politically and from a policy perspective, arguing that languages do not exist or that they are merely social constructions may raise too much resistance. As Cummins (2015) eloquently pointed out at the first-ever conference dedicated solely to translanguaging, in Falun, Sweden,

An analogy can be made with the construct of 'colours.' In western society, we typically distinguish about 7 major colours even though the human eye can distinguish about 10 million colour variations. The major colours we distinguish are social constructs that we use to make sense of and act on our world (e.g., paint our house). In the same way, it can be argued that the boundaries between different languages represent social constructions, but it is nevertheless legitimate to distinguish languages in certain contexts and for certain purpose in order to make sense of and act on our worlds.

The theoretical contributions of translanguaging and the push toward viewing language as fluid and ever-changing is helpful in understanding the variation of language; however, the strict adoption of 'languages do not exist' rhetoric could potentially alienate and distract policymakers and curriculum experts from using such practices in formal instruction.

Another challenge to the implementation of translanguaging in higher education is the *de facto* and sometimes *de jure* language policies at the macro (national), meso (institutional) and micro (classroom) levels. Bilingual or open-language policies as exemplified in Mazak *et al.* (Chapter 5) and further discussed in Carroll and Mazak (forthcoming 2017) open the door for the instructor to use translanguaging practices to augment their teaching of content and to better relate to their students. However, as was discussed in Carroll and van den Hoven (Chapter 8), there are contexts where *de facto* policies prevent the overt use of translanguaging practices because doing so could jeopardize instructors' job security. In contexts where strict separation between languages is required, it is all the more important to open the dialogue about such practices. Throughout the past year, I have had numerous conversations with my students, who are future primary EMI teachers in the UAE. The look on their faces when I say that it is a good thing to use targeted forms of Arabic in their English-medium classroom is priceless. My comments are often met with resistance and dismay, since students report that I am the only one who has ever told them that such practices were actually positive. Nevertheless, the same students, throughout their various teaching practicums and observations in local schools, have witnessed countless bilingual teachers using translanguaging practices, yet such practices were positioned as inferior when compared to the practices of monolingual English teachers. Equipping future teachers with the discourse to describe and justify their use of translanguaging practices is a challenge that must be met if we want to create a pipeline of translanguaging practices that stretches from the primary to tertiary levels.

An additional challenge toward the implementation of translanguaging practices in institutions of higher education is the recruitment of instructors and administrators who themselves are willing to use such practices in their formal teaching. Aleksandr, a student participant in Goodman's study (Chapter 4), exemplifies those students who are ideologically opposed to the mixing of languages in formal instruction, despite his admission that he indeed mixes between three languages outside of class. Unfortunately, when teachers face students with such strong language ideologies as Aleksandr, they potentially lose authority and the respect of their students.

Institutions that wish to promote translanguaging face yet another challenge when it comes to immersion programs, where students select particular classes or areas of study in which to be immersed in a target language. Doiz and Lasagaster's chapter on the use of English as the medium of instruction within the context of the Basque nation of Spain raises the question: to what extent should the two-solitudes approach (Cummins, 2008) be respected when students expect an immersion experience? The element of choice separates students in the Basque context from students around the world who are forced to study in a language that is not their first. The fact that the University of the Basque Country provides curricular options in Basque and Spanish makes the use of EMI an additive-type program where the addition of English is viewed as a resource.

How to Promote Translanguaging Practices

Despite the success and use of translanguaging practices exemplified in the diverse linguistic contexts presented in this book, there are countless contexts around the world that keep operating largely in the two-solitudes assumption, where there is a strict delineation between the language that the students come into the school with and the target language they seek to learn. Below, I summarize some of the ways in which policymakers and educators can work to promote translanguaging practices in higher education.

- Look beyond Western education models where a monolingual lens has been the norm.
- Resist the adoption of market-based teacher reform that focuses on standardized assessments and increasingly globalized metrics in which assessments are solely in one language (the Programme for International Student Assessment [PISA] and The Trends in International Mathematics and Science Study [TIMSS], among others).
- Actively look to hire professors who have similar linguistic backgrounds as the students they will be teaching and consciously assess their linguistic practices in the interview phase of hiring.
- When evaluating professors in annual reviews and for promotion and tenure, count and promote publications and work other than in English.
- Provide experiences in teacher preparation courses in which preservice teachers experience translanguaging in formal instruction firsthand.

- Create language policies that actively promote the use of translanguaging practices or create policies that are open enough that professors are not penalized for using them.

While this list of suggestions is nowhere near exhaustive, the adoption of these recommendations would provide systematic changes allowing for sustainable translanguaging practices that potentially provide more equitable access to higher education among users of non-dominant languages.

Concluding Remarks

Throughout this volume, we have presented contexts around the world where translanguaging practices are part of the fabric that makes up higher education in bi/multilingual contexts. As Makelela argues in Chapter 2, this return to *ubuntu* is really not new at all; it is acknowledging that within multilingual communities it is normal to mix codes, and the two-solitudes assumptions of bilingualism is an antiquated and deficit-minded perspective of language use. Unfortunately, given the colonial underpinnings of monolingual ideologies and their influence on systems of higher education, prestige has traditionally been granted to monolingual approaches. Fortunately, as can be observed in all the cases presented in this volume, teachers, administrators and students can benefit from translanguaging in higher education. As more students gain access to institutions of higher education, creating spaces for translanguaging practices is not only essential in legitimizing the languages they speak, it is also essential in building the prestige of non-dominant languages. Doing so will not only result in increased access to education for speakers of non-dominant languages, but the potential for the prestige of the language to trickle down into primary and secondary education will only improve literacy and educational attainment for children whose languages are not traditionally used in higher education. It would be naive to think that tertiary institutions will change their language policies overnight, but instructors and professors can and should use translanguaging to the extent that they are allowed in order to push for equity and access. Higher education is often the last place where future teachers are students themselves; if as students they never experienced translanguaging practices in formal education, how can we expect that they will use it in their future classrooms?

References

Annamaliai, E. (2004) Medium of power: The question of English in education in India. In J.W. Tollefson and A.B.M. Tsui (eds) *Medium of Instruction Policies: Which Agenda? Whose Agenda?* (pp. 177–194). Mahwah, NJ: Lawrence Erlbaum.

Baldauf, R.B. (2004) Issues of prestige and image in language-in-education planning in Australia. *Current Issues in Language Planning* 5 (4), 376–389.

Bamgboşe, A. (2000) *Language and Exclusion: The Consequences of Language Policies in Africa* (Vol. 12). Münster: LIT Verlag.

Benson, C. and Kosonen, K. (eds) (2013) *Language Issues in Comparative Education: Inclusive Teaching and Learning in Non-Dominant Languages and Cultures* (Vol. 1). Rotterdam: Springer Science & Business Media.

Carroll, K.S. (2010) Examining perceptions of threat: Does an influx of Spanish speakers pose a threat to Aruban Papiamento? *Romanitas, lenguas y literaturas romances* 4 (2). See http://romanitas.uprrp.edu/vol_4_num_2/carroll.html (accessed 4 July 2015).

Carroll, K.S. and Mazak, C.M. (forthcoming 2017) Language policy in Puerto Rico's higher education: Opening the door for translanguaging practice. *Anthropology and Education Quarterly* 48 (1).

Celic, C. and Seltzer, K. (2011) *Translanguaging: A CUNY-NYSIEB Guide for Educators.* New York: CUNY-NYSIEB. See http://www.nysieb.ws.gc.cuny.edu/files/2012/06/FINAL-Translanguaging-Guide-With-Cover-1.pdf (accessed 13 July 2015).

Cooper, R.L. (1989) *Language Planning and Social Change.* Cambridge University Press.

Creese, A. and Blackledge, A. (2010) Translanguaging in the bilingual classroom: A pedagogy for learning and teaching? *The Modern Language Journal* 94 (1), 103–115.

Cummins, J. (2008) Teaching for transfer: Challenging the two solitudes assumption in bilingual education. In J. Cummins and N.H. Hornberger (eds) *Encyclopedia of Language and Education, Vol. 5: Bilingual Education* (pp. 65–75) (2nd edn). New York: Springer.

Cummins, J. (2015, April) Translanguaging: What does it mean to teach for transfer in educating multilingual students? Presentation at the Conference on Translanguaging – Practices, Skills and Pedagogy, Dalarna University, Falun, Sweden. See http://www.du.se/pagefiles/118244/Power%20points/Cummins%20Falun%20presentation%20April%202015.pdf (accessed 6 July 2015).

Dijkhoff, M. and Pereira, J. (2010) Language and education in Aruba, Bonaire and Curaçao. In B. Migge, I. Léglise and A. Bartens (eds) *Creoles in Education: An Appraisal of Current Programs and Projects* (pp. 237–272). Philadelphia, PA: John Benjamins.

Haarmann, H. (1990) Language planning in the light of a general theory of language: A methodological framework. *International Journal of the Sociology of Language* 86, 103–126.

Haugen, E. (1983) The implementation of corpus planning: Theory and practice. In J. Cobarrubias and J. Fishman (eds) *Progress in Language Planning: International Perspectives* (pp. 269–290). Berlin: Mouton.

Kloss, H. (1969) *Research Possibilities on Group Bilingualism: A Report.* Quebec: International Center for Research on Bilingualism.

Phillipson, R. (2003) *English-Only Europe? Challenging Language Policy.* New York: Routledge.

Ruiz, R. (1984) Orientations in language planning. *NABE Journal* 8 (2), 15–34.

Smith, L.T. (1999) *Decolonizing Methodologies: Research and Indigenous Peoples.* London: Zed.

Zhao, S. and Liu, Y. (2010) Chinese education in Singapore: Constraints of bilingual policy from the perspectives of status and prestige planning. *Language Problems and Language Planning* 34 (3), 236–258.

Index